My Fairytale Divorce

My Fairytale Divorce

A MOTHER'S STORY

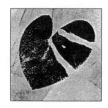

GILLIAN TUCKER

Whitecap Books

Vancouver / Toronto

Edited by Elaine Jones
Proofread by Elizabeth McLean
Cover design by Val Speidel
Cover illustration by Sheila Norgate
Interior design by Warren Clark
Typeset by Warren Clark

Printed and bound in Canada.

Canadian Cataloguing in Publication Data

Tucker, Gillian.
 My fairytale divorce

 ISBN 1-55110-505-5
 1. Divorce—Case studies. I. Title.
HQ814.T82 1996   306.89'092   C96-910363-8

❖ ❖ ❖

For Gemma and her father

ACKNOWLEDGMENTS

Grateful thanks to *Chatelaine* magazine and Ivor Shapiro, who helped bring this book to fruition.

O ❖ N ❖ E

I remember the exact moment my divorce became final. Final as in death notice final. Not the paper divorce I had agreed to eight years earlier. That was the legal severance of Howell's and my marriage. This was the visceral split, the last heartbeat of our partnership, and it came in a fraction of a second with a little click that said *this is it, this is the end, no turning back, not ever again,* almost by surprise as we sat in the front seat of his car, our nine-year-old daughter Emily in the back playing Tetris on the GameBoy her father had given her at SeaTac airport five weeks before.

I say almost by surprise, because all endings loom long before they come. Perhaps the end was right there in our beginning. But instead of packing away our marriage after we divorced, turning our backs on each other and finding other partners as soon as we decently could, we had remained courteous and amiable, fetching and delivering Emily, speaking daily on the telephone and restricting our differences to mild disagreements, chiefly because we wanted our daughter to suffer as little as possible. Now even these civilities were about to fall apart.

We had known each other for sixteen years that June morning as we sat in my ex-husband's car outside the Toronto-Dominion bank on Oak Bay Avenue in Victoria on the west coast of Canada. We had been married for five of those years, divorced for eight and for the past four had lived on opposite sides of the world. He had lived in Toronto and only recently moved to Victoria. Emily and I lived in Cape Town on the southern coast of Africa. The reason we were back together on this June day, my forty-second birthday, was that we were about to embark on an experiment for Emily's sake. Right now, she was sprawled across

1

the back seat of the car, her GameBoy bleeping congratulatory riffs as she punched up yet another record-breaking score for the morning. I glanced back over my shoulder at her, noting again how blonde her hair was in comparison to the dun brown of my own.

"How're you doing Em?" I asked her.

"Kay," was all I got back. I had read in a magazine on the flight over that electronic games, far from frying our kids' brains, might even be helping them sprout new neural paths. So what if it turned them into lab rats pulling levers for kibble? Her father's gift had turned out to be an inspired choice. Without it, Emily might have gone stir-crazy waiting around for me to make up my mind about whether we were going to stay in Victoria or not.

Four years earlier Howell had immigrated to Canada from Cape Town. The joint custody agreement we had signed entitled him to have Emily visit him in Toronto for two months of every year. She had been six years old when she made the first of these trips—still too little to know much about time and distance. We had waved goodbye and two months later magically met up with each other again, neither of us much the worse for our time apart. By the time she was seven, all of that had changed. I had stood at the check-in counter at the airport in Cape Town watching an attendant snap an outsized *Unaccompanied Minor* tag around her neck, fighting the urge to snatch her back and run from the concourse. My last sight of her had been framed by an electronic surveillance gate, a blanket and battered rabbit tucked under one arm as an airline attendant hustled her off like a piece of luggage. The separations had become a nightmare for all of us. Emily cried herself to sleep every night in Toronto, wrapping an old sweater of mine around her to pretend I was with her. Two months later, back in Cape Town, she sobbed inconsolably for her father. On the day I fetched her she tumbled into my arms, her face streaked with tears, and told me that a flight attendant had called her a "ragged muffin." With airline food in her hair and clothes she had worn for several days, I wasn't surprised. But when I wiped away her tears and she had found her voice again, she told me in a whisper that the real reason she had been called a ragamuffin was that she was "a divorced child." Only divorced children travelled without parents, she said, and that's why people called them names. Over the next week, I looked on in anguish, as she talked to her father by fax every day, trying to hold on to the bond she had established with him and with her cousins over the summer. Whichever way she turned, it seemed she was robbed of a parent. The emotional toll was beginning to tell on all of us.

We had believed joint custody was the most enlightened plan we could devise for our daughter when we divorced in 1985. A bedroom in each home. No restrictions on the time spent with each parent. And when Howell emigrated, the assurance that he would pay for Emily to visit him at least once a year bolstered our conviction that we were doing the best for her. What an adventure! we thought. Emily would clock up more frequent flyer miles than all of us put together! We had never reckoned on a seven-year-old child being forced to leave home for two months at a time. Or having to say goodbye to a beloved father, knowing she wouldn't see him again for a full year. Three years was all it took to prove to us that joint custody does not work. Certainly not between continents. We had thought we could bend the rules. That we were enlightened enough to rewrite them. But the rules are inflexible. A child needs two parents in the same place at the same time. We had failed our daughter once by divorcing each other. Now we were divorcing her in turn from each one of us. The least we could do was to attempt to live in the same city again. Which was why all of us were together here in Victoria. Only this time round, it was me who was falling apart.

"What do you want to do next?" Howell glanced at his watch. He turned over the engine of his Accord, rested his palms on the steering wheel, and waited. It was lunch time and we had achieved very little so far. I could sense his annoyance—could smell it in fact. Whenever his patience was under siege, the cologne he used turned sharp and sour like a barometer signalling a pressure plunge. He had given up his morning to introduce me to his bank manager and assist me in signing up for hydro and telephone services. Now it was past one and all I had chalked up so far was a terse refusal from the bank for a credit card, and further rejections from the utilities companies. I was in Canada on a visa, they explained. I would have to be a resident to open an account. At the bank, I had pleaded six years of a gold Visa with never a late payment in South Africa, but the manager had been crisply adamant.

"Credit records don't transfer," he told me. "We'll be happy to help you when you have a full-time job. I'm sorry but we do things differently here."

Too damn right, I had wanted to lob back at him, my patience evaporating in the face of his cool dismissal. I couldn't even read the labels on the detergents in the supermarket. Let alone figure out washing machines that loaded from the top, and post offices that lurked at the back of fruit counters. In South Africa they were proper brick and brass-rail buildings, not flimsy hutches you could mistake for display stands. Even the moon looked wrong here. The features I had counted on all my life were upside down, the new moon was back to front and the stars came out in patterns that made no sense to me at all. In the frustration that mirrored my confusion, I had taken each difference as a personal affront, a marker pointing to how naive I had been to alter the fixed points of my life with such casual abandon. In the end, Howell had agreed to open telephone and hydro accounts for me in his own name. Now, as he rapped his fingers lightly on the steering wheel and waited for me to decide what I wanted to do, I was perilously close to allowing my feelings to get the better of me.

Instead I pulled myself back to the present. "We need to find a dentist for Emily," I said. "I know it's not on the list, but I'd like someone to look at the chip on her front tooth. And she needs new sneakers. The ones I bought for her back home are pinching her." Howell glanced down at his watch again.

The words *back home* pushed a neural hot button in me every time I used them. I had yet to decide whether Emily and I were going to stay beyond the two months we had agreed to and then for how long. The truth was that in accepting Howell's invitation to accompany Emily at his expense, I had been wildly ingenuous. I hadn't reckoned that the decision to remain had been made for me even before I arrived. One look at my daughter's face was all it took to convince me that bringing her back to Canada was the best thing I could do for her. In five short weeks she had slipped back into the soft Canadian burr she lost each year under the harsh dominance of South African vowels. There had

4

been a new pink bike waiting for her as a gift from her father and she had ridden this up and down the streets until the sun went down late in the evening, a concession she would never have been allowed back home. And instead of bomb and hand-grenade drill at school she had spent most of the past month knocking a puck around Howell's backyard. Best of all, her mother and father were back in the same city again. I had looked out onto the quiet, tree-lined streets and known that this was what I had wanted for my daughter all along. Howell had played a long card and won. His gamble had paid off. In all good conscience I could not take Emily back to South Africa now. Not to the heartbreak of long separations, nor to the turmoil that was ravaging the country. Now that Howell had his daughter back, the only difficulty was what to do with me. I was the one with nowhere to go.

In the back seat of the car Emily put Tetris aside and clamped on the earphones of the yellow Walkman she had wheedled out of her father the weekend before. Ace of Base pumped out *The Sign* as I glanced down my list of things to do.

"I'm hungry," Emily said to no one in particular.

"I know, darling," I answered distractedly.

"Where to?" Howell asked, his patience thinning with every tick of his watch. I looked up from my list and out onto the manicured streets of Victoria. Midsummer and none of the blinding light of Africa that bounced off glass and metal, burning your nose and shoulders as you shopped. The houses here looked like muffins spilled from the same patty pan, the colors and scents of the season so delicate, even the leaves trembled like feathers. No gum trees in violent bloom on every corner. No clamor in the streets as people of every hue pushed, called, shouted, jostled and whistled for your attention. Caught off guard for the hundredth time since I had stepped off the ferry a few weeks before, I wondered *where am I?*

"Well, why don't you *do* something about it?" Emily asked from the back of the car.

"We will, we will," I said. I didn't want to take too close a look at the realities. I was in my forties, divorced, thinking about starting all over again in a new country, in a city as remote from home as I could get. *Come and look,* Howell had said. *You know it's the best thing for Emily. If you decide to stay, we'll go from there.* Leaving Cape Town would mean selling up everything I possessed and scraping together the little money I could legally transfer to start a new life here. I would leave behind family who had been in Africa for nearly two hundred years and say goodbye to a city and to people I had worked with for nearly a decade as a journalist and editor. Here I knew no one. No, that wasn't the problem. No one here knew *me*. I couldn't even get a credit card! There was the objective correlative of the whole enterprise. *Zero credit rating*. Howell had agreed to underwrite my expenses until I found my feet again. Eight hundred dollars a month to feed, clothe and provide for myself. And if I chose to stay, he would transport my furniture from South Africa at his own cost. The offer couldn't have been more enticing or more generous. Yet, sitting there in his car, I had an aching desire to step back into my kitchen in Cape Town again, to break open a bottle of wine, and throw together a stir-fry for three or four of my oldest friends. I thought of my good kitchen knives sealed away in a storage warehouse somewhere out on the salt flats near Cape Town. Funny how much you miss the little things, I thought. Just to close my fingers around their handles again, they would have to sail all the way across the Atlantic, on through the Caribbean, navigate the Panama Canal, call in at San Francisco and journey on up to the Port of Vancouver before they could be delivered by ferry to my kitchen here on Vancouver Island.

"I'm hungry," Emily said again, pitching her voice to compete against *Ace of Base*.

The thoughts kept crowding my head, tumbling over one another, all demanding to be dealt with and simplified then and there. How would I work? Would I ever find friends again? God, I couldn't even figure out the supermarkets. Back home *Ivory* was a shampoo. Here it was a dishwashing liquid. Nothing was labelled the way it should be and I had stood in the household goods aisle this morning as though I was in the British Museum deciphering hieroglyphs.

"*Hello-o!* Satellite station to the Mother Ship. I am not an alien. Repeat, I am not an alien, I need refuelling."

"Okay okay. I *heard* you," I said again. But with her Walkman at maximum volume, Emily did not hear me and roared in my ear.

"Mo-om. *I'm starving.*"

Startled, I swung around to face her. "*Em!* Don't *ever* yell in my ear like that again."

"Well, why don't you answer me?"

"I did. I told you we'll eat as soon as we've finished what we have to do."

"You said that an hour ago."

"That's why I wanted you to eat breakfast."

"This is so *boooring,* sitting in a car while the two of you decide what to do."

Her voice had taken on its familiar whine, a bray that had driven me mad over the last couple of months. Each time I was caught up with packing, arranging airline tickets, handing over keys, or getting us to an airport with only minutes to spare, Emily had been under my feet, demanding food, restrooms, money and attention. And always at a moment when I was incapable of giving it to her. This time, I snapped.

"Oh for *heaven's* sake, will you please *shut up!*" I yelled.

"Why do I have to be here with the two of you. I *hate* this," she shrieked back at me.

"Emily! Will you *just shut up!*" I shot back at her. She tore off her earphones and flung them across the car, snatching up her GameBoy and stabbing at it to block out my voice.

Oh God, a voice said. *That was unnecessary. Get yourself under control.* The echo of my words bounced round the car and back into the crowded spaces inside my head. Something like paralysis began to choke me, constricting my throat and numbing my legs and arms like poison. *Why did you* do *that?* I raged at myself. Whenever this happened, at times when I had yelled without thinking or my brain flooded with an overflow of stress, this was the reaction. An outburst, then crippling remorse. Fear and horror. Especially of the backlash I was certain would follow. Sure enough, Howell's voice came smashing back at me, amplified by the confines of the car.

"Do you know what a bitch you sound? If you *ever* speak to Emily like that again, I warn you I'll see my lawyers."

I swivelled and looked into Howell's face. A vein snaked along his temple and his eyes were green with fury.

"Ever since you arrived here," he went on, "I've sat by and listened to the way you speak to Emily. You have *no* sense of control. No sense of what it must be like for her to be in a new country. What kind of a mother *are* you? You're not fit to be a parent. If I hear you speak like that once more, I *promise* you I'll be speaking to my lawyers about getting full custody of her."

I turned in my seat to check on Emily and saw that she too was frozen, GameBoy in midair, sunk back into her seat as if to protect herself from the shock waves of our voices. Howell thundered on.

"She hunches her shoulders. She looks at you before she dares to answer a question. She's a shell who's had her self-esteem *destroyed* by her own mother. Do you hear me? *I will not allow you to go on doing what you are doing to Emily!*" I felt myself turn icy with shock. Everything seemed to freeze under the onslaught of his voice. Again I turned around to check on Emily.

"It's okay, Honey." I reached over and squeezed her palm in the secret way we had of saying *I love you*. But she coiled herself away into a corner of the back seat, her hands covering her ears. Howell had never done this in front of her before. I had lived through outbursts like this when we were married, but never in front of Emily, except perhaps that one time in the kitchen when she was a baby. He had always had the self-composure to leave the room before his frustration made him give way completely. This time he didn't care who heard him. Now a shutdown reaction set in as though I was walking through a house, methodically snapping off the lights. *Make it stop. This isn't happening. Pretend it never happened.*

"Stop," I found the voice to tell him. "Stop. *Stop it.* I don't want to hear anymore."

"I've got plenty more to say."

"Then say it away from Emily. She doesn't need to hear this."

"I want her to." He swung round in his seat to face me. "I want her to know what I feel about the way you treat her." From the back of the car, Emily's voice piped, "Stop it, Daddy. Please stop." Howell turned to face her and his voice instantly modulated to a reassuring purr. "You don't have to say anything you don't want to, darling," he told her.

"Howell, are you crazy?" I said, ignoring the commands in my head to shut out his words. "You make it sound as though I've done something terrible to Emily."

"That's *exactly* what you've been doing."

"This is insane."

"*Daddy, please stop!*"

"She stays loyal to you because she's too afraid to speak out."

"Howell. I don't understand this but I'm getting out with Emily if you don't stop right now."

"Go ahead. Threaten. Isn't that what you've always done?"

"That's what you're doing to me right now."

"And high time too."

"What kind of example are you setting Emily? That it's okay to scream at me like this?"

"I suppose that's your exclusive domain," he hurled back.

I searched his face for an explanation. What had I done to ignite an explosion like this?

"I've heard the way you talk to Em," he repeated. "The verbal abuse. I've heard you tell her—I don't know *how* many times—to shut up."

"Is that *all?*" I asked.

I had made the wrong admission. Howell's fury escalated. "She's my child and I will not stand by letting anyone talk to her like that. *Do you understand me?*" A passerby stopped in his tracks, trying to trace the roar from Howell's car.

"I am Emily's mother," I said, trying to hold on to one sure thing in the face of this insanity.

"Does that give you permission to do what you like?" Howell asked.

"Howell," I tried to reason. "Either we speak decently to each other or I'm getting out of this car now."

"Threaten. Go on. Threaten as much as you like. I promise you I'll do whatever it takes to make sure Emily is never subjected to your kind of abuse again. If it takes me every penny I have in the world."

I could hear the words, but my senses stuck on the meaning. Had I *really* hurt Emily? *How* had I hurt her? Howell was right. I *had* been sharp. And short-tempered in the last few weeks. Was she hunching her shoulders because of me? And under the same kind of strain as us? She *was* biting her nails again. She was only nine years old. She couldn't be expected to know when to keep quiet. My attention had been all over the place and I couldn't find the words to tell her, or anyone else for that matter, that I was about as frightened as I had ever been in my life. In the past five weeks I had made the biggest jump of my life and discovered that there might not be solid ground to land on when I finally came down to earth again.

The last ounce of my courage gave way. If there had been something I could answer to other than my own sharp words, I might have stood my ground. But the ferocity of Howell's attack, the senselessness of my own outburst and his groundless accusations sent tears of fury and exhaustion spilling over my cheeks. I found myself heaving for air as though I was suffocating. Emily leaned over and handed me a clump of tissues from her pocket.

"It's okay, Mommy," she said. "Daddy doesn't mean to be so angry." We were all of us tired, I told myself. That had to be the reason. These past five weeks had used up the last vestiges of good humor and energy left in all of us. Howell and I hadn't spent this much time in each other's company since we were married. At the same time, I marvelled at my daughter's ability to keep a cool head when her parents had completely lost theirs.

"Thanks, Em," I said. Howell had ceased his blitz and sat in frozen silence, his face averted from me. I turned to look at him but all I could see was the vein on his temple. That's when the click happened. A little switch in my head that said I would never take this from him again. He had done what I had always thought he never had the courage to do. At last he had given me a definitive reason to end our relationship. We were back to ground zero after this. That was the moment I realized with absolute clarity that I had finally divorced him.

"I need to be on my own," I told him.

He said nothing.

"Could you take me back home?" I asked. I had to think. The illusion of reuniting the family was falling apart in front of my eyes. I needed to get away to walk. To do anything that would allow me to take hold of myself again.

Howell started up the car, checked his side mirror and maneuvered into the traffic. He glanced in his rearview mirror two or three times to check on Emily, still bunched up in a corner of the car. "How are you doing, Em?" he asked, his voice a little hoarse, but otherwise back to normal.

"Fine," she said uncertainly.

We drove in silence, except for the hiccups I tried to swallow. We were making our way through the city when Em's voice piped up again from the back of the car.

"It's Mom's birthday, Dad. I'd like to take her to tea."

"I'm not coming," Howell said.

"That's okay. I'd still like to take her out."

Howell looked at her again in his rearview mirror. "Where were you thinking of going?" he asked. He made an effort to smile and catch her eye but she refused to look at either of us. We were stationary at a traffic light when Emily's glance fell on a restaurant over the road from the Empress Hotel. "There's a place over there that looks just fine," she said, leaning over and pointing in the direction of Rattenbury's. "Could you drop us off there?"

Howell swung into a loading bay.

"Come on, Mom," Emily said, putting an arm around my neck. "Let's go."

"How will you get home?" Howell asked.

"We'll take a cab," I said.

We stood on the curb watching him drive away, and Emily turned to me.

"All alone in the big city, Mom," she smiled, putting her hand in mine. That was a favorite catchphrase of ours—one we used whenever we found ourselves temporarily lost. I felt the velvet softness of her skin under mine and gave her another squeeze. She returned the compliment. She hadn't done much of that lately and the pressure of her hand in mine felt warm and comforting. When we took our seats in the restaurant she took over the business of ordering.

"I'm going to order tea and ice cream for you, Mom, is that okay?" she asked.

"Fine with me," I told her, fishing in my purse for dark glasses. My eyes, nose and cheeks were swollen to a bright pink. I hoped nobody would look closer.

Emily announced gravely to the waiter, "It's my mother's birthday and I'd like ice cream for both of us please."

"I'll see what I can do," he told her. Ten minutes later he was back at our table with two small silver dishes of vanilla, strawberry and chocolate ice cream, one of them topped by a lit candle.

"There you are, Mom," he said with a flourish. "And a very happy birthday to you!" The candle was short and squat and about to slide off the summit of the ice cream. But it made the afternoon into an occasion, compensating for the past few hours and turning my heart inside out with love for my daughter.

"Thanks, darling," I told her. "Now I feel really special." I smiled at her. "Good thing he didn't know my age."

"Would've made it look like a voodoo doll," she said, glancing at my ice cream. I had to laugh at her candor. "Now pour your tea," she said. "You know how you say it always makes things better."

Outside, the early afternoon light fell golden and mild across the gardens of the Empress Hotel. The Port Angeles ferry barked a long blast, then two short ones as it squeezed into the narrow harbor. Next door in the Crystal Gardens, a pair of sapphire macaws screamed and chattered among the palms, and along the boulevards, hanging baskets of lobelia and impatiens glowed in the clear air. In spite of the shattering row between Howell and me, Victoria still felt like a good place to be. Emily was alleviating the stress of the morning by scraping her bowl clean and sucking noisily on the Coke she had ordered. I looked around the restaurant at the tables of quiet, civil people, so different in appearance and manner from those I had grown up with back home. We were most of us from English stock, but here the men and women seemed smaller and chunkier, with fine brushes of hair I fancied they must have evolved against the harsh Canadian winter. I warmed to their reticence and self-composure—my own sense of shyness didn't feel out of place here.

"This is a good place to be," I said, thinking out loud.

"It's great. We could come back every week," Emily replied.

"Not just this restaurant," I laughed. "I mean Canada."

"Oh. Right." She laughed at her mistake.

"They're good people."

"Who?" she asked.

"Everyone we've met so far." Apart from the bank manager, I told myself.

"They're okay," she acknowledged.

"And you've got both your parents in one place."

"Doesn't count if they fight," she said.

"That wasn't much fun, was it?" I conceded.

"You frighten me when the two of you get so weird."

"I know. I'm sorry."

"So what're you going to do?" she asked.

"Some honest thinking," I said. "Figure out if there's a way to make this thing work."

She didn't reply. Her face had become grave. When I turned back to look at her a few moments later, I caught her nibbling again at the quick of her nails.

That evening, I took myself for a long walk along the waterway. Emily and I had taken an apartment in a highrise block in Esquimalt and I had discovered that the winding path at the water's edge was a quick way to reach the city. It also offered a retreat that let me pound out the fear and confusion of the past few weeks. There, at one turn in the walkway, a great blue heron perched on an offshore spur, one leg tucked elegantly under a wing. This was my favorite refuge. As I sat and watched the bird, I addressed my unquiet thoughts to him. That evening I thought especially about the advice friends had given me before I left South Africa. *You've never fully worked through your difficulties with Howell,* they had warned me. *You're giving up your trump card by taking Emily over to him. Set foot in Canada and he'll move heaven and earth to get her under his control. You'll be left out in the cold. On top of that you could end up on the streets. The country's in a giant recession and you won't find work easily. Are you seriously giving up everything here? Why don't you simply step in front of a train?* He's her father, I kept telling them. He loves her. He has his quirks, but he's never wavered in his responsibilities. Besides, she needs both parents in the same city.

We couldn't go on shuttling her back and forth like a piece of cargo. *You're making the biggest mistake of your life,* they had said. This evening it looked as though they had been right all along.

The truth was that we had never resolved the difficulties that had caused us to divorce eight years before. Both of us had simply shut the door on our marriage and walked away. With time, I had come to believe that the past had been forgotten. That both of us were now older and wiser. But I had been proven wrong. Howell had not changed the view he had always had of me as a less than adequate mother. If anything, he seemed more fanatical than ever about taking control of his daughter's life. I remembered again why we had parted in the first place. There had been our persistent difficulty in discussing problems coupled with his insistence on running Emily's life as though it were a science project. What was I doing then? Had I really believed that eight years would mellow him? Make him more amenable to reason and discussion? He had proved today that he was still the same old Howell. If anything, more irascible than ever. If I was going to stay in Canada, the choice would have to be my own entirely. I would be a fool to fall for his blandishments. All the same, as Emily's parents, we needed to pull together.

Both of us wanted to do the right thing for her. Both of us *knew* what the right thing was. But the demons that lurked below the surface of our relationship always seemed to rear up and destroy our good intentions. What we desperately needed was counselling. Some form of intervention and guidance that would help all of us negotiate this bumpy road together. Howell had always refused professional guidance before, the few sessions we had gone to before we divorced ending in strife and bitterness. He was adamant that no one was going to tell him how to live his life. And then of course there was the real worry of how to earn a living here. Under the terms of our divorce settlement, Howell did not pay me alimony or child support and that would not change now. Although he paid Emily's school, clothing and medical expenses, it was up to me to provide for her when she was with me. Until I was on my feet again, I didn't know how I could manage this. Where he was comfortably settled and worked from home, it was unlikely that I would ever again establish the contacts and circle of acquaintances I had built up in South Africa. There was also the nagging feeling that if I chose to return, I might not be able to pick up my old life again. Job trails go cold—even in the short time I had been away. And then there were the memories of Emily in the after-school daycare center I had been forced to put her into when Howell emigrated. Dropping her at school before eight in the morning and fetching her ten hours later—both of us white-faced with fatigue—had left me aching with guilt. The only time we had together was a couple of hours in the evening and a half-hour every morning. I was determined that neither of us would go through this again. I needed Howell. To be there as a parent for Emily. And to help me out as I built up my life again in Canada.

But the little click I'd heard that morning had told me that from now on, I was on my own. I was free to make whatever choices I decided were best and the single most important question facing me was *which way to turn*. A part of me was already in love with the quiet and calm of Canada. For the best part of twenty years I had lived under a pervasive anxiety like everyone else in South Africa. Here, I was hypnotized by the sight of children playing in the streets till dusk or people waiting at bus stops late at night. I was astonished by the open frontages of homes without padlocked gates, high walls and razor wire. I had seen strollers parked on front porches, garden furniture a few feet from the sidewalk, and even a house where the inhabitants hung coats outside the front door. Emily and I had lived in a war zone for long enough. At least here the country was not at war with us.

"Can we talk about what happened yesterday?" I asked Howell the following morning. I had called him as soon as I got up. Emily was still asleep—a luxury I allowed her every day now. Here in Canada the school year was coming to an end and if I stayed, she would begin school in September. In the meantime, she was on an extended holiday. While she slept, I hoped Howell and I would have time to regain some perspective on the heated emotions of the day before.

"What's there to say?" he answered abruptly.

"I could ask you to apologize. Or at least tell me what made you lose it the way you did."

He gave a short laugh. "There's no need for either. I think you know why I did what I did." I could feel a flush of fury racing through me. I gripped the telephone, took a breath and started again.

"Look Howell. It was an act of faith to come here. You've been here for nearly four years. You know Canada well. If we're going to make a go of it, I can't live with you as my enemy. We need to pull together."

"I'll do the best I can. But the real reason you're here is because of Emily."

"That's absolutely true. We both want the best for her."

Howell's silence affirmed this.

I took a deep breath and decided to go for it. "It's not going to work unless we get some help. I can't compete with a shower of gifts or a Dad who tries to be a pal. Emily needs a parent. I believe we could do with some help to find out more about that."

"She's got me."

"When she's with you she can go to bed anytime she wants. She doesn't eat properly. And she's picked up on some of your bad habits." My voice sounded more shrill than I had intended.

"Such as?" Howell's tone was defensive.

"The way you speak to me for a start."

"I speak to you the way you deserve, Gillian. If your child shows no respect for you, look to yourself." There was a faint echo in my head of someone else expressing similar sentiments. Where had I heard them before?

"We have to get help. I can't think straight. I feel as though you're the enemy."

"Just because you're falling apart doesn't mean *I* need help," Howell retorted.

"We're both Emily's parents. We have to do this together."

"Well go sort yourself out then. I'll be a parent to her in the meantime."

God I hated him. I hated myself. I took myself back to the walkway to think. I should have realized Howell would be intransigent. It wasn't only my short temper with Emily that had set him off the day before. Deep in my heart, I knew what else it was that had sent him over the edge.

As soon as I arrived, he had expected me to make up my mind about staying or leaving. He couldn't understand why I had kept my options open and hadn't hit the ground running, checking out job prospects and searching the newspaper for a permanent place to live. He had been patient and helpful during our first few weeks. He had paid all of our expenses and been an unstintingly generous father to Emily. Now he was running short on understanding. Instead of cooperating, I had dallied, then come up with a temporary plan to stay. Only until the end of summer, I told him. That's why we'd been out to fix up bank, telephone and hydro accounts. The truth was that five weeks had been just enough time to frighten me senseless about the prospect of starting all over again. I was a forty-two-year-old forced to go back to kindergarten and in every direction I turned my own incompetence stared me in the face. The humiliation of not being able to navigate my way around this new society sent me into a panic. There had been an incident on a bus, two weeks after we arrived, that still made me burn with embarrassment. Emily and I had climbed aboard and unaware of the exact fare rule I had fumbled to put together enough money, holding up a line of people behind me. "Got two loonies here?" the bus driver had boomed down at me while I flushed scarlet with humiliation. "How could he *do* that to us?" I hissed to Emily as we took our seats. "Calling us crazy in front of the whole bus." Realizing my mistake, she had grinned and pointed out that a loonie was a one-dollar coin. The bus driver hadn't been calling my mental competence into question—he'd simply been helping me find change. I hadn't known whether to laugh or cry. My daughter knew these things. Why didn't I? I had forgotten that she had been a regular visitor to Canada for several years now and that I was the learner. So, apparently, had Howell. He had been hectoring me about what sort of work I could get ever since I arrived.

"I could bag groceries," I told him. "That's about all I'm capable of doing right now." Why didn't I apply for the position of a tour bus guide in the meantime, he suggested.

"I don't even know my way around town yet," I protested. "I'd be fired in a day. Besides, I'm not a landed immigrant, Howell. I need a SIN card to work."

Late at night while Emily slept, I watched the local news on television in a futile attempt to make sense of the place names, products and even the politicians that represented this corner of Canada. There were grannies forming human chains in front of chainsaws in a forest called Clayoquot next door to a town called Ucluelet. What was that all about? And what in heaven's name was the Meech Lake Accord and the Charlottetown Agreement? Was there a local radio station that could tell me what was going on in this town? Who the mayor was? What if I needed a doctor or a dentist? Where to buy a car? I supposed I'd have to learn to drive all over again, I thought with a sinking heart. In South Africa, we drove on the left-hand side of the road. I was certain I was too old to make the transition to the right. I felt as though the part of my brain where life's most essential information was stored had been trepanned overnight.

Sitting and watching the great blue heron two days later, I knew I didn't have the courage to start all over again. I had no choice but to return to Africa. My eighty-five-year-old father lived on his own in Zimbabwe. If I moved to Harare I could look after both Emily and him at the same time. His townhouse was big enough to accommodate all of us and if I put my teaching experience to work, I could easily find work in the city. I had taken O and A levels in the country, taught English at university level in South Africa and knew the literature syllabus backwards. There would be old friends to look up, familiar places to visit, and the warm-heartedness of the people would make it easy to adjust to a new society. In my mind's eye I pictured Emily running free across the veld, just the way I had done as a child. While she and my father got to know each other again, I would be employed and useful. The more I thought about it, the more a move to Zimbabwe seemed the one sane solution to my problems.

Howell was unyielding.

"I do not want Emily growing up in Africa," he said. We had been over this countless times before. Howell loved the continent but believed that whites had no future there. Africa belonged to the Africans, he said. Whites had shown themselves unable to withstand the devastating heat, droughts, tribal conflicts and arcane beliefs of its peoples.

I argued back. We would have a home there. I could teach and Emily would have a grandfather. Zimbabwe was a peaceful, stable country. I had visited my father just over a year before and made a mental note that Harare was still a good place to live.

"We've talked this over before," Howell said to me. "You know what we both feel about living in Africa."

"I don't have a choice," I told him.

"Yes you do."

"How?" I asked.

He paused before answering. "For Emily's sake, let me take care of her."

"Meaning?"

"If the worst comes to the worst, you go back and leave her here with me."

"*Never,*" I shot back.

"Think about it," Howell said in a smooth purr. "What you want is not necessarily what she *needs.*"

I stared at him in disbelief. Had this been his plan all along? To bring Emily to Canada, then make life so difficult for me that I had no choice but to leave? Obviously he had no measure of what I was made of. No court or human being would ever separate me from my daughter. Besides, had he thought about how much Emily needed her mother?

"Have you thought about Emily?" I asked him. "Surely you understand how much she needs me?"

"I don't go along with that," he said, his voice calm and reasonable. "She needs a stable parent, that's all."

"And I'm not? Is that what you're saying?" I could hear my voice spiralling out of control and tears pricking the back of my eyes.

"Look at you. You're hardly capable of shopping for milk."

"If there's one thing you've done for me today," I told him, an icy calm keeping my voice steady, "it's to help me make up my mind." I looked him squarely in the eye. "I can't stay here with you," I told him. "Emily and I are going back to Cape Town."

The worst of it was that a part of me always caved in to Howell's opinion. Without the definitions bestowed by employment, an address and people who could vouch for me, I seemed to have lost all sense of who I was.

"You're no one and nothing," I had caught myself saying to the reflection in the mirror each morning. But that had been before I heard the click. Now, instead of faceless misery, there was something else I sensed in myself—a core, an ember, a tough little nugget of determination that refused to be doused or shattered. And the face in the mirror had lost its despairing stare. Instead, it said back to me *do what you're capable of doing. Don't put yourself down. Do the best you're capable of for both of you.*

"I want to go back to South Africa as soon as I can book our air tickets," I told Howell resolutely, a day or two later. "I've thought it through and I have no choice. I can't work here. I have no use in this society. I must get Emily back before the July school holidays end in South Africa."

The agreement was that if things didn't work out, Emily and I could return to Cape Town as soon as I wanted, and I knew that Howell could not dishonor this.

He said nothing for a moment. He looked at me steadily, then stood up and walked over to the window.

"Are you doing this to hurt me?" he asked.

"Of course not," I said.

"Then why?"

"Because I have a home there. And work. And most important of all, friends. They're like family to me."

He turned to face me. "You'll find all of that here in time," he said. "That's not the real reason, is it?"

I chose my words carefully. I didn't want this to escalate into another argument. "The real reason is that it's just too hard to make a go of it when I have you against me," I said. "I thought it would be best to have both of us in one city again. But I feel as though you're out to keep Emily all to yourself and make me into the enemy."

"That's nonsense."

"It feels that way, Howell. I want to go."

"If that's what you want I can't stop you," he said.

When he turned back from the window, it looked as though there were tears in his eyes. For a brief moment I thought he might relent and tell me I had a point. I stepped towards him, but he backed away. "Light from the water's pretty strong this afternoon," he said gruffly. I should have known that Howell never cried.

Neither of us knew it at the time, but the moment marked the beginning of the first real relationship that was to grow between us.

T ❖ W ❖ O

I broke the news to Emily the following morning. We would be returning to South Africa as soon as I could book our air tickets to Cape Town. She said nothing. Her head sank onto her chest and tears rolled down her face, pooling into dark stains on her T-shirt.

"You promised me. You *promised,* Mommy," was all she would say.

"I promised I would do my best to make a go of it here. You saw what happened between your father and me. I can't do it without his cooperation."

"Yes you can. You just have to make more effort. Isn't that what you're always telling me?" She lifted her face to mine and the depth of pain and betrayal in her eyes hit me like a blow.

How had we done this to her? This was our daughter, our long-awaited gift from God, our golden child like no other. We had sworn she would never experience the hurts and frustrations of childhood that Howell and I had known. She would never want for anything, neither in love nor in material goods. We would shield her from the humiliations, the stumbling blocks, the moments of fear and loneliness that had scarred our early years. I remembered the prayer I had written for her, the week after she was born.

Now God,
While all is gold within her
And not the common red of our existence,
Set Your seal on her,
Stay my hand from harm.

23

All we had seemed to do since then was to hurt her. I sat down on the chair next to her and leaned closer, offering a hug, but she tore away from me.

"Leave me alone. I hate you both!" She pushed away from the table and ran from the room, slamming the bedroom door to mark her anguish. From the kitchen I could hear her muffled sobs. How in the name of God had we done this to her? I thought back to the night she was born, her solemn little face and the love and wonder that had welled up in me as I looked into her eyes. I saw Howell cradling her in his arms, walking up and down the delivery ward, talking to her all the while. I remembered the flowers he had strung over her baby carriage and how he walked her down to the water's edge, showing her how to put first one foot and then the other into the surf. She was surely the most beloved child in the universe, perfect to us in every way. There were other pictures as well, not as idyllic. Of Howell flying her to London to see *Cats* as a sixth birthday present. Of the lavish birthday parties he had thrown for her, with ponies, circus clowns and magicians. Of times when I was caught on overseas assignments and had wandered around shopping centers in Rio de Janeiro, Tel Aviv, London and New York, picking up expensive peace offerings for her. After our divorce both of us had become relatively successful and she had never wanted for anything. But the gifts masked our guilt and she was quick to pick up on this. She did not want another new bicycle, doll's house or designer outfit. What she needed most was a mother and father, a place of her own, and the reasonable expectation that each day would be as predictable as the last. I had been overworked and burdened with too many responsibilities after our divorce. Howell had done his best to make it up to her. But when he emigrated, we may as well have abandoned our daughter to the daycare center I had to put her into. Now, as I folded clothes and packed shoes, I berated myself yet again for failing her. The single-parent family is a travesty of human needs, I told myself for the thousandth time. Never mind what it does to adults. For children, it is nothing short of a catastrophe. If Emily slammed doors and refused to eat, she was not to blame. We were.

How could the couple who had clinked champagne glasses on that blustery wedding day in 1980 have turned into the bitter, foul-mouthed war veterans we had become? If you asked Howell, he would say with characteristic reserve that we were merely incompatible. All his disappointments, the souring of every dream could be fused into that single adjective. If pressed, he would admit that I had been pathologically critical, a world-class whiner, a pennypincher who worried and fretted about money and a stick-in-the-mud who was abnormally afraid of taking chances.

"You're not adventurous," he had said to me a year or two into our marriage, and in those few words he had summed up everything he was, and I was not. Folding clothes from the laundry and turning out drawers, I tried to trace how we had ever reached this low point in our lives. We had been written up as the *Couple with Everything* when Howell's documentary on Soweto was nominated for an award. We had been young and filled with ambition and nothing had stood in our way. But the truth was that as long as things went well we had had a good partnership. When difficulties arose we had no idea how to negotiate this new and uncharted territory. We fought bitterly to protect our vulnerabilities, both of us living in an emotional vacuum, unable to share fears and failures. Then there had been Eleanor's interference in our marriage. Howell's mother had never wanted me to marry her son and I could still see her cool, disapproving eyes when I thought back to our first years together. And there had been years of living hand-to-mouth. Years in which we had become stubbornly entrenched in different patterns of parenting. Both of us used Emily as the battleground on which to prove our own theories about everything from evolution to the correct pacifier. Somewhere along the way, in the manner of many of our generation, we had stopped questioning ourselves. Weren't we the most enlightened, privileged, well-educated age group of all time? Weren't we entitled to the best that life had to offer? If we messed up, the fault had to lie somewhere out there. Not with us. The only trouble was that the pain felt like it was right here inside me. This was the impasse we found ourselves in on that June day in 1993. Once again, I had failed. I had wanted to do the best for Emily, but I had arrived in Canada stupidly naive about work prospects. I had forgotten the difficulties of negotiating with Howell. I had been grateful to leave a country that was in full-blown political turmoil and happy to turn my back on a relationship that had blown up in my face. But the bottom line was that yet again I was trying to sort out my own confusion on Emily's time. The sense of self-disgust I felt as I packed that June morning plunged me lower than I had sunk in days. Much later, I would think back to the ringing telephone and laugh out loud. Howell's sense of timing when he had a pitch to make had always been impeccable.

"Gillian?" Howell's voice over the telephone sounded as though he hadn't had much sleep.

"What is it, Howell?"

"Can I talk to you? A few minutes is all I need."

"Sure."

"No, I mean can I come over and see you?"

I glanced at my watch. It was seven A.M. "If it's that urgent, come on over now," I said. I had got up early that morning to make a phone call to Cape Town. My apartment had been standing empty since I'd left a month before and I had called an old and close friend to open it up for me. I'd probably be back by the end of June or the middle of July at the latest, I told her. She had been tactful enough not to ask what had gone wrong. "You can tell me everything when you get back," she said. "I'll meet you at the airport."

Howell arrived fifteen minutes later, unshaven and with deep rings under his eyes. He had a paper bag filled with fresh bagels, cream cheese and lox, Emily's favorite breakfast, in his hands.

"Is the kettle on the boil?" he asked.

"I've just made fresh tea," I told him.

He sat down at the kitchen table and I put a cup in front of him.

"So," he breathed. "Everything all right?"

I nodded. He glanced around the room at the open suitcases and small piles of clothes next to them. "Em still asleep?"

"I can't seem to wake her up these days."

Neither one of us wanted to express the suspicion that she preferred sleep to the realities of her waking life.

"I'll come straight to the point," he said.

"Please do," I invited.

"I have a proposition to make."

"Howell, please . . ."

He held up a hand. "No. Please. Wait. At least until you've heard me." We had been through this before. I had been led by the nose with so many of his promises in the past. Not another one. Not now.

He looked at my face, waiting for my cue. "What is it?" I asked.

He leaned forward and chose his words slowly and carefully. "If you consent to stay for at least another couple of months, I will agree to go into counselling with you to figure out how we can become better parents to Emily."

"Howell . . ." his name came out in one long sigh. "Look. We've done everything we can. Nothing has worked. We've got to do damage control. When we're apart, we get on just fine. Together, it's war."

"Gillian. You didn't hear me. I'll do *whatever it takes*." I looked into his face for the first time since he had begun talking. There was something like a plea in his eyes. I had never seen that before.

"For Emily?" I said.

"Of course, for Emily. She's our daughter. I think you know that aside from all my other failings, I've been a pretty good father to her. I love her dearly. I know you do too. But we've made terrible mistakes and I don't really know why. She doesn't deserve to be the scapegoat."

"Counselling. You said you would actually go into professional counselling?"

"Yes."

"You. You who said you would never see another therapist in your life after Kate Lyons."

"I who said I would never see another therapist in my life after Kate Lyons."

"Who? Where? How do we even go about finding someone?"

He stopped and put his hands palm down on the table. "Well. As a matter of fact . . ."

"Howell Edwards," I said. Somewhere deep inside I could feel something like a grin starting. I should have known. Howell's little black books. Filled with the telephone numbers of contacts in every city of the world. His *World Directories*. His lifelines. "You've already lined up whoever this person is going to be," I said. "How did you manage to do all of this in the space of one day?"

27

"Do you agree? Say you agree and I'll tell you," he grinned.

I poured myself another cup of tea. Emily appeared around the door, hungover from too much television the night before. "Want a bagel, darling?" Howell asked.

"Okay," she said listlessly. She didn't bother to greet either one of us. She slumped into a chair and began to tear at the fresh bread.

"Here. Let me help you." Howell took a knife and deftly split a bagel in two. Then he spread cream cheese and layered lox on top. "All that's missing are the capers," he said. When she was tiny, Emily had fallen in love with the sour little berries and she could eat a jar at a time. She bit in and jiggled a foot, still not looking at either of us.

"Tell me first who you've lined up. Then I'll give you my decision," I said.

"Her name's Alma Newman. I called friends of mine in Santa Barbara yesterday morning and asked them for the name of a licensed family and marriage therapist here. They're both practicing psychiatrists at a family clinic down there and they called back yesterday afternoon with a name. I spoke to her last night. I've set up a session for tomorrow morning."

"What're you talking about?" Emily asked sullenly.

"Better tell her," I said to Howell.

"You mean you agree?"

I had forgotten this aspect of Howell. When he wanted something, he would move heaven and earth to get it. Everywhere he went, he carried a briefcase of little black books, indexed for every continent in the world. He had friends in Moscow, New Zealand, Tierra del Fuego and Greenland. "There's no one in the world who isn't a phone call away," he liked to say. And I remembered how I had marvelled at the way he could call friends around the world, picking up on conversations he had left off five years before as though they had simply been temporarily interrupted.

"You know, Em," I said to our daughter, "there are times when I still have to bow to your Dad's ingenuity."

"What does *that* mean?" she asked.

"It means your Mom has agreed to stay on indefinitely," Howell grinned at her.

T ❖ H ❖ R ❖ E ❖ E

Alma Newman's consultation room was small and welcoming, with sisal mats on the floor, beamed ceilings and a window that opened onto lopsided tomato vines in her backyard. The sagging bookshelves were filled with battered sets of the Russian novels she loved to read, and the sofas against each wall were faded and comfortable, as though they had absorbed all the indignities of a lifetime and were impervious to further insult. The single jarring note was the hot pink of the tissue holders planted next to a wastepaper basket at the foot of each sofa. On our first visit, Howell had presumed that Alma provided these as a thoughtful gesture for clients suffering from summer allergies. It was only after he had glanced into a basket at his feet and recognized tell-tale traces of mascara on a wad of tissue that he realized the boxes were there to help exorcise the diverse array of human miseries Alma dealt with on an everyday basis.

But aside from that single sign, the room felt as safe as a nursery. And in a sense that is what it became for us—a protected place where, with time and a growing sense of trust, we felt secure enough to examine the beginnings of our bitter feud and to unravel the tangle of disappointments and anger that had destroyed our marriage.

In our first session, Alma wasted little time in getting to the point: Why had we married in the first place? she asked. Could we remember how it felt to be in love all those years ago? That was easy, I jumped in right away. I had very much wanted to be part of a family. And Howell's mother and father, his two younger brothers and the easygoing, rambling seaside house they called home seemed to embody everything I had ever wanted in a family.

"Are you saying you married Howell's family and not Howell?" she asked me.

"Isn't that what people do?" I said. "You marry a man, you marry his family?"

"Perhaps," she replied. "But usually we choose our partners first. The family comes along as part of the deal. What happened to your own family?"

I told her that my parents had decided to leave South Africa for Zimbabwe when I was nineteen. My mother could not tolerate the injustices in South Africa and Zimbabwe, newly independent and familiar to both of them from the sixties when we had lived there as a family, seemed a good place to settle. I had a sister in New York whom I saw every two years or so. I did not tell her about the cool relationship I had with my parents, or that my sister and I were too different to be close.

Howell's reply made his disappointment in our marriage explicit. He had been under the impression, he told Alma, that there was plenty we had in common. We both loved movies, held the same political convictions and liked to travel. But aside from these early attractions? Well, he shrugged, a dozen years of arguing about almost everything had made it difficult to remember what little he liked about me in the first place. Alma nodded. Was there anything else?

"I soon found out what she felt about a whole lot of other things she never mentioned before we were married," Howell added.

"Can you say what they were?"

"She can be pretty rigid about things," Howell said. "If you put a jar back in a cupboard with honey on it, she'll blow up. If I was late for meals, it drove her mad. She couldn't understand that if I was out on location, I was working and that was all there was to it. She used to wait up until I got home at two in the morning and then *wham,* let me have it!"

Alma looked at Howell. "One of the things I'd like both of you to do when you're in here is to address your feelings to each other," she said. "Not to me. In here you both have names. Gillian is not *she* and you are not *he*." Then she turned to me. Did I want to comment on what Howell had said? I shrugged. There was little point in contradicting him. Everything he said was true. Right after we married, Howell had gone off to shoot a documentary that had kept him away for days on end. I had given up lighting candles and putting out our wedding china each evening. For the first two months of our marriage, I hadn't eaten a proper meal with him. But what had hurt me most was the way he had belittled my loneliness, calling me selfish for being unable to cope with his absences. He'd added that if I really wanted to be supportive, I could be a little more courteous to the crew members he brought home after night shoots for planning sessions.

"You've got a wildcat in there, Howell," I heard his cameraman tell him once while I scrambled eggs at two in the morning. "She'll have you punching a time clock unless you make it clear who's boss around here." Within a year, while I continued teaching literature at our local college and Howell made two more documentaries, our arguments had scaled up into bitter conflicts about money (never enough, I told him), sex (too little, he complained), time together (nonexistent, we both agreed) and children. Howell wanted to start a family immediately. I wanted more time to establish a home, get on our feet and test our strengths as a couple before we became parents. I had begun to feel I hardly knew the man I had married. The free spirit I had known who would take off to explore locations at the drop of a hat had become an exhausted grouch who slept all of Sunday and suddenly scrutinized bills for evidence of my spendthrift ways. In fact, every penny of our salaries went on strict necessities and my sister had taken to parcelling up old clothes for me so that I could save on clothing bills. By the end of our first year together, I was asking myself over yet another meal of hamburger and chips how we had ever agreed to spend the rest of our lives together.

"Sounds as though you're carrying a lot of excess luggage there," Alma summed up. "I realize that both of you are here to find out more about being better parents to your daughter, but the point I want you to think about," she went on, "is that couples choose each other for very profound reasons. It's never a random choice. Even after divorce, the pulls are still there." If we really wanted to clear the air between us and go on to find successful partnerships elsewhere, if we wanted to become better parents, we would have to understand why we had chosen each other in the first place.

"Think of this as a debriefing period. Perhaps even a de*griefing* period," she said. "When I listen to both of you, I hear that neither of you has let go of the angers you stored up during your marriage. You won't let go—you *can't* let go—until you know yourselves and each other very well indeed."

Howell was skeptical. And fidgety. He wanted immediate results. Couldn't Alma give us a couple of suggestions we could put into practice right away? We were here because we wanted to be better parents for Emily. Not to repair the relationship between us. What had happened long ago no longer interested him. He wanted to get on and make a new life for himself as quickly as possible.

"There's no quick fix," Alma told him. "If you stay with counselling, you'll learn more about yourself than you ever thought possible. In six months' time, you'll have very different opinions of each other from the ones you hold now." Howell bridled at the suggestion. Six months was an eternity to invest in a relationship he had no interest in maintaining.

"We have no intention of getting back together again," he told Alma firmly. "Six weeks seemed to me long enough to find a way of getting along." Alma listened without comment and turned to me. How did I feel about committing myself to a period of intensive self-examination? I didn't know. I was worn down by the petty squabbles and unspoken fury that seemed to characterize our every encounter. Worst of all was the effect this was having on Emily. Just nine years old, she could not remember when her parents had ever been married and she had never seen us get along together. Her face often reflected the tension she picked up when Howell and I argued over mealtimes, bedtimes, even what shoes she was allowed to wear. Lately she had refused to wash or to take a bath and at every opportunity she would sneak away to slump in front of the television. Our brave experiment had failed. We both loved our daughter dearly and it was with the hope that we could make a new life for her that all three of us were in Canada in the first place. But there had simply been too many unresolved differences between Howell and myself to allow this to work. If we were unable to find a way of respecting each other's differences, or of cooperating as parents, I told Alma, I would leave Canada and return to

South Africa as soon as possible. Howell knew he would be separated once more from Emily and that she would have to revert to the old system of travelling the punishing distances between Cape Town and Canada to spend two months of each year with him.

It was the specter of yet another parting in the soulless surroundings of an airport that loomed in front of us now. No matter how tough things had become, I did not want to inflict this again on Emily, Howell or myself. I still felt great unhappiness about our breakup, but my deepest feelings of guilt were reserved for the memory of Emily, just seven years old, looking back at me as she was hustled off to board her plane. If I could make sure this scene was never played again, a few months with Alma was a small price to pay.

"Well, it's up to both of you how long it takes," Alma concluded. "My job is to help you understand what got you here in the first place. We'll work on how you deal with each other and understanding yourselves better. The insights and skills you'll pick up here are powerful tools. You'll use them in other areas of your lives as well. But," she warned, "there's plenty of painful work to do, and at times you'll be tempted to give it all up." Six months, I was thinking, a minimum of six months before we can begin to function as normal human beings again.

In fact, we were to spend a full year with Alma. At times, when our arguments escalated into fierce battles leaving us incapable of settling the simplest disputes, we saw her twice a week. Howell paid for the sessions, often writing out a $900 check for the month. Outside of Alma's rooms, his manner continued to veer between cool formality and sharp impatience. He had been as helpful as he could be in settling us in during our first two months in Canada. But money was running low and he wanted finality. Was I going to apply for landed immigrant status or not? As an act of faith in the outcome of our sessions, I formally lodged my application to remain in Canada soon after we began seeing Alma. But a small calcification in one of my lungs delayed acceptance and I was unable to look for work. Coming from Africa, my state of health made the examining doctors understandably cautious. I was tested for cancer, for tuberculosis and finally for AIDS. I had never really been ill in my life and the lengthy tests I had to undergo reduced me to floods of despair. Without money to live on or friends to confide in, I found myself splashing tears of self-pity over spaghetti boxes in the supermarket or snivelling into sodden tissues in the anonymous safety of buses.

"What you need is someone to play with, Mommy," Emily told me in all seriousness one afternoon. And as always there was wisdom in her words. Was I crazy to give up friends, work and a home to bring her to Canada, only to put myself through the torture of excavating a dead marriage and picking over the corpse? There were days when it was all I could do to slice an onion, cook up a plate of spaghetti and heat a jar of pasta sauce for Emily's dinner.

F ❖ O ❖ U ❖ R

"My wife watches Oprah Winfrey."

Howell had kicked off a joint session with Alma by listing some of my shortcomings as a parent.

Alma nodded and indicated for him to continue.

"Well, that says a lot about her, doesn't it? If you have to watch Oprah Winfrey to figure out how to be a good mother, I think there's something seriously wrong with you."

Howell glanced over at me and back to Alma.

"She's forever picking up on these wild theories," he continued, "then testing them out on Emily."

Again, Alma gave no more than a nod.

"For instance she's got this system," he cleared his throat, "where she doles out fourteen jujubes a week to Emily. Like money or something. Then she adds and takes away from them for good behavior and stuff. It's degrading."

At last he drew a brief response from Alma. "I don't quite understand," she said. "Can you explain why that's degrading?"

"Well, she picked up this idea of making a 'candy bank' from one of these shows she watches. She keeps a supply of candy and Emily can earn stuff if she does chores without being told to. She has to give back stuff if she forgets to make her bed or leaves wet towels on the floor."

"And why is this bad?" Alma repeated.

"I think it encourages the wrong values."

"I don't understand. You mean you're rewarding good work with a visit to the dentist?"

Howell grinned. "That too. I don't encourage sugar in my house. But at least I don't believe in *paying* a child to learn."

"How do you think it should be done?" Alma asked.

"With lots of explaining and patience. It's a process."

"Do you find that's what works for you?"

"Not always. I like to say something, then consider Emily's reaction. Gillian's way is like rewarding a dog for sitting up. It debases a child's instinctive feelings."

"Go on." Alma had not looked at me yet and I was beginning to squirm in my seat. She had warned us that this would happen and her rules were firm. No interruptions while the other was talking.

"I believe in the dignity of feelings," Howell went on. "Appealing to a child's best instincts. I have a lot more patience with that idea than Gillian does."

"How do you measure Gillian's way?" Alma asked.

"I've seen her in action. She asks Emily to do something and then she expects her to do it immediately."

"How does she ask?"

"She just asks," Howell said.

"Doesn't bully her? Yell?"

"Well . . ."

"Is that a yes or a no?"

"Well, it's a close call. I've heard her get pretty impatient. She expects Emily to do what she tells her to do right then. Even when Emily is doing something else, you know, like drawing or reading. If she tells her to come to the dinner table, she expects her to come right away. Isn't that imposing her will?"

"If those are the rules of the household, I expect she's showing Emily how to get on easily within the system."

"It's just her manner I don't like," Howell said. "The reason we're here is because I couldn't take her telling Emily to shut up anymore."

"What was it like for you when you were growing up?" Alma sat forward a little.

Howell gave a short laugh. "My father was impossible. I could be in the middle of putting the last strut on a model airplane and if he called we had to drop everything and run." He looked to Alma for a response. She said nothing and waited for the parallel to sink in. Howell did not respond immediately. When he did, he twisted away with a quick, sharp grin.

"Oh I see," he said. "It's going to be all about me and how *I* was brought up, is that it?"

"Too quick for me," Alma smiled.

Howell shifted in his seat. "Well come to think of it, Gillian *is* a lot like my father," he said. "I felt like a toy soldier when I was a kid— always being ordered about, never having a chance to say what I liked. If I didn't jump to it, I got locked in the garage." He took a breath and added, "I can't bear to see a child being bullied." He stopped abruptly, glancing over at me. His last words hung in the silence that followed. Finally he said to Alma, "Are you telling me this is more about *me* than it is about Emily?"

"I haven't said a word yet," Alma remarked innocently. "What do *you* think?"

"Well I've seen Emily look pretty miserable when she's been told to do this or that by Gillian."

"You feel badly for her," Alma stated.

"She's just a baby. There's still time for her to learn, isn't that right?" Howell appealed.

"She's nine? No, ten? Is that right?"

"She's about to turn ten."

"She's no longer a baby. By five, most children have a clear idea of how they fit into the family and what the outside world looks like. By eight they have a fair sense of right and wrong. By ten, a kid as bright as Emily should be building a sense of how the world works, and taking on small responsibilities."

Howell looked somber. "I don't agree," he said.

"Which part don't you agree with?" Alma asked.

"This whole idea of taking on responsibilities too young. Buckling down. Becoming a grownup before your time. Being trained to do *the right thing*."

"What do you feel that does to a child?"

"Crushes them, no question about it."

"I agree. If it's done harshly and with no empathy for a child's rate

of learning, you can destroy his spirit, make him into a mindless, con-
forming puppet. If it's done consistently and without punishment, it
teaches him to become competent in the way he handles his world."

"Exactly," Howell jumped in. "And I feel that Gillian manipulates
Emily into doing what Gillian thinks is best by using a primitive system of reward and punishment."

"Something like your father did to you?" Alma said.

Howell shifted uneasily in his chair. "I don't think that's *entirely*
true. Well, okay, maybe."

"Howell, I want you to know that I'm not siding with Gillian's way
of handling Emily. You both have different styles of parenting. Neither
is wholly wrong nor wholly right. And I suspect that when you're around,
there's a completely different interplay between all of you than when
Emily is alone with her mother."

"What do you mean?"

"Kids are as sharp as razors. Emily probably knows you don't ap-
prove of the way Gillian does things. She probably plays this up to get
out of doing things the way her Mom wants her to."

"I know Emily. She doesn't do that."

"Oh, come on. She's a kid," Alma said. "She knows exactly how to
get around her parents. Especially since she's cottoned on to the fact
that both of you feel as guilty as hell about what you've done to her."

"I'm just asking for fair treatment, that's all," Howell fumbled. But
Alma had driven a crucial point home. For the first time, he had made
a connection between his own disapproval of my parenting and the
anger he had never expressed at the way he had been brought up by his
father.

We were forty minutes into the session and I had nearly bitten through
my tongue obeying the rule not to interrupt. Howell had always made it
clear that he thought I was a poor mother and this had become a bitter
battle between us. Apart from my failure to stay calm under pressure, I
often drifted off into spaces of my own when I should have remained
focussed on Emily's needs. In the year after she was born, he complained that I slept too much, that I bought processed foods instead of
making her meals from scratch, and that I was so inept as a mother that

I had had to learn how to take care of her out of a book. He berated everything I read on baby and child care. If I had been a born mother, he told me, my instincts would have been enough. I told him there were no instincts to cure diaper rash. Secretly, I wondered whether other mothers possessed magic hands that soothed away rashes and fevers. But at two in the morning, suffering from cracked nipples and sleep deprivation with a baby who was cutting a tooth, I believed in all the help I could get. When all else failed, I resorted to tucking Emily into a kangaroo pouch and carrying her wherever I went. I had grown up alongside black women who carried their babies everywhere on their backs and I had never heard a black child cry.

All right, so I consulted books when Emily cut a tooth or got a rash. But there was one area I had always been sure about as a mother. No amount of persuasion would make me turn my child over to a caretaker or go back to full-time work while she was little. Nor was I going to follow the fashionable practice of "breaking her in" to an inflexible routine that suited me and no one else. And yet, it was in this area that I ran across the fiercest opposition. From Howell's mother, from friends, even from Howell himself. Other women were getting back to work, he reminded me constantly. Why couldn't I? Heaven knows, we could have done with the extra money. I had no idea how other mothers did it and castigated myself unendingly for the lack of organization in our life. There were days when I would mark off a time—three days away—as the first chance to take a bath. When the time came, I would forget to brush my teeth. Every other mother I had met in the nursing home had established a routine that ran like clockwork and loudly trumpeted her success at the get-togethers we arranged on Saturday afternoons. Most of these women were already back at work part-time and I marvelled at their stamina and ability to perform two jobs at once.

"Oh yes. I'm the meanest mother on the block," one of them crowed proudly. "If Tyler isn't down and out by six in the evening, I shut the door until the next morning. He soon cries himself to sleep." I was appalled. Surely this wasn't the way to treat a baby who simply needed comforting?

"You've got to establish who's boss from the word go," the same woman told me. She had gone back to a full-time job when her baby was three weeks old, carrying a breast pump in her briefcase.

"But who looks after him?" I asked. Why had she gone to the trouble of having a baby if she was going to hand him over to a stranger as soon as he was born?

"I've just taken on the most marvellous nanny," she said. "Besides, I don't have a clue what to do with a screaming scarlet brat. On the *one* occasion I took him to the office, I flung him into a corner and let my secretary take over. I just don't have the right genes to handle diapers." My tolerance—irrevocably damaged from lack of sleep—snapped.

"You have *no* right to do that to a baby," I blurted out. "I don't care how good your nanny is, your child is not her child. Besides, what happens when you let her go one day and the only parent your child has ever known will be taken away from him? What then?"

"My wife gets very hot under the collar these days," Howell apologized, stepping in to smooth things over. This had been our Saturday to host a gathering of mothers and babies and Howell was revelling in every minute of comparison between Emily and her peers. At eight months, our preemie was bigger than most of the children born at the same time, with a full head of blonde hair and an insatiable curiosity for exploring the corners of our rambling old house.

"They say the hormones in a breastfeeding mother are lethal," he added. "All Gillian needs to do is to get herself organized." It was true that most of the women were more rested and even-tempered than I. I was the only one screaming like a banshee. But when all was said and done, what they advocated *felt* wrong to me. Perhaps I was simply envious that they had got it right and I hadn't. I longed for someone to tell me I was doing okay. In spite of my exhaustion and lack of order, I *liked* being Emily's mother. My heart leapt through the ceiling when she stood up in her cot and shimmied her shoulders when I walked into the room. She seemed to think I was doing all right as a mother, even if no one else agreed.

Besides, I argued with Howell. What was the "quality time" these polished office harpies spoke about so smugly? An hour in the evening getting to know their babies all over again? What about the dozens of moments during the day when a child needs a mother to pick her up after a fall, to wipe her face, hug her, laugh with her, discover an ant, hold hands and look into her eyes? How did you program all of that into "quality time?" "That's all been disproven time and time again, Gillian," Howell's mother told me. "Look at my three. I was always busy when they were tiny—they had frauleins to look after them. I don't see any lasting damage." I was torn between guilt about not getting back to full-time work and doubt about my abilities as a mother. I saw myself as a disorganized, inept housekeeper who had failed miserably, not only in the eyes of other mothers, but also in the opinion of my husband and mother-in-law. All the same, I refused to give up being Emily's full-time parent.

"I may be a lousy mother in your opinion, Howell," I told him when he scorned my ham-handed attempts to run the house smoothly and belittled my exhaustion, "but at least I'm here twenty-four hours a day for Emily. She trusts me to be there for her and that's what counts." For the first three months of her life, our daughter had hardly cried and I had finally asked the district nurse if this was normal. "Don't worry," she assured me. "When you foul up, your baby will let you know."

"The point is that you slept so much of the time," Howell said. "It was left to me to take over." Alma watched our interaction closely. "And in my opinion," he went on, "you weren't focussed enough because of this depression thing you had."

Alma looked at me for an explanation. "You had postnatal depression?" she asked.

"I didn't *know* . . ." I began to defend myself.

"No. No need to apologize," she held up a hand. "Does that mean a yes or a no?"

"It means I don't know," I said. "I didn't know till years later that I must have been depressed. Emily came six weeks early. It took a while for me to get back on my feet. And," I looked across at Howell, "although Howell was very good about helping me with diapers and taking Emily for walks, I knew just after she was born that I no longer meant anything in his life." I heard my voice break. "Sometimes I think this may have affected the way I did things." I sounded more bitter than I intended, surprising myself. All of this had happened so long ago. Yet here in Alma's rooms, fragments of those times could come flooding back in seconds. I remembered how from the moment Emily was born,

Howell had spent hours helping her grasp a bottle, climb stairs, or explore the garden. He videotaped her every move, but was reluctant to share these moments with anyone else. At first, my heart had swelled with pride as I watched him shower Emily with affection. Then, as time went on and his criticism of me became more frequent, I couldn't help remembering Kate Lyons's ominous warning. I couldn't deny that Emily blossomed under his attention, but there were moments when I wondered whether Howell's devotion to his daughter wasn't obsessive. Whether what he really wanted was to have me out of the way altogether.

There had been one morning when Emily was five months old that would stay in my mind forever.

She still spent most of the day asleep in her baby carriage, I explained to Alma. That morning, I had wheeled the pram out onto the front lawn overlooking the ocean. I had stretched a cat net over her, tucked in the down comforter and hung a length of ribbon strung with big plastic beads above her head—she had already begun to explore everything within her grasp. Leaving her safely within my line of vision, I returned to the kitchen to make lunch. Twenty minutes later, I glanced up to see Howell checking on his daughter. First, he bent down to examine the brakes on the carriage, then he peered under the net to make sure Emily was covered. Next, I saw him remove the beads above her carriage and disappear around the back of the house, carrying them in his hand. I thought he may have found a bird dropping on them and taken them away to wash them. But later when I went outside to bring Emily back indoors, I found that the plastic beads had been replaced by a garland of fuchsias strung on a length of garden twine. Wide awake and kicking aside her covers, Emily was gurgling with delight as she reached up to explore the scarlet and purple blooms. At lunch, as we sat down to share a salad, I had remarked on Howell's inspired handiwork.

"Did you see how much she liked your flowers?" I asked. "Much better than the beads," his reply had been. "From now on, leave these things to me. I only want her to contemplate perfect form." I stared at him in surprise.

"Perfect form?" I repeated.

42

"That's right. It's a Platonic concept."

I broke into giggles. "Oh Howell, you can't be serious."

His expression when he glanced up at me was close to hostile. "Sometimes I think you're so off-beam, Gillian, you don't deserve to be Emily's mother," he said.

"And I suppose you're the arbiter of all that's good, right and pure?" I snapped back, stung by his insult.

"I'm a hell of a lot more concerned about what goes into Emily's head—and into her mouth—than you are," he shot back, his voice rising.

"You're nuts," I barked.

"And you're—oh what the hell. I can't talk to you. It's impossible. I don't think you understand anything." He flung down his napkin and stalked out of the room.

I still wasn't sure whether Howell was the most conscientious father in the world, a raving eccentric, or like me, a little around the bend after having a baby.

Yes, I watched Oprah Winfrey—she had been a lifeline to sanity in my first few months in Canada. But the jujube bank was all my own idea. Undisguised barter, to teach Emily the value of consequences. In the years that had intervened since our divorce, Howell's and my parenting styles had consolidated into violently opposing points of view. He still allowed Emily to do things in her own sweet time. When she was with me, this would push my patience to its limits. Back in South Africa she had dawdled so much in the mornings that unless I hollered myself blue in the face, she was always the last child in class. She insisted on going to bed as late as she pleased because that's what she did when she visited her father and because he had never used the word *no* to her, she found it difficult to accept a refusal.

When she was with me, I tended to overcorrect these habits, and naturally she had balked at the tougher standards of discipline. Shortly after I arrived in Canada, during one of our most difficult periods of adjustment, I had hit on the simple idea of using her favorite currency as bribery.

Jujubes happened to be what she liked best, especially the sour berry kind I could buy in bulk from the supermarket. I stocked up on these, keeping them in big jars in the kitchen and doled them out in payment for good behavior. She got fourteen every Sunday and if she ate all of her allowance at once, she had nothing left for the rest of the week. But she could earn more. For every two jujubes she saved, she earned one in interest. I told her this was what the banks did with money. If she saved most of them, she could actually end up with more than she had been given in the first place. The other side of it was that if she forgot to hand me summer camp notices or didn't mind her manners, she paid a forfeit or didn't get her full share of candy on Sunday. This was how the real world worked, I explained. For me, for Daddy and also for her. And through this simple method, she had begun to understand that she had the power of control over her actions. I hadn't thought my system degraded Emily until Howell had brought it up in the session with Alma.

"The two of you can certainly be tough on each other," she laughed. "It's like watching Betty Hutton and Howard Keel in *Annie Get Your Gun*. There's a song they sing when they're trying to outsmart each other. Each one does something better than the other." She looked from Howell to me and back to him again. "Both of you want the best for Emily. But you're still not willing to accept each other's differences. It seems to me both of you are vying to be seen as the better parent, the one who automatically knows best, instead of acknowledging that you are both repositories of different but equally valuable points of view." Both of us fidgeted, avoiding the other's eyes.

"The battle here is not who is the better parent," she went on. "The battle is with the ancient grudges neither of you will let go. Neither of you is operating rationally. Both of you are operating out of emotional pain. We need to look more deeply into that."

She was right, of course. I criticized Howell for allowing Emily to get away with murder when my real fury was directed at him for allowing our marriage to disintegrate. He felt my strong views on morals, manners and responsibility were tyrannical because they were uncomfortable reminders of his own harsh upbringing. Neither of us had the skills or insights to separate the issues or to understand how powerfully long-buried angers still drove us. Without Alma's intervention, and our own determination to get it right for Emily's sake, it's safe to say we would have remained deadlocked forever.

Suddenly Howell turned to me with a grin. "Can you bake a pie?" he asked.

"No."

"Neither can I."

"By George, you've got it! I think you've got it!" Alma clapped her hands. "Gillian," she turned to me, "neither you nor Emily are up before the Examinations Board. You can afford to slack off once in a while. Howell, Gillian is not your father's *doppelganger*. You confuse her methods with his—we'll look more closely at that when I see you on your own. And guess what? Only Emily seems to have caught on that neither of you is concerned with setting a consistent example for her. Both of you are trying to win a war. While you're wasting your time, she's playing the two of you off against each other and having to be a parent to herself and to both of you." She looked intently at both of us. "Will you think about that?"

The line of Howell's mouth tightened. He never welcomed altering his opinions. But Alma had not finished with him yet.

"There's one other thing, Howell. You're not off my hook yet. I want you to think over something you said about your relationship with Gillian."

"What's that?"

"Do you remember saying *my wife watches Oprah Winfrey?*"

Howell blinked. "I said *my wife?*"

"You did."

He crossed his legs. "A slip of the tongue. I didn't mean anything by it," he laughed.

"Not consciously, no."

"That's ridiculous. Everything I say gets twisted into another meaning."

"Do you hate revealing yourself?" Alma asked. "Or do you hate having to look at what you say?"

"Both."

"Most men do, if that's any comfort to you."

"It's safer to keep my mouth shut."

"Again, a guy sentiment."

"I feel under attack by you two women."

"Now you're really opening up," she beamed at him. "Good work. I haven't heard you express yourself so openly yet. That's *very* good progress." Howell gave her a sheepish grin. The easy rapport between Alma and himself was the key to our continued presence in her rooms.

"Perhaps there *is* something there, Howell," she continued. "I mean with a slip of the tongue like that. I don't believe either of you is properly divorced from each other yet. In spite of what you tell me, Gillian. Howell, you still want to control Gillian's way of doing things. She's still justifying her choices to you. And to me. You," she said, turning to me, "need to take a little more responsibility for who you are. You don't have to explain or excuse your choices to Howell, to me or anyone else. If there are ideas you value, take responsibility for them and by all means pass them on to your daughter. Having principles and people to value is the greatest gift you can give her. And one other thing. Just remember that as parents, we are infinitely more scary when we *don't* yell at our children. Next time you're tempted to bellow, try it. You'll see what I mean."

I sneaked a glance at Howell. As he wrote out his weekly check for Alma, I couldn't help wondering what it might have been like for us had we had these few simple skills at our fingertips a dozen years ago.

F ❖ I ❖ V ❖ E

But the business of reconstruction was exhausting. Without insight into what drove us, we fell back into our old behaviors as soon as we left Alma's rooms. I bridled at Howell's manner of giving in to Emily. He tensed every time I asked her to do something. She responded by chewing her nails down to the quick. We tried desperately to abide by Alma's primary admonition to stay polite. All the same, I would flame with fury at the slightest provocation.

In our early meetings with her, Alma had suggested that we spend one evening a week in each other's company, taking in a movie or sitting down to a meal together. These were family times that would allow us to practice her rules and to model them for Emily. We had nothing more to do than listen attentively when one of us spoke, watch our manners and monitor our responses. But I was still caught in a spiral of irritation and anger with Howell that betrayed itself in my voice, my abrupt gestures and the way I locked onto small things as an excuse to criticize him. Did he *have* to spend ten minutes haggling with the unfortunate waiter about whether the salmon was wild or farm? Did he have to tell Emily it was okay to follow up ice cream with a chocolate shake? Emily rode us like a bareback rider, having her own way at every turn. To break the deadlock, we inevitably ended up seeing the movies she had chosen, eating at McDonald's and coming home exhausted.

Howell and I were still the victims of forces beyond our reasoning. With our emotional thermostats always on high we had no idea how to keep our discussions focussed, nor to empathize to reduce tension. As a result, the evenings were barely controlled disasters, leaving both of us in a worse state of shutdown than before.

"What did you fight about when you were married?" Alma asked us one morning in a joint session.

"Everything!" Howell said.

Alma laughed. "Most people say that. Be specific. I want to hear the details."

"It's over. I don't want to think about those times," Howell said.

"I'd like you to remember because I want to see what drove them. Both of you are still reacting like hair triggers to each other—you're both finely tuned to lash back, instead of hearing what the other person is really saying. When Gillian criticizes you for letting Emily have ice cream and a shake, she's saying she knows more about nutrition than you do and she doesn't want you to give Emily permission to make herself sick. When Howell chivvies you to make up your mind about staying here, he's really expressing the fear that you're falling apart and he doesn't know how to cope with that. We've heard how strongly you feel about your position as Emily's mother, Gillian, but I still don't hear that you're acknowledging Howell in the same way. When you understand what the other person is *really* saying, you're in a much better position to respond coolly. This may take some time to achieve. You're going to have to practice it over and over again. You're going to have to check things out with each other. You're going to have to ask *Is this what you're saying?* You're going to have to stop yourselves from kitchen-sinking—dragging in irrelevant arguments. Remember we only hear the negatives people give us about ourselves, not the positives. And remember, too, stress can make you say stupid things. Watch for that. You're going to have to modulate your voices and watch your body language. Howell, you jiggle your foot a lot when Gillian is speaking. Gillian, you get a look on your face that says Howell's talking hog-wash. You're going to have to rewrite the neural circuits in your brain. Rewire yourselves. When you've achieved that, you'll be well on your way to regaining control over your relationship." She cocked an eyebrow. "Okay. Was it money? In-laws? Sex? I'm giving you a head start. Those are the sort of things people fight about. What was it with you?"

I kicked off, sounding awkward and priggish. "There was a time when we went away together and Howell flirted with a woman at the table next to us in the dining room." Alma nodded. "Howell?"

"For heaven's sake, Gillian," he shot back. "I was just being friendly. *I* remember a time you threw a tray of eggs at a wall I'd just painted."

"Why did you do that, Gillian?" Alma asked.

"I was furious with his mother," I admitted.

"Rubbish," Howell retorted. "You were jealous because Vanessa was having dinner with her." Vanessa was Howell's ex-fiancée and a source of unending friction between us. Howell's mother had always preferred the patrician blonde to me.

"Howell. Do you hear how you discounted Gillian's explanation?" Alma orchestrated. "I want both of you to monitor how you respond when you talk about these things. Gillian?"

"Well, there was a birthday cake I made for Howell that he refused to eat. He threw the whole thing in the garbage can."

She looked back at Howell. He shrugged. "She was trying to kill me with cholesterol. I've told you I don't want to bring this stuff up." We sat staring at the floor in uncomfortable silence.

"Is that all you can come up with from the years you've known each other?" Alma pushed.

My heart was hammering.

"Or all you're prepared to come up with?" she said.

"I don't think it serves any purpose to dredge this stuff up," Howell said.

"So both of you store up anger, then blow like a volcano when you're good and ready to."

Neither of us could deny the pattern. "Well, isn't that it?" Alma persisted. "Isn't that what happened in the car the other day, Howell? Isn't that what you claim Gillian did throughout your marriage?"

"The past is the past. Let's stay with the present," he said.

"The past is here in this room today. The same forces drive the present. Where do you think they changed direction?" Alma asked him.

"I don't like living life through the rearview mirror," Howell was emphatic. Alma turned to me. My heart was thudding hard enough to make the pulse in my ankle jump.

"Why are you breathing so hard?" she asked.

"Just remembering stuff," I said. A torrent of images had flooded my brain as she prodded us to remember our marriage. *Howell's mother, Eleanor, telling me to get "some polish," Howell turning away from me after Emily was born, Kate Lyons's warning that I came low on the list of people Howell cared about, Vanessa at the front door, coolly asking for Howell. And finally, Howell's cold-blooded acceptance when I decided to leave.* The legacy of anger was stifling. Alma might as well have invited us to face off in a pit of rattlesnakes.

"The two of you don't really have much choice about getting on with each other," she went on. "You're stuck here for the time being. Both of you know the right thing to do for your daughter's sake. But I'm concerned about the stuff buried between the two of you. I think it's time to bring it to the surface."

"When I listen to you, I hear a very angry woman," Alma reiterated at the first session I had alone with her a few days later. "I don't think you can do the best for yourself or for Emily until you untangle yourself. I'm not talking only about your marriage. The anger goes back a long way—probably to the first few years of your life. The defences you put up, for example, when Howell talks about your mothering skills tell me that this is a very painful area for you. Am I right?"

"I talked a little about that in our first session. I don't want to go over it again."

"That's fine with me. We'll get there. What I'd rather do is get to the bottom of the rage you keep bottled up inside you."

"Rage? *Me?*" I looked at her in astonishment.

"Oh yes," she smiled. "A few megatons worth."

I flushed with discomfort. I, who always presented myself with a pleasant smile and a polite word, just the way I had been taught to do as a child at the Convent of the Holy Family in Johannesburg. Before this moment I had never thought of myself as a particularly rageful person.

"Just presuming I'm correct," she went on. "Tell me what you'd have to say about your own anger."

"I really don't think I'm angry," I said. I was surprised at the irritation in my voice.

"Just as an imaginative exercise," she pushed. "Try to believe you were. Tell me what it feels like, where it would come from, where it would go."

I remembered how my heart had thumped in the session Howell and I had together and the itch in the palms of my hands as I remembered scenes from our marriage. "Okay," I said, plunging right in, "I'll admit that sometimes I think I hate Howell violently."

"What do you mean by 'violently?' "

"Enough to smash his head in with a baseball bat."

Alma nodded. "*That* violent. What do you do with the feelings?"

"Nothing much."

"That's where you're wrong. You do plenty. If they stay, they're going to come out somehow, somewhere."

"I get hives on my arms and hands."

"That makes sense. It would be your arms you'd use if you were going to act on your feelings."

"I never would, of course."

"Oh? What stops you?"

"Well, it's not in my nature."

"But you've just said it's what you want to do."

"Yes, but . . ."

"You've been taught that acting on feelings is wrong?"

"Of course. I've got enough self-control not to indulge in every whim."

"Self-control is crucial. But so is the *healthy* expression of your feelings."

"You're going to tell me to bash a ball to displace my anger?"

"That's a big part of why people play. Keeps excess testosterone on the tennis court. Where it belongs. But I want you to think about how *you* handle your anger. How do you express it? Tell me what happened the last time you were angry."

"As a matter of fact, it was just a couple of days ago."

"Go on."

I had to catch my breath as I recalled the scene. It was Sunday evening and we had gone to a choir concert at the small Anglican church Emily and I sometimes attended. Emily hoped to sing in the choir one day and both of us enjoyed the rousing hymns and gifted organist who played there.

"We both love singing," I told Alma. "But Howell is not a regular churchgoer. All the same, he agreed to come along for Emily's sake. She was singing in the youth choir that evening." I told her how we had arrived late for the service and had to take a pew at the back of the church where we couldn't see Emily well. "And then when the plate came round for the offertory," I went on, "I fumbled in my purse and found I had left my money at home. I asked Howell to put in something for me but he only had a twenty-dollar bill and refused. I was furious. I was so choked with anger, I could hardly sing."

Alma listened attentively.

"I couldn't understand where all this fury came from so suddenly," I went on.

"How did you express it?"

"I froze. I couldn't talk to him. I stood next to him hating him so much I was shaking."

"And ruining the choir concert for yourself."

"*He* ruined it for me."

"No he didn't. You ruined it for yourself. Remember the first rule in here is that you take responsibility for your own emotions. No one forces you to feel anything except the programming inside your own head. Remember that you're working towards *choosing* how you feel about incidents and how you respond to them."

"Well, then I didn't do too well the other night," I told her petulantly.

"Apparently. Let's start from the top. You got there late. What was that all about?"

"Howell arrived very casually to pick us up and said we had plenty of time. I knew we didn't, but I went along with him. I was angry when we arrived, but then when I saw how few decent seats were left, I was furious."

"What could you have done to take control of the situation?"

"Gone on my own. Insisted we go earlier," I shrugged.

"Why didn't you?"

"It was more convenient to go with Howell."

"So you played possum rather than initiating a plan of your own. No excuses," she held up a hand as she saw I was ready to spring back with a defence. "Think about it, Gillian. Is this a pattern from girlhood? Going with the flow? Don't be a leader, be the follower, the supporter, never criticize? Make a man feel he's right at all times, then kick his butt when he does things his own way?"

"You're saying none of this was his fault? It was all my own?"

"You should have made your own arrangements, yes, instead of blaming him for being late. You could have saved a seat for Howell and you would have been in control of your own movements. But there was plenty more happening with the money thing. Tell me about that."

"When I thought about it afterwards, I knew it was my fault. I reminded myself in the shower to put money in my purse but I forgot."

"Intentionally?" she cocked her head.

"No."

"Yes."

"Why would I do that?"

"You tell me."

I had to think about that for a couple of minutes, an uncomfortable prickle inching up my arms. "I think it's wrong for a woman to pay for things when a man is with her," I said at last.

"Where did *that* notion come from?"

"I don't know. Just a belief that a man should be the one to pay on behalf of his family."

"But Howell doesn't even go to church. Why should he pay on your behalf?"

"I realize that."

"What else?"

"What else *what?*" Wasn't that enough? God. Everything I said here was being turned upside down! Alma's relentless probing had begun to take on the attributes of a dentist's drill. "I'm sorry," I said "I know you're helping me understand. It just feels as though I'm in the wrong all the time."

She gave me no quarter. "The money thing. Let's get back to that."

"You're making such a big issue out of it," I said, annoyed that she still refused to let up.

"Not me. You're the one who was furious. Fury is a lot stronger than *pissed off* or *mildly peeved. Fury* is the word *you* used."

She was right. I could hear my voice bouncing off the walls as I spoke about the evening. What was going on deep inside? I remembered the pounding of my heart as I belted out *Crown him, Crown him,—* bloody apt choice of hymn, come to think about it now.

"Shall I tell you when women are most angry?" Alma asked.

"When?"

"When they wear that beatific smile of theirs. You know the ghost smile? *All's well in my private Disneyworld?*"

I flushed in recognition. "Why do we *do* that?"

"Because most of us are afraid of showing how we really feel. We've been taught it's wrong and ugly to show anger, jealousy, hate, fear."

"That's me," I confirmed miserably.

"Want to go over everything we've talked about so far?" Her voice was more gentle than before.

"I'll try." But the words didn't come easily and I had to think about them. "I didn't take charge of my own time. I blamed Howell for being late. I was furious that he wouldn't put in money. And you want to know something about that? I was embarrassed because I thought the people next to me would notice."

"Did they know you?"

"Not from a bar of soap."

"What does that mean?"

"An expression. Never saw them in my life before."

"So why did it matter?"

"Oh, you know. Appearances."

"So. A new element. Blaming Howell for refusing to put money into the offertory plate. Then taking it out on him because you were embarrassed."

"Guilty to both of the above," I said. I felt curiously lighter for having it all out there on the table.

"Okay, that was one incident," Alma summed up. "Are there any other concrete behaviors you hate about Howell? Is he immoral? Perverted? Underhanded? Violent? Does he drink, do drugs, fornicate?"

I laughed. "None of the above."

"What drives you mad about him then?"

"Well, he has a grin like a Cheshire cat," I said lamely.

"You can do better than that. What do you most dislike about him?"

"His stupid ignorance and his . . ."

"No abstracts. Give me the concrete stuff."

"I hate it when he pretends he knows something he doesn't. I hate it when he storms out of a room. Or when he wolfs down his food. You want more?"

"Go on," she urged.

"I hate it when he walks ahead of me—he's always doing that. Oh God. This could go on forever. I hate the way he drives, ignoring signs and refusing to look at a map. I hate his snobbery. The huge gaps in his knowledge he refuses to admit to. And on and on and on."

"You *must* have been tough to live with." Her grin was sardonic.

"He hates as many things about *me*."

"No. You hate as many things about *yourself.*"

I was caught off guard. I didn't understand what she meant.

"Take any one of those things on your list," she said. "Let's say snobbery. How do you fare in that area?"

"I'm probably a snob," I admitted.

"About what?"

"Oh, good manners. Education. The way people speak."

"So when you're with people who might have a better education than you, how do you react?"

"I try not to let it worry me. But I guess I feel they're assessing me."

"You feel uneasy?"

"Sure. I'm judging. They are. It's the way of the world."

"Is it?"

"Of course. You know that."

"So in your pecking order there are always going to be those nearer the top, those at the bottom and the vast majority of mankind in the middle."

"I guess. I'm only talking about superficial traits here."

"How do you behave when you're on the middle rung? With all those people above you?"

"I keep my head. I stick to my principles. I try not to be starstruck."

"But you are all the same."

"Sometimes." Where was she leading me?

"What happens then?"

Oh God. I started to fidget, and then to giggle. I had a horrible habit Emily continually pointed out to me. Growing up all over Africa, I had picked up a grab bag of accents. I could slip in and out of them the way a chameleon changes his colors. "I change my accent to suit the occasion," I confessed.

"So you're *not* yourself all the time?"

"Oh no."

"Is that fawning on the person you're with? Or perhaps speaking down to them?"

"I don't seem to be able to help it," I squirmed.

"No. And that's why you hate it so much in Howell. You're projecting onto him the way you feel about yourself."

"You're not saying that *all* those things I hate . . . ?"

She nodded. "The stuff you hate in him is the stuff you most hate about yourself."

"Are you playing straight with me?" I asked her. "Is this one of your own sacred theories or a generally accepted principle?"

She shook her head. "We most hate in others what we cannot accept in ourselves. We bury these feelings about ourselves because they are too painful to acknowledge. But they never go away. They get split off and projected onto others. The most convenient 'other' is usually a spouse."

"Oh shit," was all I could say.

"So you see if you're serious about being Emily's parents, you're going to have to reconstruct your relationship. I can't provide you with china glue," Alma reiterated to Howell and me, in a joint session a week later.

"What about if one of us meets someone new?" Howell asked. We had been seeing Alma for just under two months now, and both of us were still ambivalent about having to reinvent ourselves. In spite of my last session with Alma, I still found it difficult to control my responses to Howell and he in turn was reluctant about taking on more work than he had at first committed to.

She looked at him hard. "Did you hear what I said? If you're serious, you're going to have to rebuild your relationship for Emily's sake." There was a long moment of silence before her words struck home.

"You're saying we have to put aside any other life for ourselves?" Howell asked.

"If you want the best for Emily, yes."

"You're not saying we have to get back together again, are you?"

"In a way you do. You will have to relearn how to see each other by seeing yourselves anew. I'm not talking about a physical reconciliation. I'm talking about the rehabilitation of your roles as parents."

"But don't I have the right to a life of my own?" Howell asked. "Surely one of the best things I could do for my daughter would be to reestablish myself, remarry, perhaps even give her a stepfamily?"

"But you wouldn't do that," Alma told him. "You'd simply repeat your errors. You don't know what a stable family looks like."

"How do you know that?"

"It's my job to see these things," Alma said. "When I talk with you, I'm aware of some of your defences. I understand that you have not been in any long-term relationship since you and Gillian divorced. I'm aware that you married relatively late in life. These are all indicators that you're in no hurry to become a family man. Until you understand what prompted you to make those choices, you will have no place better to go than back inside yourself. Until you understand what that looks like, you're only dealing with the external and largely superficial Howell."

As much as Howell balked at the task, I too wasn't sure whether I was up to the full breadth of Alma's challenge at this early stage. My weakness was that I often gave in to black despair when life looked tough or bleak. Finding the raw energy to face each day had not been my strong suit lately. In the past, I had pulled back into myself, put on as cheerful a face as I could muster and ridden out the dark periods, however long they lasted. There was no room for that now. As parents we came second to Emily's needs and rights. I had no right to wallow in self-pity. I had a job to do. And the same went for Howell. In Alma's book, the primary covenant was with our daughter and no matter how we felt or how much we fought and disagreed, that was all that mattered.

"So you're saying that if we buckle down to the responsibility of being good parents, we cut through the obstacles and life becomes a whole lot more simple," I clarified with Alma in a session on my own with her.

"Go on," she urged.

"You shut off other options, accept the duty and get on with it."

"Exactly."

I hung back searching out the flaw in her argument. "It also means you close off all sorts of other paths," I hedged. "You can't follow your dreams. You can't even go back to work with any kind of commitment if I understand you correctly."

"Those are negotiated choices. But once you put the foundation stone in place the rest of the house builds itself." She drew a breath—heaved a sigh, if I remember correctly. "You and Howell have a daughter whom you brought into this world with the best of intentions. You are honest enough to admit you had no idea how to turn those intentions into good parenting. You probably did not know how. I don't know about the parenting in your own life. We'll come to that. But you're beginning to understand the responsibilities that go with being a parent. You wanted your child. That should have meant that you were ready to put aside your own needs and give yourself up to starting her off in life. You're beginning to accept that being a good parent means giving up the daydreams you had of having it all."

"You're saying that every child should be the center of their parents' life?" This was certainly not the case in the family where I had got my start.

"Isn't that what you would have wanted?" Alma asked. "At least for the first decade of your life?"

"Wouldn't that have made me a spoiled brat?"

"Perhaps you could have done with a little of that. But of course you don't breed brats if you temper love with wisdom and discipline."

"The way you make it sound, it appears I've never known how to love properly."

She drew in a breath, and I was quick to catch its implication. "What

I see is two very needy people who took refuge in each other's company," she said.

"Isn't that a form of love? Taking care of each other?"

"I'm always worried when I hear people telling each other *now we are one,* or all that 'stand by your man' nonsense. What if he's violent? What if he plays around and can't stop? What if he can't give up drugs or alcohol? Those behaviors do not represent love. Real love comes from a place of strength. And that strength comes from knowing intimately who you were born to be and where your own unique abilities lie. All of us have places in the heart that should be filled by other's wisdom, other's strengths. But you must know your own first."

"What you're asking is very hard for both of us," I told her. "We're going to have to do this on our own. If we manage that, we may be able to find a way of doing it together. That's a tough request."

"Let me understand what you mean," she persisted. "Which part is tough? Being a parent or giving up the unfettered freedom you thought you had?"

Shame made me blush from head to toe. "Both."

"It's hard because you haven't been shown how."

"I'm not sure I would have wanted this if I'd known what it entails."

"Too late to debate. You're a mother. Howell's a father. Emily is as complex and as needy as you are. The only difference is that she has a *right* to expect your care."

"That's the part I find hard. How do I give her something I don't seem to know much about?"

"I challenge you on that," Alma gave back. "You know what you wanted from your own parents. Where's the difficulty?"

"I'm not sure."

"You're playing games here, Gillian. Do you want someone to tattoo the rules on your forehead?"

Perhaps I was playing around. Still waiting for permission to take time-out when the going got rough. I hadn't had much input from my own parents, that was true. But that excuse wouldn't wash with Alma. This wasn't a practice run or dress rehearsal, she was saying. There was no downtime, no respite. This wasn't just about being a parent. It was also about discarding a lifetime of buying time, soliciting sympathy, sneaking through the day on half-owned principles. *Damn,* I wanted to yell at her. I had two degrees, I had helped run a company with a turnover of twenty million a year. I had put myself through university, given birth to a child, emigrated and supported myself for over twenty years. The gall of it was that none of this meant a thing to her—she didn't give a tinker's curse for my hard-won accomplishments. She was telling me in plain language that the only worthwhile diploma I could earn as bona fides for time spent on this earth was being a decent parent to my child. Hadn't I done my best? Not good enough, she was saying. Didn't I have a right to protest the past? Old grievances condemned Emily to inherit them as her own. You've got to reach beyond yourselves, she told us again and again. Scour out the past. Even more so since you broke your primary vows to each other. I sulked and glowered through our sessions, hating her unruffled dismissal of my excuses. Then, as I mulled over her admonitions, a pinprick of insight, the countermand to my first response of *what about me?* took a halting hold of my conscience. What if this were my chance to have it all over again? To relive my childhood. This time getting it right for Emily? What if I gave her the security I had never had? Gave to her what I had always wanted from my parents and never found? If we succeeded there, it would be like shattering a curse, breaking the cycle of failure and heartbreak that had been bequeathed over generations to her parents. Doing this for Emily would be my own replenishment. Helping her succeed where we had failed would be better than having it all myself. And what about Howell? However much he and I had grown apart, he *was* the father of my child. He had been an honorable parent, as committed as I was to Emily's well-being. Neither of us possessed the mystical blueprint to perfect parenting, that was obvious, but if I understood Alma correctly, she was saying that even after divorce, our chief responsibility was to parent our child together. What intrigued me even more was just how we were going to achieve this feat.

"Your face tells me there's something you'd like to say," Alma invited at our next session. "Take a chance and tell me what it is."

"Oh I'm just wondering about you," I began. "You seem to have all the answers. Was it ever this difficult for you?"

"Yes, it was."

"Is it simply that age mellows a person? I don't mean to be rude. It's just that—God—I wish I could get to that place of wisdom sooner rather than later."

She did not smile at my self-reproach and I was grateful for the fact that she did not try to humor me with a glib reply.

"What if I'm just genetically bad-wired?" I went on. "If I'm never going to grow up and feel the right things?"

"It takes time."

"What if I don't care?"

"You do. Or you wouldn't be here. You're exhausted by everything that's happened in the past couple of months. And the stress of that makes us all feel stupid. But remember you are not the only one that counts here. You're doing this for your child and the generations of children who come after her." She cocked an eyebrow at my surprised expression. "Don't you believe that?"

"I hadn't thought of it that way. But give me a start. How do *you* do it?"

"I have a foundation of principles and beliefs I've put together over a lifetime. That's the container. Then I keep filling up every day with good moments."

Oh spare me, I thought. She's going to break into Hallmark verse. Instead, I heard myself asking, "Where do you find them?"

"When I was younger, I had to look harder," she said. "Now they're all around me. Do you see my tomatoes through the window there? When the sun shines, there's a gold dust on them. I wouldn't have seen that when I was younger. I have moments of joy all the time when I'm with my grandchildren. Sometimes just sitting with a friend does it. My books give me great pleasure. My first cup of tea in the morning. You get the idea?"

I remembered, in a rush, a rock I had picked up in the veld one afternoon when I was five years old and walking home with my nanny. There, in the dust among the stunted bushes was a lump of amethyst, its shattered sides glittering, nearly blinding me with light as I turned it this way and that in the sun. Nothing I owned had ever given me greater pleasure than that piece of quartz and the solid weight of it in my hand.

Throw it away, Miss Gilly. Put it down. It's dirty, Josephine had said to me. Many years later I realized that I had held the fragment of a geode, its ragged crystals spilled a hundred million years after its creation by bulldozers excavating a new housing development in the veld. As impressed as I was by the fact that I had held a jewel nearly as old as earth itself, nothing could supplant the surprise and joy I felt at the play of violet and rose light in the depths of that stone.

"I think I know what you're talking about," I told Alma. "But what if you had a rackety upbringing. You know. Not much affection. All the rest of it."

"No one on earth has had a perfect childhood," she said.

"What about your own? Did you have a good start in life?"

"I had an excellent start. I had a mother who was completely unselfish."

"Oh, well then . . ." I began.

She held up her hand. "I'll tell you about her some other time. Let's get back to you."

"No. Tell me about yourself. Is it okay to ask?"

"Of course. If you'd like a quick summary, I'll give you one. Some of my story has shaped the way I am. But I like to think I'd still be who I am even if I hadn't been given a good shove to get me started. I was born in Lithuania in 1928 and sent out of the country to live with an aunt in Toronto when I was eight."

The first thing she remembered about Canada was the glorious aroma of roast chicken from her aunt's kitchen. "She'd used a whole pound of butter," Alma recalled "and the smell was so rich, so delicious, it made me ill." Back home, she and her family had lived on not much more than cabbage and potato soup for most of the previous year. She remembered her mother walking her to the railway station on the day she left the village where she was born and how the snow had blinded them both, halting their steps and allowing only enough time for one or two admonitions to keep her coat buttoned and a few hurried goodbyes. For her pilgrimage to Canada, she had been given the best of everything her mother owned—a cashmere shawl, fur-lined gloves and a coat purchased three sizes too large so that it would last her several seasons. There was gold money sewn into the lining of the coat, as well as a gold locket that had belonged to her grandmother. The lesson Alma had brought with her to the New World sixty years before was that no matter how much a family had to sacrifice, its children had to survive. Children were the treasured future. Nothing else mattered as much as helping them overcome the obstacles that had prevented their parents from achieving success in life.

"Did you see your mother again?" I asked.

She shook her head. "She wrote to me every month. But by the end of the thirties, she had disappeared in the purges. I live as fully as I can now, to make up for all of those who did not survive."

For a moment, I sat stunned. Unable to answer back or excuse myself for the doubts I had allowed myself about my role, I compared my life to hers and saw only a succession of stops and starts, roles and poses, patched together by times of anguished indolence. I had dawdled over decisions, indulged in pained debates at every turn, believing my so-called education would help me to arrive at the best of all possible solutions. Worst of all, I had toyed with the fallacy that a compromise could be reached over any issue. I was simply looking for a comfortable way to ease the responsibilities that stared me in the face.

I looked over to where Alma sat in her faded pink chair, her head cocked to one side, a bright query in her eyes. "Does it all make sense now?" she asked. She looked like a shrewd bird, talon in mid-air, an all-knowing sentience in her brilliant eyes.

"Right now, I don't know whether to hate you or thank you," I told her.

"Good. That means we're on our way," she said.

I took myself down to the water's edge to think. There with the wash of the tide against my feet, I saw with sharp clarity what I had to do. Counting angels on the head of a pin had been a delicious pastime when I was an unencumbered dreamer. Now these fancies were unusable. There was no question about the work I had to do. I had a child. And she in turn had a father who loved her. If our commitment was to give her the best start in life, our task was to help rebuild the family structure, to bury our differences and to take on our full roles as her parents. We had to become a community of three again, whatever our living arrangements turned out to be. Howell might hate the way I did things, as much as I disagreed with him. But our personal differences no longer counted. We would have to make this work.

The water slapped against my sandals and sucked back at the shore as it retreated. Why hadn't I seen any of this before? I had wanted so badly to get out into the world and to become someone. I was never going to be bogged down by bills and kids the way my mother had been, forfeiting all her girlhood dreams as soon as she became pregnant. I could see her now, the light spilling on the nape of her neck as she darned and sewed, turning old sheets sides to center. She was always on the move, her feet swelling in the heat of summer, her face harried and unsmiling even when we reached up to hug her. She gave herself fifteen minutes to sit down on the veranda in the morning and perhaps another break in the afternoon. For the rest of the day she imposed a routine on her household that kept it running like an army base. Dinner was on the table at seven sharp every night of the year. Lunch was soup in winter; avocado and papaya salad in summer, the fruits picked from trees in the backyard and served with brown bread and butter blended with margarine to make it go further. Thrift and order were the watchwords of our childhood. My mother had been an orphaned child at the end of the Great War, a young woman with babies during the Depression and a widow with two teenage boys at the end of World War Two. She had never known a time when need and exhaustion did not rule her life. From the time she was a young woman she had worked compulsively, going to night school to master bookkeeping and squirreling away money in secret accounts and stocks all her life. When she died, my sister had found ninety thousand dollars in her household account alone. Yet, to her thinking she had always been poor, and she had allowed herself few indulgences. The crystal flacon of L'Heure Bleue my father brought her from Brazzaville, the "Paris of Africa," had turned rank and cloudy at the back of her bedroom cupboard, its seal unbroken after fifteen years. She had washed her face in Sunlight soap and dismissed gifts of chocolates, silk scarves and hand cream as wanton extravagances. On the other hand she had a horse trader's eye for value. She could put an accurate price on anything and believed that good looks were a woman's only asset if she had neither education nor a place in society to advance her in the world. When I was a teenager, she had made it clear that I would have to fend for myself, as she had done for herself: I did not have the kind of personality or looks that men fell for. Along with my cornflakes, I had accepted that I was to be my own guardian and keeper.

Later, Gloria Steinem, Fay Weldon and Kate Millett had aided and abetted my tortuous independence. I had promised myself an education, money in the bank, and then, only then, if I was lucky enough, a well-chosen husband and a carefully spaced family. My university background had taught me to be a rigorous thinker, to worship logic before all other gods. But my emotional IQ had been allowed to shrivel on a starvation diet of punishing self-criticism, my parents' cool disregard and the treacherous delusion that education would liberate me. Nowhere had anyone warned me: *none of these choices has prepared you to be a good parent, let alone a half-way decent mother.* The feminist movement had never given me permission to abandon my hard-won freedom when a small bundle of anarchic energy sabotaged every theory they had ever propounded. Weren't we all in revolt against the unfulfilled lives our mothers had led? Didn't we have a right to participate in the good life men had enjoyed for so long? I, along with other women of my generation, had grown up believing we had a duty to have it all, if only to avenge our tired, disappointed mothers.

When the time came, I had thrown myself into motherhood as though it was a business project, worrying all the time because I was not back at work earning money, and feeling guilty for every delicious, extended moment I spent with my daughter. I had defended myself weakly against the shrill admonitions of other women to get a nanny rather than care for my daughter myself. In truth, I was hopelessly ill prepared for the exhaustion and emotional demands that motherhood brought, and terrified of ending up like my own mother. In the end, trying to do it all had left me a burned-out divorcée wondering how it had all blown up in my face. Now the time for self-absorption was past. When all was said and done, when the briefcase was back in the cupboard, the power suits zipped away in dry-cleaning bags, the divorce papers signed and the tears dried, I had a child in my stewardship. And if Howell and I were to repair the damage we had inflicted—on ourselves and on her—if we were to attempt to pass on to her the trick of living life to its decent fullness, we had to discard personal grievances, get over our grudges, understand the mission and get on with it. There was no other way.

"Okay," I told Alma the next time I saw her. "I'll do whatever it takes to get us up and working again. Where do we start?"

"Tell me about your marriage to Howell," she said. "I want to know where the anger comes from."

S ❖ I ❖ X

My sister had introduced us. She was twenty-two at the time and at the top of her profession as a model. One afternoon in early February, Howell had happened to walk by a city fountain where she was working on a *Harper and Queen's* fashion shoot. He stopped to watch her work in front of the camera and a week later met her again by chance at an art gallery opening. With her cloud of red hair and high cheekbones, she resembled the young Katherine Hepburn, and Howell was quick to tell her so. Encouraged by her response, he had, with characteristic cheek, gone on to introduce himself as a television producer and suggested she should think of a future in front of the camera. In spite of the transparency of his pitch, she had sized him up, told him she liked his smile but that, in fact, she was engaged to be married. Undaunted, he asked, "Do you have a sister?" Much later, she wondered why she had made the split-second decision that was to change all of our lives forever. She put it down to an underlying vulnerability she perceived in Howell, a guess that behind his easy exterior he was looking for something more substantial than the feverish glamor offered on Johannesburg's social circuit. Howell's charm, I told her. That look was his specialty. Even she hadn't been immune to its effects.

"Well, as a matter of fact I do have a sister," she had told him. She took his business card and the following day called the company where he worked. Speaking to his immediate boss, she told him she was calling from the credit company through which Howell wished to purchase electronic equipment. Since he was new to the country, she wanted a character reference as well. "How could you *do* that?" I shrieked at her when she told me.

"You need to get out of that library," she said, matter of factly. "You could do with some fun. Besides, his boss was very complimentary." When she went on to describe Howell, my heart sank. He sounded like every other well-connected young man in advertising, film and social circles—a dedicated pleasure-seeker, whose only goal was to crash the city's fiercely competitive social scene and whose idea of a serious relationship was what you had with your beer. "He's just what you need," she said, undeterred. "The contrast alone between the two of you would appeal to your sense of the ridiculous." She was right about the disparity. On our first date, Howell arrived wearing a red paisley waistcoat, a green velvet jacket bought on sale at Ted Lapidus in Paris, jeans, old boots and a ten-foot-long red scarf wound round his neck and trailing over his shoulder. His voluminous hair was Afro-frizzed and when I opened the door, I thought for a moment he had electrocuted himself on the doorbell. Just another poseur, I thought with a sinking heart. This was going to be a disaster. He peered shyly at me and said, "Gilly, is it?" and I knew immediately he was comparing me with my sister. She was four inches taller and the only thing we had in common was our unusually pale skin, a legacy from our Scots grandmother. "Not Gilly," I said stiffly. "Gillian." If he was disappointed, he had the grace not to show it. He'd heard from my sister that I was organizing a course in film studies at the university, and a mutual interest in old movies had eased us through the first awkward hour together. I was as stiff as a board and humiliated that he might be thinking of me as a second-best choice. All the same, I admired his willingness to ride out my prickly queries and the fact that he didn't automatically order a drink to loosen me up earned him points as well. Instead, he answered all my questions with the same self-deprecating diffidence I'd first heard on the phone when he called to ask me out. Would I risk having dinner with him? he had asked, immediately after the initial pleasantries.

"Why would that be a risk?" I had answered testily. "Have you got a record you aren't telling me about?"

"No, no, I don't mean that," he laughed. "It's just that I haven't been here long enough for you to check up on me. With friends and people, I mean." I let that ride for the moment. He didn't try to fill up the silence and I stalled. Why, I wondered, would a man my sister described as a living dish call a stranger for a date? I hedged further. Didn't he know people in television he could go out with? Well, yes he did, he told me, but he had exhausted the party scene. After months of trying to make himself heard above the din, all he really wanted was a quiet dinner with someone he could talk to. "If you think it's too much to take me on all at once, we could always go to a movie first," he suggested.

I was still not sure. Eight months earlier, I had found out that the medical student I had had a three-year relationship with was more interested in scoring drugs than in keeping me. The wounds were still raw.

"I'm sober, I have my own teeth and hair, a driver's license and I love Italian food," he went on. "I've never been married. No children I know of. I'm not gay. I pay my taxes and I've never been arrested for anything. If you were my sister, I'd say take a chance." *When*, I asked cautiously. "Oh, tonight. Tomorrow night. Friday. Whenever you like," he said disarmingly. "I'll keep them all open for you."

I took the chance. And there we were that Friday night in the Toucan restaurant lingering over the first of a thousand Italian meals we would eat together. He told me he had worked in Hollywood with Sam Peckinpah on a film called *Killer Elite* and had decided to return to South Africa to work as a documentary director in television. At present he was putting together a story on nightlife in the shebeens—the beerhalls of Soweto. Already he'd run up against government opposition to showing black life on white-owned television screens and was finding it difficult to keep his liberal views to himself.

"Did you know I'm not allowed to shoot a black man and a white woman in the same frame?" he asked me. Yes, I knew about the ridiculous laws, I told him, but putting that aside for the moment, what had he done while he worked for Sam Peckinpah?

"I was third assistant director," he replied.

"There's no such thing," I told him.

"Well, there's a second second assistant director," he said.

"Is that what you did?"

"Well, okay," he said, "I kept back the crowds."

Both of us laughed and that broke the ice between us. He asked me what I was working on at university and how come my sister and I had chosen such opposite careers. That was obvious, I told him. I was shy. She was an extrovert. She loved city life. I liked wide-open spaces and my own company. I told him about growing up in the countryside outside Johannesburg and how my father had travelled through Africa on business while my mother stayed home to bring up six children. There had been my father's two sons, her own two, my sister and myself. "We had to be out of the house by eight every morning," I told him, "so she could restore order in her domain. When I wasn't in school, I was in the veld. And the habit has stuck." He understood that, he said. His own parents had given him great freedom to explore the countryside in South West Africa where he had grown up. I told him how I would take a book, ride into the veld, climb a tree and read all afternoon. He stared in surprise. "I did the same thing!" he said. Somehow I couldn't see this charming gadfly up a tree, but years later, he took me to the secret dugout he had made for himself at the base of an acacia tree on a rocky knoll above Windhoek. It was one of the rare moments when I sensed how close we were to a common center within both of us, one that had built a small, tentative universe out of the scraps of affection that came our way in an emotionally sparse childhood.

We talked until midnight and he asked me out the following night. And the next. In fact, we never stopped going out with each other. We discovered a passion for European movies and signed up for every film festival on the circuit that year, often crowding eight movies into two days, and keeping ourselves going on Coke and pizza. I organized a campus festival of Chaplin movies and he came along to help run it. Then we hit on the idea of starting up a film club to see every movie made before sound came in. He rounded up six or seven colleagues at work, I put up a notice in the English department and twenty people signed on. Every Friday night, I hung a sheet on my living room wall and we assembled to watch the great German Expressionists and Russians and all the Keaton, Chaplin, Harold Lloyd and D.W. Griffiths masterpieces still in existence.

All the while I kept asking myself if there were other women in his life. I wondered why he chose to spend so much time with me, but had enough sense not to ask. I knew I would ruin it for myself if I did. Best enjoy his company while I had it, I thought. Sooner or later, he'd show his real colors and that would be the end of it. Sure enough, after we'd been seeing each other for about four months, Howell announced out of the blue that he was taking time off to go sailing in Mauritius. I'll see you in a fortnight, he said breezily, and left. That was short and sweet, I thought, a little bruised but not battered. I had grown used to his company but at least I could get back to some hard work on my post-grad degree. All the same, I missed him terribly. At the end of the week, I was reaching into the mailbox hoping to find a postcard from him when, without fanfare, he appeared at the front door.

"Got bored," was all he said. "What are you doing tonight?"

Not a good sign, I thought to myself. He's obviously impetuous and restless. Nevertheless, I was elated to see him again. And flattered that he had come straight from the airport to find me. Encouraged by this, I decided that before we went any further, I needed to know whether there were other women in his life. Although we spent so much time in each other's company, there were still enough gaps for me to wonder what he was up to when he wasn't with me.

"Howell, I need to ask you a question," I began, my voice shaky with nerves.

"What about?" he asked.

"Other women," I said. My back felt like a ramrod. I searched his face for the usual grimace that came in response to this question. Did he see other women when he wasn't seeing me? To myself I thought, *you're every bit as handsome and charming as my sister said you would be.* To him I said, "Why isn't every available woman in Johannesburg after you?"

"Well, as a matter of fact, they are," he said candidly. He simply never spoke about them. And he was masterly at keeping them out of sight. I learned later that just before me there had been a heartbroken production assistant who still trailed him, hoping for a reconciliation. There was a female director who had dedicated a short film to him and a gallery owner who showered him with invitations to her society get-togethers. There was also his landlady, a Marlene Dietrich double, who had established first call on him to fill up numbers at her elegant dinner parties. And of course, there was the photograph of his ex-fiancée that he still kept in his wallet. I couldn't help noticing her waist-length blonde hair whenever he hauled out a credit card to pay for dinner.

Living on my own, on a postgraduate scholarship at university and emotionally naive, I knew next to nothing about how to conduct a relationship with a playboy. I believed Howell kept seeing me because I was an easygoing companion who was happy to talk movies and made few demands on his time. But, as we spent more and more time together, I became painfully aware that wherever we went, there was always a chorus of women, older and younger, who appeared to have strong prior claims on him.

"Howell, darling. How *are* you! I haven't seen you since varsity days," was the frequent greeting. One of his old skiing companions had pulled his head down and cooed into his ear, loud enough for me to hear, "Oh Howie, I've *so* missed your profile." Another, a blonde fitness instructor (blondes held sovereignty in his life) had taken hold of one of his hands and kissing each fingertip in turn, ticked off the parts she most missed about him. "This one's for your charm," she fluttered. "This one's for your eyes, this for your toes, this one for your wonderful hair, your gorgeous chin," she went on, "and last but not least," holding his thumb high in the air, "this one's for your legendary stamina." The crowd around us had erupted into laughter, and Howell had ducked his head under his arm to escape the obvious inference. Hypnotized by these encounters, I hung back and wondered about this mythical creature and what he was doing with me. I had no plans to settle down until I had finished a postgraduate program that would lead to a doctorate and with luck, a secure teaching post at the university. Was I throwing this all away by hanging out with a man who appeared to be more of a desirable accessory than a partner for life? Then there were other stories, almost as enthralling as the accounts I heard from the legion of blonde handmaidens. This time, they emphasized Howell's extraordinary sporting prowess. There was the day he had exited noisily from a final-year economics lecture, taking half the class with him when he forecast that the perfect, once-in-a-lifetime wave was waiting for him out there in the surf. Reading the direction of smoke coming from the canteen chimneys, he had persuaded his lecturer to abandon leveraged buyouts in the interests of allowing the class to experience the rare occurrence of this phenomenon. Later, he had thrown a legendary party to celebrate the accuracy of his prediction. There were stories of Howell negotiating mountain passes in his Morgan sportscar without fear of momentum or speed restrictions and tales of Howell skiing black diamond paths in Switzerland and off-piste in France. He still held the record for the fastest one-hundred-yard sprint in South African running history as well as a brace of swimming records that had never been broken. I couldn't help but be awestruck.

"You should have seen him," one of the women who had been in his final-year class told me. "He had the most perfect body I ever saw. And that smile. He melted every girl's heart. And then went on to charm our mothers as well."

When he returned to South Africa, eight years after leaving for Paris and other capitals of the world, he hadn't changed much, other than to acquire the polished exterior that comes with working in an investment bank in London and running its Paris branch for four years. He still preferred people and parties to work, although he claimed differently. His charm had been honed to glittering efficiency. His smile may have been a little too facile and the opening gambits in flawless French or German too easily managed. But it was the disarmingly frank moments when the facade dropped away that made me fall in love with him. It was then that I saw someone as alone and uncertain about life as I was. In truth, I was probably as bedazzled as any of the happy-go-lucky blondes he attracted so easily. But his touching eagerness to learn all he could about filmmaking was what finally bound me to him. The film course I had helped launch as an adjunct to advanced English studies was now up and running and Howell plied me with questions about technique and theory. He had never been to film school and was frank about the fact that his only expertise had been picked up on the job in London and Hollywood, and was owed in large measure to his ability to talk himself into anything.

"Tell me about Eisenstein," he asked me one night in the middle of a party. "Tell me everything you know about the Russians and the way they changed film." He borrowed books on seminal filmmakers and annotated them in his careful script, writing out long passages that he kept on filing cards before returning them to me.

"I love you," I told him one night without thinking. I couldn't believe that the words had left my mouth. Involuntary statements had always betrayed me when I was overcome by the moment. I had always wished I could stuff them back again. But they seemed to come out of nowhere and had a life all their own. The only difference was that this time I meant what I said. I *was* in love—with Howell's carefree way of handling life, with his refusal to bow to convention or to government decrees that threatened his documentaries, with his insatiable curiosity and surely, too, with the fact that so many other women had failed to pin him down. I knew by now that I was the peahen to his more glorious bird and, as is so often the case with supremely handsome men, that both of us were happy to have it that way.

"Thank you," he said gravely. And nothing else. He did not say he loved me in return. Not even as a kindness or a nicety. In fact, he never did. Not once in the twenty years I have known him. Once or twice, he wrote to tell me how much I meant to him. But he never spoke the words. And a part of me continues to admire him for the fact that he has never used them lightly.

He also did not tell me that there was only one woman he had ever loved and that was Vanessa—his ex-fiancée whose photograph resided in his wallet. I heard from old classmates that Vanessa and he had met in their final year together at Cape Town University and that the ring he gave her when they became engaged had been so massive it had dwarfed her fingers. No one, not even Howell himself, could tell me why their engagement had ended. All I knew was that Vanessa was still out there somewhere and that now and then Howell called her "just to find out how she was doing." She was at Cambridge, he told me when I asked. She had gone there some years before to complete a postgraduate degree but the "sodding English weather" had got her down and she found it difficult to make friends. She was working now for an art dealer in London.

"Do you miss her?" I fished, trying to find out where she still fitted into his life.

"I miss certain things about her," he replied.

"What about her? What do you miss?" I asked.

"Oh, things. She was sharp. Didn't have much of a sense of humor, though."

I locked on to this hint of disloyalty. "Why won't you tell me what went wrong between you?" I demanded.

"She wasn't right for me," he hedged. "I've told you that."

"Do you think she misses you?" I pushed.

"Quite possibly," was all he would say.

"So you broke it off and she met someone else?"

"Something like that," he answered. I continued to live in anxious fear that at any moment Vanessa would reappear to claim Howell again.

By now, I was supplementing my university paycheck by researching and outlining ideas for him for future documentaries. Late one night while we were working on a rough draft together at the cottage he rented, the telephone rang and he took the call in his bedroom. Afterwards, when I found out it had been Vanessa, I remember thinking that anyone who called at that time of night still had rights and privileges in Howell's life. She was in the middle of a crisis, he told me, a personal dilemma of sorts. He had reversed charges, talked her through what was bothering her and restored her spirits before joining me again. He had been on the phone for just under an hour.

We had recently begun spending the weekends together at his cottage and I was still not sure this was the right thing to do. That night I felt as vulnerable as a baby.

"You're still attached to her, Howell," I said when he came back into the room. "You haven't broken away from her and I think until you have, we need a break from each other."

"Don't be silly," he insisted. "Vanessa's the past."

"That's not true," I shrilled at him. "How come the two of you are still in touch?"

"I've made it clear," he replied. "I always stay friends. I never turn my back on anyone I've been close to and walk away. It's not in my nature. I can't change that."

That was what finally won me over. If I'd been as smart as I believed, I might have savvied up to the implications of his statement. *Why* couldn't he let go of Vanessa? Did he hate resolving problems? Would he rather put a relationship on ice than confront what was wrong and work it through? It was only after twenty years of knowing him that I understood the merits of his statement. At the time, I ignored every misgiving and saw him only as a safe haven. My parents were living in Zimbabwe, a thousand miles away, and my sister was planning to leave for the United States with her husband. The man I had loved before Howell had descended into a full-scale cocaine addiction, abandoning our relationship without conscience. Here was Howell making it clear that he never let go of anyone. Not Vanessa, not his mother whom he called every weekend, not even the swollen-eyed production assistant whom he had had promoted to field producer since the end of their brief fling. We crossed the barrier between companionship and what was to become a bitter battle because, despite believing we operated out of educated choice, we were in fact emotionally blind to who we were. I believed I was enlightened and independent, but deep down I was riddled with the fear of being alone.

By December, nine months after we met, we were ready for the next big leap into our entangled future together.

"I always spend Christmas at home," Howell had told me. In early December, he mentioned that he wanted to spend the holiday season with his family at their house in the Cape. I know what's happening, I thought. He's pulling out. He's had a wonderful year with me, but now it's time to bring down the curtain. This always happened. Just as I was beginning to build a pinch of trust, I would find that the other person had been simmering with plans entirely opposite to my own. My characteristic reaction was to shut down, withdraw and stay there for weeks. Just then he had added, "I wondered if you'd like to fly down and join us after that? I think it's time you met my family."

S • E • V • E • N

Howell pushed through to the front of the crowd at the airport to meet me. He was wearing denim shorts and a T-shirt and had acquired a deep tan in the two weeks since I had seen him. I noticed too that he had cropped his hair. He looked pleased and shy when I flung my arms around him, as though not quite sure whether I should be here or what he was going to do with me next. I felt a similar sense of displacement.

I had travelled to Cape Town only once before, when I was nine years old, to meet my mother off the old *Pretoria Castle*. We had stayed in a drab hotel near Table Bay before driving the thousand miles back to Johannesburg, and I had been too young then to perceive how different Cape Town is from other cities in South Africa.

Those who decry its aristocratic, old-world society contend that living there is tantamount to retreating behind "the cabernet curtain"— an allusion to the lush vineyards that once supplied Napoleon Bonaparte and still flourish in its gentle mediterranean climate. Even the light falls differently in Cape Town. Under a white glaze of heat, vegetation and people alike shimmer, as if wrapped in an unearthly dust. In the distance, the hard-edged monolith of Table Mountain looms over a city that began as a refreshment station for sailors rounding the Cape in 1652 and is still clustered around its star-shaped castle. Unlike the thin, dry air of Johannesburg, five thousand feet above sea level, Cape Town's air is soft and heavy, anointed by the Indian and Atlantic oceans and three thousand species of flowers—the richest floral kingdom on earth. Here, after nearly four centuries of intermarriage, Afrikaners, blacks and the descendants of Malay slaves all have extended blood ties with each other. One branch of a family might call itself white, another might officially be designated "colored," but everyone knows that their children are cousins. In a city where apartheid was always impossible to enforce, Cape Town's small clannish society is steeped in a rich and intricate past, whose secrets and snobberies go with its members to the grave.

I was the child of an altogether different culture. In 1886 my family had helped found Johannesburg, erecting the city over the richest seam of gold in the world. My forefathers were pioneers and frontiersmen, my great-grandfather one of the first mayors of the vulgarly rich new metropolis. I could not come to adulthood in South Africa without re-alizing that Johannesburgers are dismissed as brash and characterless upstarts by the patrician families of the Cape. This beautiful, decadent world was Howell's home town. This was where he had spent most of his childhood, and attended school and university. Suddenly, confronted by the formality of his manner, and his altered appearance, the differ-ences seemed forceful and unsettling. I couldn't help turning my head to catch the high-pitched lilt of Cape "colored" speech, a ringing and picturesque argot unlike any other in the country. Whether it was a combination of the city's striking differences, or my own awkwardness at being so far from home, I found myself taking a step backwards to check out Howell on that hot January afternoon. And he did the same with me.

He had borrowed his mother's 1964 white Mercedes coupe to meet me and as we drove back along the shore to his family's home, he tipped back the hood to allow the cool sea breeze to stream over us. At the first pair of crossroads, he stopped the car to buy me a basket of straw-berries. Each fruit, as big as a baby's fist, was so ripe and so red that flocks of birds hovered above the hawkers' heads, ready to dive-bomb the unattended crates for their share of the bounty. Farther along the road, gulls wheeled and screamed around fishermen who sold their catch-of-the-day from the back of battered trucks, singing out their wares and tap dancing in the dust to catch motorists' attention. Every-where, children, dogs and casual strollers played in and out of surf that frothed and creamed at their feet. Even the light lingered, leaving a violet glow till late in the evening that seemed to extend all the way down to the ice floes of Antarctica, a thousand miles to the south.

A half hour's drive from the airport, Howell turned into a brick courtyard ablaze with hibiscus and bougainvillea flowers. Stepping round to my side of the car, he reached forward and opened the door with a flourish.

"Welcome to Omutara, 'place of rest,'" he smiled. "This is where the world congregates and all important decisions pertaining to the family are made." I looked up to gauge whether he was being serious, aware that I was here on trial and there might be obstacles to overcome.

"I've been a little nervous about you meeting the family for the first time," he said, ushering me into the cool, white house. "But only my mother and father are here, so it shouldn't be too bad. My brothers are off diving on the West Coast." I wasn't sure whether this would make the ordeal easier or not. As he led me through the wide, high rooms, I tried to fix a floor plan in my head. In front of me, in a brilliant orange dining room, the long white table was already set for the evening meal with candles, baskets of yellow hibiscus and wine glasses. Beyond there seemed to be some kind of a sauna, a door leading through to the butler's pantry and the kitchen. I caught a glimpse of wine cooling in buckets, and a further array of crystal decanters lined up on the sideboard. I thought back to my mother's starched napkins and polished dining table at home, the careful servings of green beans, mashed potato and stewed beef apportioned as standard fare on Wednesday evenings. In our home, wine was served only at Christmas and then limited to a single glass per person. It felt delicious and heady to be in a home where rules like these obviously did not apply.

"This is where we spend most of our time," Howell said, standing aside as I followed him into a room painted a deep forest green. The living room stretched the full length of the house, one of its walls swallowed up by a painting of two male gorillas sparring for dominance in the African bush. Other walls were hung with paintings of the desert and men in agony, which I later learned formed a triptych by Francis Bacon. At each end of the room, deep sofas echoed the green of the walls and were offset by pale cream curtains that pooled on the floor. The white marble fireplace was stacked high with Christmas cards and invitations and, although this was early January, the height of the southern summer, firewood and coals had been laid in the grate to extend the impression of seasonal cheer.

"Why don't you make yourself comfortable while I see if my mother's still resting," Howell said. He pressed a jade button on the wall and ordered tea for me from the kitchen. Then he disappeared upstairs, taking the stairs three at a time and leaving me to breathe in the intoxicating mixture of sea air, cigar smoke and fresh flowers. A portrait of Howell's mother hung in an alcove above the fireplace and adjacent to it was the maquette of a Henry Moore sculpture. Mahler was playing on the stereo and the hardback books piled on every side table were this season's bestsellers—an unimaginable luxury in my world. I sat with my feet pressed together and my hands folded in my lap, overwhelmed by the light pouring through the windows and the opulent disorder of the room.

One of the black women who helped run the household came in on silent feet and placed a tray of tea in front of me.

"Are you Miss Gillian?" she asked with a shy smile.

"Yes I am. And who are you?" I asked.

"I am Carsalina," she said on a long outbreath that made her statement sound like an apology. "I cook here and also run the house."

"How do you do," I said and held out my hand to shake hers. She put her hand in mine with a light touch and then withdrew it quickly. "I'm sorry," I told her. "I don't drink Earl Grey tea. Only ordinary Joko if you have it."

"Shoo!" she said, her eyes wide. "I thought all the Madam's friends drank Earl Grey. Just like the Madam does."

I laughed. "The flavor is too strong for me. Can I have plain tea instead?"

"No problem," she said. "I'll fetch some from my own room. Where did you say you come from?"

"Johannesburg," I told her.

"I was there once. In nineteen sixty-one." She shook her head and made a clicking sound that indicated the place was a cesspool of sin and damnation. "And you're here to visit Master Howell?" she asked.

"Yes," I told her, knowing that this was the polite way of saying, *so you're sleeping with him and you're here to be presented to the family.*

"*Ai, ai, ai,*" she said and shuffled off on bare feet to make another pot of tea.

Twenty minutes later, after strong tea and two chapters of *The Thorn Birds* had revived me, a rustle like the sound of a curtain rising snapped me back to the present.

"So you're Gillian," Howell's mother said as she swept into the room. She stood in front of me, hand outstretched, wearing a flowing white caftan pinned at each shoulder with an aquamarine clasp. Her eyes, an unusual shade of sea green, were too astute to be immediately friendly, but her smile was brilliant and I stood up to shake hands with her.

"How do you do, Mrs. Edwards," I said.

"Welcome to Omutara," she replied. "The word means 'place of rest' in the language spoken in Namibia, but of course that's a hopeless misnomer as Howell no doubt has told you. I see you already have tea. Carsalin-ah!" she raised her voice just a fraction, but immediately the woman was at the door. "Bring me fresh tea," she said, "and a cup for Master Howell as well." Howell had come in behind his mother and stood in the doorway, grinning broadly. This was the crucial moment of meeting and I hoped he had put in a good word for me.

"Mom, this is Gillian. Gillian, this is my mother, Eleanor Edwards," he said.

"I'm trying to make out whether Gillian matches your description of her," his mother said as we arranged ourselves around the table. She leaned forward to make space on the table for the new tray of tea, and instinctively I straightened my back. The bracelet on her arm glittered with raw gemstones while she herself seemed to crackle with energy.

"Howell has said so much already about you," she said. "But of course, the real thing is always more interesting." She smiled again at me, taking in my floral dress and plain brown sandals.

"So tell me about yourself," she invited. I looked over at Howell for enouragement and began by talking about the postgraduate work I was doing in nineteenth-century British literature. "I did the whole thing back to front," I explained. "I worked first, saved up enough money to go back to university and then got my degree. I'm finishing off now, and teaching part time."

"Good for you," she said, reaching for the teapot. "Howell says you're going to be working on a script with him. Do you know I wrote *my* first script when I wasn't as old as you are now?" She stopped what she was saying to direct the pouring of tea and dispensing of cups, then propped a saucer on her palm and stirred as I talked about the research I was also doing for Howell on what made happy marriages work. But before I could get very far, she held up her hand and called for more hot water from the kitchen. Howell took up where I had left off, but before he could get anywhere, his mother excused herself to take a phone call she had been expecting. I wondered whether I should continue when she returned. I had overheard the call she had taken from an opera singer friend in Vienna who would be performing in Cape Town and staying with her at the end of the month. Suddenly, our news sounded dull and ordinary.

"So the thing about this script," I fumbled, "is that Howell has this great idea of getting the people we want to interview to talk into the camera when we're not there."

"Who asks the questions?" she asked.

"No one. That's the point," I said. She broke into a tinkling laugh and turned to Howell. "Well, I've never heard of *that* in all my life," she said. She turned back to me and said, "It won't work of course." Howell, who had propped himself on the edge of the sofa next to me, smiled indulgently.

"No, you don't understand, Mom," he said. "We give them the questions before we leave them to talk, and after that, they speak off the top of their heads. They'll say whatever comes to mind instead of being tongue-tied because there are people in the room. That way, we hope they'll really open up." But his mother's attention had already wandered. She was riffling through papers on the table in front of us.

"I'm sorry, darling," she said. "I know I had some papers here for the piece I'm writing, and now I don't know where they've gone." She called again for Carsalina, to ask whether, by chance, she had removed the papers from the table.

"Of course not, Madam," Carsalina said and, breathing heavily as proof of her innocence, stooped to gather up the tray. Eleanor turned back to me and was at once attentive and enquiring. Where had I said my parents lived? she asked. And what did my father do there again? A chartered accountant! How useful, but why on earth did they live in Zimbabwe? What was up there except the Victoria Falls? My mother's political views, I told her, had made them leave—that and the chance my father had to run his own accounting practice in Harare. Oh I see, she said. Well, that's very interesting. I tried to think of something I could tell her about my mother that might interest her, at the same time wondering what my practical, hardworking mother would think of Eleanor. I put both thoughts out of my mind and asked her instead about her art collection.

"Howell's told me a lot about your art collection," I said, trying to revive her interest. "I'd love to see more of it while I'm here."

"Oh this is the fun stuff," Eleanor said, laughing off the landscapes and animal studies around her. "The really valuable pieces are up at the castle." The castle was Howell's childhood home in Namibia, a miniature crenellated folly built in Windhoek at the turn of the century and now the family's principal residence for seven months of the year.

"If I have some time tomorrow, I'll dig out one or two of the books I've written on some of the artists I own. Now you'll have to forgive me," she said, standing up to leave, "but I've got to get back to putting the finishing touches to a piece I'm writing for *ArtWorld*." She pressed the jade button for Carsalina to remove the remaining cups and smiled sweetly at me. I jumped to my feet like a schoolgirl in the headmistress's study.

"We'll see you again at dinner tonight at about eight. Oh, by the way, we've put you in the red room down the hall. You'll have to use the guest bathroom next to the sauna. I'm sorry there isn't one just for you. And if you feel like a midnight snack, well, the kitchen is right next door."

I quickly learned that the running of the household revolved around Eleanor's breakneck schedule of breakfast dates, lunches and dinner parties. As early as seven in the morning, guests would start to trickle in to join her for her morning swim in the ocean, and during the day a constant stream of people rang the front doorbell or simply walked in through the back patio to pay their respects to her. Many were visiting writers and artists who scribbled or painted greetings in her bulging visitors book. Others sent her miniature "works in progress" as bread-and-butter notes for her lavish hospitality.

Howell's father, Leo, was nowhere to be seen. He limited his appearances to the early mornings, when he accompanied Eleanor to the beach, and to dinner, when he polished off a gargantuan meal and a Cuban cigar. During the rest of the day, he preferred to remain invisible, poring over newspapers and stock reports or sleeping as far away from the bustle of the house as he could get. He was a gruff, handsome man whose shock of white hair and melancholy expression gave him the look of a lion with toothache, and no one seemed to think it important to introduce us formally before his first encounter with me at the dinner table on the night I arrived.

"Are you Howell's friend—Gillian?" he enquired, taking his seat at the head of the table. From the way in which he hesitated when he spoke my name, I knew he had had to be prompted by Howell. So many guests passed through the house, it would take him a full week to realize that I had become a permanent fixture at the dinner table.

"What do you want to drink?" he asked, and without waiting for a reply filled a wine glass to the brim and set it down in front of me. "You could do with more meat on your bones," he said, appraising me over his reading glasses. "Do you eat lobster?" I turned, following the direction of his gaze and watched a platter laden with the spiny carapaces making its way up the table towards me. I thought it best to be honest from the start.

"No, I don't," I said, turning back to him.

"You don't eat lobster?" he asked. "Why not?"

"Where I come from, they're the cockroaches of the sea," I said. To my horror, all conversation at the table died away. Eleanor turned towards me and asked if I would repeat what I had just said. Had she heard me correctly? I felt myself flush scarlet with embarrassment. What had made me say something so blatantly tactless? The words had spilled from my mouth as though my brain were disengaged, as indeed it was in this unfamiliar and disconcerting company. I looked over to Howell who was sitting at the opposite end of the table, praying for him to come to my rescue.

"Just a joke, Mom," he said. "You know we've all got to become more environmentally aware nowadays." Then he lifted his glass to me in mock salute.

"Haven't you ever eaten lobster before?" Eleanor asked, turning back to me. There was a second's silence while I scoured my head for the appropriate reply. Then she broke into her silvery laugh. "Well, never mind, we shall all savor them with new appreciation tonight." The table plunged back into conversation and the moment passed. I reached for the bowl of salad in front of me and glanced back at Howell's father. He had said nothing in response to my remark and appeared to be engaged in cracking a claw and dipping it into the sauce boat filled with lemon butter beside his plate. He sucked out the flesh, raised his head and gestured towards my plate.

"It won't fatten you up eating stuff like that," he said. "But I'll tell you what. I'll eat your cockroach for you. I've got plenty of room for another one."

We were allies from that night on. I never minded his gruff ways or blunt refusals to mix with Eleanor's friends. In many ways, we were similar souls, pragmatic exiles in Lotus Land. There would be times in the years ahead when he and I would escape to the veranda at the top of the house to get away from the throng downstairs. Both of us were shy people at heart, and once, when I had suggested that he could save money on electricity bills by lowering the thermostat on the fifteen hot-water heaters in the house, he had turned to me and said, "Thank God my son has chosen a sensible woman." I wondered whether this was a reference to Eleanor's spendthrift ways. Howell had told me that his father sometimes confiscated his mother's checkbook when her spending exceeded his frugal limits.

"He gets *that* mad at her?" I had whispered when he gave me this astonishing piece of information. Still under the spell of Eleanor's charismatic presence, I caught myself whispering even when she was nowhere within earshot.

"Oh, well, you know," he said vaguely. "She certainly knows how to spend."

She certainly knew how to tell a good story as well. She was a born entertainer whose only fault lay in her refusal to yield the floor once she got going. On the day I arrived, she had spent the morning with Princess Alice of Athlone, Queen Victoria's last surviving granddaughter.

The old lady, now in her nineties and increasingly frail, was on holiday nearby in the house she had been visiting for nearly half a century. Eleanor had become a friend of hers many years before and would drop in to pay her respects at the start of each season. At the dinner table that night, she regaled us with an account of their meeting, beginning with the fall that had nearly tipped her into the princess's lap as she stepped forward to curtsey.

"Well, how was I to know the Persian rug was rotten?" Eleanor laughed. "Can you imagine what might have happened if I had been pitched headlong into her lap? In her condition, I may have finished her off right then and there. Imagine a long and glorious life snuffed out in a trice because of a frayed carpet!" She had gone on to recount how the notoriously irascible old woman had responded when Eleanor had asked whether she remembered her illustrious grandmother.

"She looked at me as though I had uttered high treason!" Eleanor recalled, digging the flesh from her lobster. Adopting her most imperious manner and drawing herself up to her full height, the old lady had boomed back, "Well, don't *you* remember *yours?*" Eleanor had done a brilliant imitation of the princess's high Victorian accent, mimicking the way she pronounced *yours* as *yewers*.

"And can you *imagine* what wonderful memories she must have locked away in her head?" she went on. "I'd give anything to steal inside for a rummage."

Suddenly, while still in midsentence, she had ducked under the table to locate the floor bell that summoned the servants. "This *darned* bell," her muffled voice rose from under the table. "*Forever* sliding around somewhere down here. Can't we get it fixed to the wall? Leo? Do you hear me?" she said, popping up again. Without missing a beat she continued with her account. "Yes, I do think I should approach a publisher with the idea of writing her memoirs for her. Of course, if I'm going to do it, I'd have to get started pretty darn quickly because the old gal's bound to pop off soon and then it's Kaiser Wilhelm, all her Russian cousins, the world at Osborne and Sandringham all gone, like snapping off a light with the flick of a switch. *Tempus fugits* I'm afraid, even for royalty." Like everyone else at the table, I sat speechless and spellbound.

But life with Eleanor was not all entertainment. What Howell had neglected to tell me was that the family had long ago devised a private code to determine who was eligible for election to their circle and who this coveted position would always elude. One of the more simple marks of favor Eleanor bestowed on aspirant insiders was to invite them to join her for her morning swim. Only those who were *One Of Us* regularly attended. I had not yet realized that the hour on the beach in the morning was more sacred to the family than any other time of day. This was when all policy was decided, when Eleanor canvassed opinion, planned and organized the lives of everyone around her and *in* and *out* votes were cast. If I really wanted to be a part of Howell's life, my presence on the beach in the mornings was not optional, it was required. But apart from being good form, it was also one of the family's acid tests of character. This was where I was to fail so miserably.

Eleanor was wonderful in the mornings. She awoke without a yawn and immediately plunged into the business of organizing her day. First there was a forty-minute ritual during which she made and took the first of the three or four dozen phone calls that punctuated her day. Then she lined up guests and family to load them down with towels, beach umbrellas, Thermos flasks, surfboards, inflatable rafts and instructions. Though the sun had barely appeared over the horizon, every inch of bare skin had to be slathered in sunscreen before we left for the beach. With hats assembled, sunglasses found, more sunscreen applied, hair slicked, shirts donned, lipstick on, scarves tied, sandals buckled, and last-minute telephone calls made, the slow crocodile, led by Leo, finally made its way to the tidal pool a hundred yards from Howell's home. This was where I first discovered I was a poor candidate for taking holy orders in Howell's family.

The first time I plunged into the freezing Cape waters, I lost my breath for a full minute.

"This is the bravest thing you'll ever see me do," I told Howell after testing the water with my toes. I walked into the pool up to my waist, then flung myself forward into the frigid water. That was when all breath exited me, leaving me speechless with shock. All I had on between me and the bath of icy salt was a thin nylon bathing suit. Around me, beefy characters in wetsuits were applying vaseline to their faces and hands to keep out the cold. But Howell's family threw themselves into the stinging water as though it was a pond of warm chocolate. They floated on their backs and laughed uproariously as high tide smashed over them and the salt water stung their eyes.

"Isn't this wonderful?" Howell laughed. "Makes me feel I can take on the world."

I looked around to see Eleanor and Leo bobbing on their backs, calling to their guests to join them. Howell applauded me from the side of the pool and plunged in over my head, completing two or three lengths before climbing onto a wall that separated the pool from the Atlantic current. As the huge breakers broke over him, he turned his body sideways to their force, finally flinging himself into the water and riding the length of the pool on the swell of a wave. By this time, I had swum back to the shallow end, my teeth chattering like castanets and every hair on my body standing upright from shock.

"Wasn't that wonderful?" Howell said, slicking back his hair from his face.

"Exhilarating," was all I could manage. There was too little fat between me and wherever my core temperature was located to survive the shock of this icy baptism. All the same, I was determined to prove I could withstand the ordeal. The second morning out, I stayed in the water for a full fifteen minutes, and shivered for an hour afterwards in spite of black coffee and a hot shower. The third morning, I had an even more startling reaction. My body turned bright red and erupted in weals all along my legs, torso and arms in response to the extreme cold. On the fourth day I told Howell I was staying in bed.

"Don't be silly," he said, standing in the doorway of my bedroom in his trunks. "*Everyone* is down there. You know you'll love it as soon as you get used to it."

"No I won't," I told him. "This is not about character. This is about survival. I'm not built to withstand eight-degree water."

"Suit yourself," he said. "But you're going to miss out on all the fun." It took me a while to realize that not only was I guilty of a flagrant breach of manners, but that my refusal to brave the water was proof enough that I did not possess the right stuff to make a good match for Howell. In failing, I had put all my other flaws under scrutiny as well.

Later that week, Howell and I had gone for a long walk along the beach. For the first time since I had arrived, the benefits of long carefree days and glorious weather were beginning to work on me. Books and lectures, students and timetables were a world away.

"There's something I want to talk to you about," Howell said, linking his arm through mine as we walked.

"Oh yes?" I said. The afternoon was a rare break from Eleanor's relentless round of activities and I hoped he was going to tell me how much it meant to him to have time alone with me. I missed the easy days we had spent together back home. Instead, he launched without ceremony into what he had to say.

"When you dress for dinner tonight," he said, choosing his words carefully, "you may want to put on something more formal than you wore last night. My mother's having in some old friends for dinner—I think the German ambassador is among them—and a couple of local artists. Oh, and I hope you don't take this badly. But when you live by yourself, as you've done for so long, you may get a little careless . . . well, you probably don't have to worry about your manners very much. So when you're talking to my mother, try to keep your elbows off the table and don't pick at the salad with your hands. Just a couple of points, okay?" He jostled my arm as if to say this was all between friends.

Hot shame flooded me and rooted me to the spot.

"Your mother doesn't like my manners?" I asked him, as he, too, stopped short.

"No, it's not exactly that." He examined a stick he had picked up on the beach.

"Howell, look at me. Is this you? Or is it your mother?"

"It's me," he said, looking me in the eye. I refused to accept this and turned on him in humiliation.

"If your mother doesn't like the way I act or dress or talk, tell *her* to have it out with me," I said, rounding on him. "I don't understand why it's you who has to tell me I don't match up to her standards."

"Rubbish," he said. "I'm just saying this for your own good."

"You sound exactly like her. Do you realize that?"

"Don't take it so personally," he said.

"How much more personal can you *get?*" I asked him.

Howell stared down at his feet, uncomfortable for me and embarrassed by my outburst.

"I know what it's about," I said as the thought suddenly hit me. "Your mother's been bitching to you about me, hasn't she?"

"Don't talk about my mother like that," he snapped.

"I'll tell you what, Howell," I said, with more bravado than conviction. "Both of you can go and *shove* your opinion of me down your royal throats. If your mother doesn't like me in your life, you know what you can do about that too." He was silent.

"Well?" I yelled at him. He looked at me planted in front of him, hands on my hips, face ablaze with humiliated fury, and suddenly he began to laugh—first a chuckle, and then a full-throated roar that brought tears to his eyes.

"Gilly, Gilly, Gilly," he said. "Now don't get yourself so upset. You know my mother. She . . . well, she is who she is. What can I say?" He threw his arms up in the air and then out towards me. But I jerked away angrily.

"I don't know what to make of all of you, Howell," I said. "I don't understand how you operate. You're a different person when we're alone back home or you're working. Here, with your mother, you're different. What *is* it with you?"

The playfulness was gone from him now. His face was somber and his mouth a tight line. "I can't reason with you when you're this way," he said.

Suddenly, he turned and began walking away from me along the beach. I didn't try to catch up with him and he did not look back. I felt furiously ashamed. And furious with myself that I cared so much. I felt that he was seeing me through his mother's eyes and had been doing this from the day I arrived. There had been that stupid remark at the dinner table and then my refusal to swim in the mornings. And now the domino effect was that everything I said or did was under scrutiny. I remembered how distant, polite, even formal he had been with me when I arrived. On my first evening, he had kissed me goodnight and left me to find my own way to bed. The following day he had pushed away my arm as I put it around his waist.

"Not the time or place for that now," he whispered.

"What's the matter?" I hissed back. "You're not a teenager. We're grownups. We don't have to ask your mother's permission."

"We're in her house," Howell whispered back. "Let's show her some respect."

For the first time, I had wondered what a man of nearly thirty was doing under his mother's roof if he had to watch what he said and how he could behave with a girlfriend. I had also thought back to that first meeting with Eleanor many times since I arrived. I was reasonably confident about getting on with people. But with her, I had been flustered and stupid, as though I possessed no social skills at all. Eleanor's cool, beautiful eyes had rested on me briefly at the dinner table that evening and drifted away, as though there was nothing at all I could say that might be of interest to her. Once or twice I had seen her clamp her jaw when I spoke, as though she was stifling a yawn. I was too naive to read the signals correctly, to understand that this might be a power play on her part. Instead, I had fallen right into her trap, feeling intimidated and stupid. And she had seen it. In her eyes, I was an upstart who talked too much, had no social connections of any importance and dressed like a peasant.

Standing there on the beach, watching Howell disappear, I realized that some of my own shame derived from the fact that I was as much of a pretender as he was. As his mother was. I *cared* that she thought so little of me. I wanted to feel as assured as they did, to fit in, to be accepted. The part I had not foreseen was that I could be dismissed so lightly. In spite of Eleanor's airs, I respected and admired what she had worked for. I hoped she would feel the same about me. I had put myself through college, looked after myself and did well at my job. In my book, that gave me some points. In Eleanor's, it simply made me certifiably naive about the real ways of the world.

Howell was a dot at the end of the beach by now. As I watched him disappear, another tiny voice in my head said that if that was all he wanted from me, then screw him too. The first serious doubts I had about us as a team were hammering in my head. I could have walked away then, but I didn't. And the psychological moment passed. The only thing that was clear to me was how horribly confused I had made myself by coming to this "place of rest."

"Howell dear," Eleanor called out from her bedroom towards the end of my second week at Omutara, "do come in here for a moment."

When he emerged twenty minutes later, Howell looked uncomfortable.

"What's up?" I asked him suspiciously. I was still smarting from the talk about my manners and wondered whether I had yet again transgressed some unspoken code.

"My mother's just had a phone call from Vanessa," he sighed. "She's out here from London and wants to see us. We've invited her to dinner tomorrow night."

"We?"

"Well, my mother."

"Look," he conceded, "I know this is going to be a little uncomfortable, Gillian, but surely you can cope."

I wasn't sure I could.

Blessed with the right provenance and bones, Howell's fabled ex-fiancée was still welcome whenever she visited Cape Town. The photograph of her that Howell carried in his wallet revealed a sophisticated waif with ragged blonde hair and the wide-eyed expression of a kitten. The photograph, along with the nearly talismanic importance she seemed to have had in Howell's life, made me intensely curious about the end of their affair.

"Just exactly what went wrong?" I nagged Howell once again. I longed to be assured that it was all over between them, but Howell evaded my questions.

"It wouldn't have worked out, that's all," he mumbled. "She was too difficult." Then why keep her photograph so close to his heart?

"Well, she *was* my first real love," he fenced.

"Then mount her and frame her," I said, immediately regretting my choice of words. "But for heaven's sake, empty out your wallet."

I also wanted to know why she persisted in seeing his family every time she made her annual pilgrimage back home. Howell's mother was the first person she called every January, and it was curious that her visit always coincided with the week Howell was in town.

"I guess my mother believes Vanessa is still part of the family," Howell said. I seethed with envy.

She had heard about me, that's what it was. And if anything, she was here to cause mischief. Worst of all, I had no advantages over her. As I ransacked my wardrobe for something different to wear, I realized it was useless. In this company, I was going to be outclassed and outsmarted at every turn.

Even the menu was different on the night Vanessa dined with the family. Carsalina had pulled out every stop in her formidable array of cooking skills. Tonight she had produced a salmon soufflé, rack of venison and homemade ice cream served with fresh mango and kiwi fruit. Instead of wine, we drank champagne.

Vanessa had arrived just before dinner, wearing a simple sheath in pink silk with strappy sandals to match and huge gold bangles stacked up to her elbow. Her blonde hair was piled on top of her head and she wore little makeup other than loads of mascara and a glistening lipstick. I heard Howell's voice catch as he stepped forward to peck her cheek.

"Nessie," he said. "Welcome back."

"How are you, Howell?" she asked, placing her hands on his shoulders and surveying him. "A work of art, signed by two maestros— bound to appreciate in value as the years go by." She turned back to Eleanor and they pecked each other's cheeks. Then she turned towards me and extended her hand.

"You must be Gillian," she said, her gaze never shifting from my eyes. Her touch was as light as a feather. No grip there, I thought. Bones like a bird. But she was every bit as lovely as the photograph I had seen in Howell's wallet. And there was a stillness about her, as though she was measuring everything you said against a little private storehouse of her own thoughts. She said very little in reply to my questions about the work she was doing in England. Instead, at dinner she had deftly turned the conversation back to me.

"Let's talk about you instead," she said. "I hear you've started up a film course in your department?" Film history was a passion of mine and I could talk about the great age of silent movies for hours.

"That's how Howell and I . . ." I faltered. I had wanted to say *became really interested in each other,* but I cut myself short. How did she know that?

"How did you know about my film course?" I asked.

She laughed. "Oh I have friends in the department."

"Who do you know?" I went on.

She swirled the champagne round in her glass and leaned closer to me. "One of them told me a very naughty thing about you," she said.

"About me?" I was flattered. But her next words caught me completely off guard. She leaned closer and whispered in my ear, "They say you slept with every one of the professors in the department to get your First Class Honors."

I sat back and searched her face to see if she was joking. But she was not. She was deadly serious. It was then that I had a swift realization of why Howell had given her up and the relief made me throw back my head and laugh out loud. She kept on smiling.

"Oh Vanessa," I said, laughing till I could feel tears in my eyes, "I can't tell you how relieved I am to hear you say that."

"Relieved?" she said. The smile never left her face.

"Whatever have the two of you found to laugh about?" Eleanor asked from the other side of the table. I couldn't stop laughing. If only I had been able to say out loud to the assembled company that I knew at last why Howell had given up this gorgeous creature. The reason was simple. She was clearly insane.

"Come on you two. You can catch up on shared interests later on," Eleanor said. "Let's go through to the living room for coffee."

Howell had not said much through the meal, but had kept the champagne flowing with a flourish. Now, to my embarrassment, he put one arm around each of us and said with a grin, "I want to know exactly what the two of you have been saying about me." Fortunately, the three of us could not squeeze through the door frame together and I freed myself.

Later, when we had finished our coffee, Vanessa sprang the surprise of the evening on us. She sat back on the sofa, crossed one leg over the other, snapped shut her purse after reapplying lipstick and smiled up at Eleanor.

"I can't let the evening go without sharing my best surprise of all with you," she said. "I've been saving it up for now and you're the first people to know." All eyes in the room were on her. I glanced over at Howell and noticed that he had frozen in mid-stance, just as he was about to pour a brandy for his mother.

"What is it, darling?" Eleanor asked. "Come on. Don't keep us in suspense."

Vanessa folded her arms around her knees and beamed directly into Eleanor's eyes. "I'm going to be married!" she said. A chorus of cries went up from Eleanor and Leo and in the middle of them, a stifled "oh" from Howell.

"This calls for more champagne," Eleanor said, expertly covering up the tension in the room. "Who's the lucky man, darling?" she went on. Vanessa looked at Eleanor with a satisfied smile.

"Langley Carlew-Scott," she said. Eleanor nodded, mentally placing the name in her scheme of things. Her own sisters had all married well and she had an encyclopedic knowledge of who was who, both in England and South Africa.

"But where *is* he?" Eleanor asked. "Why isn't he here to celebrate with us tonight?" Howell still said nothing. He and Vanessa were deliberately avoiding each other's eyes.

"He's coming out on Monday," Vanessa said, her cheeks flushed with the impact of her announcement. "We're having a week together on a farm up in the Drakensberg, and the official engagement party will be in London on the eighteenth of this month."

"Well, you two," Eleanor said, turning around to Howell and to me. "What do you think of that? Come on, Howell. Don't hold back. Let's drink a toast to Vanessa and Langley."

Well, that takes some cheek, I thought. Not only is the woman clearly off her head, but to make your engagement announcement in your former fiancé's home, with his mother and girlfriend in the same room, certainly takes the cake for nerve.

It was only then that Vanessa looked up at Howell. There was something like sly triumph on her face. He put down the champagne bottle in his hands and stepped over to peck Vanessa on both cheeks.

"Well," he said softly, "tell him he'd better take good care of you." She put one hand up over his and looked down at the floor. Every gesture she made was studiedly gracious, as though you would never catch her with her mouth askew or her eyes wrinkled up at the light.

"Thank you, darling," she said softly. She kept Howell in front of her just one second too long, and in that moment I knew that there had been much more of a bond between them than he had ever let on. Vanessa was not out of our lives yet.

Much later, when she had left, Eleanor turned from the window and smiled at us. Then she directed her attention to Howell.

"I thought Vanessa looked lovely tonight, didn't you?" she said. "Well, they say all brides-to-be are radiant. But I do think England has done her the world of good. It's given her a place in the world. And some polish." Then, without warning, she turned to me and said sweetly, "You might think about that some day, Gillian." The remark was a mild slap, but enough to make me stare long and hard at myself in the mirror that night. So that's what they wanted, was it? Polish. An exterior veneer. Well, that was easy enough to put together. The question was, did I want to? It seemed it wasn't enough to be yourself in this milieu. If I wanted Howell—and I still wasn't sure I did—I would have to learn to play their game. No. Better still. Understand their game but never play it. I was too young, too under Omutara's spell, too in love with Howell to know that the only way I could have saved myself was to walk away then and never look back.

One night towards the end of my first week at Omutara, I had gone into the kitchen to fix a late-night snack. As I reached into the back of the grocery cupboard, my hand had closed over a small package crudely wrapped in newspaper. I drew it out, tore away the newspaper, noting the date—1967—and pulled out a small silver teapot, milk jug and sugar bowl. Blackened with tarnish and disuse, the items had lain at the back of the cupboard for at least ten years. But underneath the tarnish, the teapot was beautiful. As round as a melon, with a short, straight spout and ebony handle, its only flourish was a tiny ebony knob on the lid. Salt air had begun to pit the metal but I was sure it was sterling silver—it was too light to be plate. Rummaging under the sink, I found a box of Calgonite powder and poured its contents into a basin of hot water. Then I soaked the pot, jug and bowl in the solution overnight. The next morning, while the family was down at the beach, I found an old cloth and a tin of Silvo and set to work. The metal was black with oxidization and it took a full day of rubbing before the first tiny circle of silver shone through. I told no one about my find, but whenever I had time on my own late at night, I took the pot from its cupboard and worked at removing the years of tarnish. Little by little it lifted and the metal was restored to its original condition. By the end of my stay, pot, jug and bowl shone like newly minted coins. Even the silver screws that held the ebony knob in place gleamed like water.

"Why it's absolutely lovely, Gillian," Eleanor said, holding the little teapot in the air. "You *are* a clever girl to find this for me. Thank you." She turned to Leo who was passing through the room on his way to their suite. "Leo, do you see what Gillian's found for us? Take a look, darling. Isn't it lovely?"

He took the cigar from his mouth, grunted in our direction and walked on. I quickly realized her mistake. She clearly thought I had bought the set as a gift for her.

"No, it's yours," I laughed. "I mean it's *always* been yours. I found it in the kitchen, in a cupboard."

"Oh you did? What was it doing there?" she said. The smile was fading from her face.

"You don't remember having it?"

"Well, now that you say so. Yes, of *course* I do. But I haven't seen these little darlings for years!"

"They must have been in there for some time. They were black with tarnish. I used up two cans of Silvo getting them clean."

She looked at me and laughed. "But the servants could have done that for you. You didn't have to waste your holidays polishing silver!"

"I like restoring things," I said.

"Well, in that case, I can give you the sheets to mend and you can get started on the shutters to the windows as well."

Howell laughed and I did too, although I couldn't figure out why I felt furious. It seemed that every time I spoke to Eleanor now, my voice wound up tighter and tighter like a watchspring. What made me hate myself even more was that I was still trying to win her favor. Perhaps I hadn't realized yet that everyone always tried to win her favor. And that's how she kept us all rolled up in a confused little ball in the giant sticky nexus of her web.

"When you talk about this time to me, Gillian," Alma commented, "I can't help thinking you saw too many of those silent screen melodramas you love so much."

"You don't think I'm making this up, do you?" I asked.

"Well, you tell me."

"It all happened. And the stories I heard about Howell's days on campus were told to me by several people who couldn't have known they were repeating each other."

"But you *do* like to tell stories."

"Well? What of it?"

"And you do see that Howell had a ready-made audience in you? The way you make him sound, he was irresistible. A Harlequin character come to life."

I thought about her words for a couple of seconds. "You mean I collaborated in making him who he was? Who he still is?"

She nodded. "You ignored the reality of the relationship he had with his mother. You chose only to see the dashing, glamorous man-about-town. And what else do you think you did in setting up your own destiny?"

"Surely you mean my own downfall? Well, for a start I failed to read the signs correctly."

Again she nodded. "*Refused* to read the signs would be more fair to the situation."

"If my emotional IQ had reached room temperature, I should have chartered a bullet train out of there after that first holiday with his family."

"But you didn't."

"No."

"Why was that, do you think?"

I let myself think back to the warm evenings and the phosphorescent breakers under a full moon. The guests in their evening gowns and the bustle before they arrived. The picnics on the beach when we stood knee-deep in icy water tearing mussels off the rocks and cooking them in gallons of white wine. The strawberries by the side of the road, the walks along a five-mile-long beach, the sheer hedonism of having people to look after you and cook for you and cater to your every whim.

"Because I liked the drama too much. And the glamor," I said. "Coming from my home, it felt like being part of a film set. And I suppose it evened me up with my sister and in my mother's eyes."

"So you got what you wanted and you walked into the partnership with your eyes open."

"No," I disagreed with Alma. "No, my eyes were not open. All I could see was the illusion."

"Yes," she agreed, "that *was* part of your error. But you bought it and you knew that it entailed closing your eyes to what was going on."

But what about Howell, I asked her. Why did he keep me in his life? "He says he never loved me. Why did he marry me then? What was *he* doing?"

Her answer was to raise her eyebrows in surprise.

"Both of you married what you didn't allow yourselves to be. You married the dashing playboy. He married the hard-working lecturer. You wanted each other's talents. You wanted to be more of a glamor puss. He would like to have had your commitment to hard work. And perhaps for telling stories," she added more slyly. "If that was all you wanted, the marriage may have lasted indefinitely. Working partnerships often do. You tore up the contract by asking for more."

"Yes, but he didn't have to *marry* me. And risk his mother's disappointment. That's the part I don't fully understand."

"Well," she looked thoughtful. "Perhaps it was one way to get his mother's attention, wasn't it? I'm quite sure there is a degree of ambivalence and anger towards his mother that Howell will never allow himself to feel fully."

"Why?"

"I don't know the reasons for that. He and I would have to explore it together. But I imagine that she was caught up in a world that espoused position, fame and possessions. And that her children never quite matched up to the men and women she showered attention on."

"Howell must have seen that. Why won't he admit it?"

"Fear of being seen to be disloyal. Self-protection. And denial, of course. It's very difficult to dismantle the illusions we form about our parents. When we're forced to see them as mere human beings instead of gods and goddesses, it's one of the most painful losses we ever go through. It means we give up cherished beliefs that they are invincible, all-powerful, all-protective."

"So he's been misplacing the anger he felt onto me these past years?"

"Perhaps. His outburst against you in the car was chiefly directed towards his own childhood demons. And that works both for you and against you."

"How's that?"

"I imagine that now that his mother is no longer here, you might have stepped into her shoes for him."

"I'd hate to be anything like her."

"Well. Think about that. There was a great deal that you admired about her and I'm sure you learned much from her that was good. And Howell could not have turned out to be the committed parent he is without some excellent input in his own childhood. If you've stepped into her shoes, you'll come in for some of the same heroine-worship he bestowed on her. Of course, that doesn't allow you to be entirely human either. Howell doesn't like to be confronted by too much reality— and he will have to look into that. His ex-girlfriend sounds like an icon, not a human being. He stayed loyal to her as long as she was only a photograph in his wallet. Her real problems were too human for him to take on. Rightly so, I believe. She really does sound as though she might have lost touch with reality. But do you see the pattern? Howell likes his women perfect, unreachable and not quite human. When you showed your frailties to him, his own insecurities were deeply disturbed. You reflected back to him many of his own fears. To really function here, both of you would have to tear down your facades and be prepared to accept each other for the essentially flawed and vulnerable human beings you are."

"Where do I start?"

"You've got to get past the blocks first. In your case, you've got to get past your anger with him. I'm beginning to understand where it began. I can't understand well enough yet why you didn't walk away from him. I suspect you needed to have him to build a case against. And of course the perfect arena to work through all the unresolved battles from childhood is marriage."

E ❖ I ❖ G ❖ H ❖ T

I married him because in my plainspoken world he represented everything I wanted to be and never could. I married him because what I knew about marriage and men was meager and skewed by fantasy. There had never been much discussion about what made a good life-partner at home. Loyalty and responsibility were bandied about as concepts, but the face they wore at the dining-room table was grim and unloving. I can't ever remember my parents hugging each other or showing enthusiasm for their life together. By the time my sister and I were born, both of them were exhausted by life. My mother had been left a war widow with two teenage boys. My father's first wife had left him, abandoning their two sons to his care. Each of them married again out of desperate necessity and it showed in every gesture. When they argued, my mother's voice would escalate into an accusatory whine that dumped all of her bitter disappointments on my father's head. I learned early on that it was she who laid down the law and that my father, meek and good-natured, would fall in with her decree. In the soft, silly words he used to placate her, the gifts he bought to mollify her and the manner in which she turned these down, I discovered the universal law of marriage: always there is one who loves and one who is loved in return.

Armed with this flawed perspective, I had no idea how husbands and wives found one other. How would I choose when the time came, I badgered my mother. "Marry a rich farmer," was all she would say. When I nagged further, she added that one day a man would come along who would sweep me off my feet and this would let me know he was right for me. Not happy about falling into the arms of a stranger, I persisted with my line of reasoning. So the way a man made me *feel*

103

would make him right for me? Was that what she meant? "You'll know when the time comes," she said cryptically. But *how?* How would I know, I pestered. The stronger your feelings, the more certain you would be he was the right man for you, she repeated. *Really?* I didn't like intense feelings, I told her. When they wore off, they left you feeling foolish and exhausted. "You're going to have a very dull life if you question everything to death," she said. When I think back to those words, I realize how bitterly shortchanged she must have felt by marriage. In spite of her own failures, she was still willing to believe in fairytale endings, though a thirteen-year-old girl could figure out that they were intrinsically flawed. Burying my own skepticism, and blind to the fact that my parents' partnership was the damaged blueprint on which I based my great expectations, I waited for a man to come along who not only would sweep me off my feet but also allow me to lavish all my pent-up girlish dreams on him.

When Howell came into my life, I breathed a sigh of relief. My mother had been right after all. Here was someone who ignited all my fantasies, made me feel funny, needed and useful. Blessed with charm, vitality and good looks, he was everything an emotionally naive young woman could ask for. He even made me feel that if I spent enough time in his company, some of this magic would rub off on me. So what if he didn't feel the same way towards me? I had enough love for both of us. Wasn't this what made good partners? It never occurred to me that I might have made things too easy for him. That he was happy to have me along simply because I required so little effort. Like many women with little understanding of their own worth, I was awestruck by my good fortune, willingly blotting out my other ambitions to keep Howell at my side. He never set out to demean me, but right from the beginning I was a willing volunteer for the string of abasements that came my way in later years.

For the time being, I was a full-time lecturer with a gold-lettered name plate on my office door and a heavy schedule of lectures and tutorials each week. I could barely hide the pride I derived from my new position. My mother had thought I was fit to be an excellent secretary and no more. Howell laughed when I told him this, the irony of our situation escaping both of us. He was even more scathing when he learned how many classes I was expected to give each week. "You're nothing better than a postulant in a medieval convent," he told me. "A lackey. A lickspittle. You're kowtowing to a bunch of tyrannical dinosaurs. All because you're trying to prove something to your mother." He was right. My paycheck was pitifully small in spite of filling in for senior staff who refused to be taken away from research. Too timid to question the system and wanting to prove myself an uncomplaining workhorse, I worked a sixteen-hour day, hoping the professors would notice my efforts and reward me accordingly. Howell prodded me into protest. Unless I ordered my life in the way *I* wanted it to go, why bother working at all? Surely that would be self-indulgence, I objected. People worked to keep a roof over their heads—not to have things their own way. Howell spluttered with laughter. My unpoliticized views made me an obvious target for exploitation. No wonder people took advantage of me. At his instigation, I asked for a pay increase, at the same time refusing to take on more work. When my salary had been hiked two or three notches, he pushed me to speak up for changes in the archaic syllabus I taught. And when I was tactfully requested to desist from teaching structuralism because it was "too radical an approach" to English literature, he urged me not to comply. "Trust yourself," he told me. "Defy them. To hell with their outdated ideas." Over and over again I congratulated myself on finding him. Not only was he the most supportive and inspirational man I had ever known, he was also the mentor I had always longed to find. Here, all in one person, was the wise strong guide I had looked for. A man who would bolster me to stand my ground, take charge of life and, perhaps, one day even elect me as his partner.

Within six months of meeting him, he had also persuaded me to try my hand at scriptwriting. Two years later I had written five documentaries for him, each one earning nearly three times the salary I was paid as a lecturer. But it was difficult to hold down two full-time jobs at once, as well as put in work on a doctoral thesis. I was beginning to feel the strain. When I told Howell I would have to give up outside work because my supervisor had suggested my doctoral work was going too slowly, he persuaded me that the work he was doing was worth it. He had tirelessly investigated forbidden subjects such as life in the townships and the country's abysmal rates of heart disease, alcoholism, murder and divorce—the highest in the world. This alone was worth any amount of discomfort. Because we were both committed to seeing change in the country, I agreed to continue working with him, although it meant giving up sleep and precious weekends. After all, even the most mundane outing could turn into an adventure when Howell was around. There had been the dizzying time we had begun to hallucinate from thirst while searching for an ancient *Welwitschia* plant in the Namib desert. And another when we spent days tramping the Mozambique to Knysna coast searching out a rare bird said to pluck its own feathers rather than be slain for the glories of its plumage. On other weekends, Howell had taught me the rudiments of flying, how to stalk and hunt for the pot, and on one unforgettable occasion, while camped next to a lake teeming with hippos, how to dive for cover when the wind changed and two of the beasts came rooting after us like pigs hunting for truffles. Nothing fazed him or got him down. In his company, life stretched away in all directions, timeless and limitless, an illusion so addictive it took me nearly a year to learn that there was another, darker side to his nature as well.

I saw it for the first time when he was stuck at home with two weeks of leave and little to do. I had looked forward hungrily to the break, happy to do nothing else but read and sleep. Howell, on the other hand, had turned edgy and bored almost overnight. He hated being confined, he said, and as I watched in fascination, he had lined up his black address books and begun rifling through them with all the fervor of an expedition leader planning an assault on Everest. "I have to get out," he told me, "even if it's just for a few hours at a time." There was no shortage of parties in Johannesburg to which he was welcomed and he would line them up—sometimes three to an evening, swiftly checking out the company and moving on if there was no one who caught his attention. Back among a crowd, he was his old affable self, his formidable charm drawing people to him and charging him with a palpable energy. Back home, he retreated into himself. "Oh lighten up," he snapped when I asked him what brought this on. "You can be so intense." I was becoming increasingly artful at juggling the anomalies of our situation. If Howell had somber moods, they were merely a facet of his Byronic personality. If he hated me asking questions, I would put them out of my mind. In time, I was sure that as I proved supportive and understanding, he would understand the value of our relationship. Looking back, I realize the Faustian bargain I had struck was that I hoped to become indispensable to him. That way, he would never abandon me.

Now, back in Johannesburg after our first holiday at Omutara, the relationship between us had undergone a subtle shift. Two weeks of observing Howell in the company of his family had given me an altered perception of his strengths and weaknesses. The man who thumbed his nose at government strictures, laughed off warnings from his boss and wore clothes that would electrify a gypsy couldn't put a word in edgewise when his mother voiced her opinions. "She has her way of seeing the world. I have mine," he said, when I remarked on this startling change. "I listen to everything she says. But I keep my own counsel when it comes to making decisions." I had also come to understand that Howell's ill-starred relationship with Vanessa had foundered for good reason. "She was always brilliant and unstable," he confirmed after I relayed to him the contents of her startling remark at the dinner table. "And always had difficulties with the truth. However," he added, loyal to the last, "that's all in the past. I prefer not to talk about it." Then he had added in a hollow voice, "She was my first love. And the last woman I'll ever allow to break my heart." In a rare moment of lucidity, I had broken into peals of laughter. "That sounds like a line from a bad novel," I told him.

Now that we were back home, my opinion of him was not quite as worshipful as it had once been. Howell reverted to the person I had known before, except that to me he was shadowed by the other Howell I had seen with his family. I had also decided to put Eleanor out of my mind, remembering my mother's advice about handling difficult people. "All you have to do is be polite," she would say. I won't let her get to me again, I vowed. But I hadn't reckoned on how much she still wanted me out of the way.

Shortly after we arrived home, she made a last-ditch attempt to pair Howell off with a more suitable partner. She wrote that the daughter of close friends (who just happened to own vineyards in the Constantia Valley) was arriving in Johannesburg. Would Howell see to it that she met all the right people? The young woman—just out of a rehab clinic for heroin addiction—was the heir to her grandparents' fortune as well as to the Cape vineyards and in Eleanor's estimation would make a "lovely companion" for Howell. I decided to take things into my own hands. *I* would fetch Dorey from the airport, I told Howell, and I would see to it that she met the right people in Johannesburg. He seemed relieved—even happy for me to make arrangements on her behalf. When I met her I realized why. Plump, dark and a heavy smoker, she hardly conformed to his ideal of the blonde sex-kitten. On the way into Johannesburg she chattered without pause about a Rastafarian she had met in Jamaica, who wrote inspired music and possessed other divine skills as well. In turn, I told her about the documentary Howell and I were writing and the trip we were planning to take at the end of the year. She understood immediately that we were a pair and confided that she had no intention of playing along with the matchmaking plan dreamed up by both sets of parents. She had known Howell from childhood and hugged him affectionately when she saw him, begging him not to divulge her secret when he spoke to his mother. We spent several evenings together while she was in Johannesburg, and when she called to say goodbye, I felt as though I had won an arm-wrestling contest. Eleanor was disappointed. She told Howell he might have thrown away "a gilded future." The incident sharpened my determination all the more to hold on to her son. I was no longer the wide-eyed girl who believed that true love was unassailable. The holiday at Omutara had given me a clearer idea of my own worth and a sharper reading of Howell. It would have been a simple matter, I thought, for him to tell his mother clearly that he was no longer in the running for a new relationship when she wrote to him about Dorey. But to my disappointment, he did not. And I filed away that piece of information for use later on. In the beginning, it was nothing more than a tiny spark that flared up, then smoldered. But my anger against Howell had begun to find fertile ground in which to flourish.

There was one other factor that sealed our fate together. We had come back to a city where I now had no close family living nearby. My sister had immigrated to the United States six months earlier. My parents, who lived a thousand miles away in Harare, no longer wanted to make the journey to South Africa every other year. They were getting to the age when they wanted to stay home rather than "gallivant," as my father wrote. Then my father's sister, whom I had loved dearly as a child, died of a heart attack early in the year. My uncle left to live in Natal and suddenly I no longer had close family at hand. I found myself thinking back to the get-togethers around the dining table in Cape Town, the constant flow of people in and out of Howell's home and the intense interest members of his family took in the projects they were involved in. I was willing to overlook every misgiving for the chance to be part of a circle as close-knit as theirs. Reshaping events to create the fairytale I longed for, I saw Eleanor not as a tyrant, but as a matriarch firmly in charge of family affairs. Howell was not so much her compliant son as the family's easygoing foot soldier. As for myself, perhaps Howell and Eleanor had been correct about my gauche manners. I had probably been more childishly thin-skinned than I ought to have been. With a little patience and generosity of spirit, it was amazing how much more positive things looked.

Back at work, Howell was deeply involved in a documentary that would follow the trials of the early British settlers in South Africa. He had assembled a hand-picked crew and together we spent long hours poring over details of the shooting script and commentary. He was intent on doing his best work and to this end devised a punishing schedule for himself. The logistics would call for him to haul his crew through some of the most rugged territory in the country so that conditions that had prevailed in 1820 could be accurately re-created. My own family had been among the men and women who had emigrated from Britain to South Africa in 1820, only to discover that they would be used as human barricades against marauding tribes. I couldn't pass up the opportunity to write the script for Howell, filling in details that had been passed down as part of family lore over generations. To celebrate the nomination we earned for best script and best documentary, we gave ourselves an extended holiday in England and Scotland and, in a hired car, lost ourselves on back roads up and down the country. Despite discovering I was allergic to every grass and weed in sight and sneezing my way through the British Isles, the four weeks on our own was the happiest time we had yet spent together. On the flight back home, just as dawn came up over Mount Kilimanjaro, Howell leaned over my seat and nudged me awake, suggesting it would be a good idea if we were married later in the year. "You're mad," I told him, believing he was under the influence of the glorious light flooding into the cabin. "I mean every word," he said, looking grave. It took me a while to think about the implications of his proposal and when I accepted, we toasted our future together in airline orange juice. As soon as we landed in Johannesburg, we called both sets of parents to give them the news. Mine were delighted, but Eleanor was guarded and said very little. Leo congratulated us warmly and welcomed me into the family without reservation.

"At the end of the year," I heard Howell tell his mother on the phone the following evening. "We were planning to have a small wedding here at the end of the year." When he came back into the kitchen where I was chopping vegetables for dinner, he looked unduly sober.

"Anything the matter?" I asked.

"Not really," he said.

"Your mother's not happy, is she?" I guessed.

He pursed his lips. "Well, there's one way to get around her."

"Oh yes? What's that?" I asked, thinking nothing could put a damper on our happiness now. Howell looked me straight in the eye and said steadily, "I've agreed that we'll be married in Cape Town and that the reception will be at Omutara."

I remember the ceremony well but very little of the reception. Howell, as a non-believer, did not want a church wedding. I wanted a simple service. We compromised with a civil ceremony at the magistrate's court in Simonstown on a blustery day in January 1980. My sister flew out from New York to be my matron of honor and left immediately afterwards to get back for a photographic assignment. The reception at Omutara was a crush of nameless faces, all friends of Eleanor's whom I hardly knew. She had selected and ordered our wedding cake—a three-tiered confection topped by a champagne bottle and a bouquet of sugared roses spelling out *La Vie en Rose*. "Life through rose-colored spectacles," I heard one of the guests laugh and wondered in a moment of prescience whether the joke was on me. Howell declined to make a speech, so Eleanor and I did the honors. I thanked her for organizing our reception and for giving me Howell but remember nothing of her reply. Late in the evening, Leo drew Howell and me aside and presented me with a golden tourmaline pendant, his wedding gift to me. Then, salvaging a bottle of Veuve Clicquot from the dining room, he invited us up to the veranda where he broke open cigars for Howell and himself and we had a few moments to ourselves before escaping for the night to a country hotel twenty miles outside Cape Town. I remember sitting on our bed and staring at my wedding dress, wondering how a hole could have been burned into the silk of the bodice. Someone smoking a cigarette had stood too close, and yet I hadn't even smelled the scorching fabric, or felt the burn. I called my parents to tell them that we were now a married couple and turned back to Howell only to find him fast asleep from exhaustion. The following evening we returned to Omutara for the rest of our two-week stay in Cape Town.

Immediately after we came home in late January, Howell began work on a new film. This time he would be shooting in Soweto, following a company of black actors as they put together a musical called *Hungry Spoon*. The company performed in makeshift halls every night, so most of Howell's shoots were organized between six in the evening and four the next morning. At two in the afternoon, he would meet his crew to go over a schedule. At four they would drive out in convoy to the sprawling southwestern townships where a million black people had built a city of their own. There, for the next eighteen hours, he was at the mercy of weather, temperaments and budgetary allowances. The schedule was gruelling, but I worried more about Howell's safety. In 1976, four years earlier, schoolchildren in Soweto had led a riot protesting the use of Afrikaans in their schools. Violence had exploded in nearly every black township in South Africa and by October 1977, over seven hundred people, many of them schoolchildren, had died in the subsequent confrontations with police. Since then, whites had been warned to stay away from black townships. Howell had deliberately defied this ban, determined to film conditions in the townships under the guise of following the fortunes of a band of black actors. With his gift for getting on with people, he formed a close friendship with Gibson Kente, "the Shakespeare of the townships" and creator of *Hungry Spoon*. Within a few weeks, they had become inseparable and over the next four months I saw very little of my new husband.

We had known each other for just over three years at the time and, although there were difficulties, I thought we had discovered everything there was to know about each other. Over the next six months, this perception changed. In the first four months of our marriage, I never saw Howell at all at night. When I protested, he had rounded on me with a fury I had never seen before. "What do you expect?" he said. "I have a job to do and neither you nor anyone else will stop me from doing it." All I wanted to do was eat a meal with my new husband once in a while, I told him. "I'd like to use some of our new wedding china and share a glass of wine with you in the evenings," I whined. He looked at me hard and told me that if I knew anything about the conditions people lived under in Soweto, I would know how petty my concerns were. Deeply ashamed, I stopped asking when I would see him again. But despite my best efforts to stay cool, it was Eleanor who finally succeeded in getting me to explode. This time it was not against her, but against Howell.

He was in the final stages of wrapping up his documentary when she announced she was coming to Johannesburg for a visit. Naturally she would be staying with us. Howell was too distracted to suggest otherwise. Material that should have been shot on location was not in the can, soundtracks were missing and his crew was exhausted from their long shoot in the townships. Just when I looked forward to having my husband back to myself, I would have to share him with his mother. To make matters worse, we were not geared for guests. The spare bedroom at the back of our house was still bleak and uncomfortable, boasting little more than a single bed, a side table and chest of drawers on an uncarpeted floor.

Eleanor was quick to express her discomfort. At dinner on her first evening with us, she announced without preamble that we should start looking for a new place to live.

I looked at her in surprise. Howell tactfully ignored her. I decided to go ahead and answer for both of us. "Are you offering to buy?" I asked as pleasantly as possible then went on to make it clear that we were really very happy where we were.

"Well, it's very inconvenient when you have people to stay," she replied. "Especially since you only have the one bathroom."

Again, I looked to Howell for a response but he was busy with a loaf of French bread, a look of dedicated attention on his face.

"If we ever make enough money," I told Eleanor, "I've figured out a way we can add on another bathroom by going through our bedroom wall."

Eleanor ignored me. Instead she added, "And the other thing is that you could do with some help around this place."

"I *have* help," I said in surprise.

"Oh. I didn't notice," she smiled at me.

"I have Lucy," I told her. "She lives in the outside bedroom. We can't afford to pay her much, so we give her the room and bathroom we have outside, and in return she works for us one day a week."

"But she should be paying *you* if she lives there all the time," Eleanor said.

I could feel the blood beginning to pound in my head. We had had conversations like this with several of our friends. Most of them felt we were being too kind to give a room and bathroom to a woman who worked for us just one day a week. I wondered what Eleanor would say if I told her that besides giving her the outside room and bathroom, Howell and I had agreed to pay double the going wage for a day's work, not through nobility or self-sacrifice, but simply by gearing it to the cost of groceries, transport and school fees. Again I decided to take a chance on explaining the way we felt.

"Lucy lives away from her two daughters all week," I said. "She works from seven in the morning till six at night to pay for their school fees. She often comes home after dark, and the most she can count on for company is a friend who comes over to visit her a few nights every week. Otherwise she leads a pretty lonely life."

"We've leased a television for her," Howell put in. "It was the least we could do to make her life more bearable."

Eleanor put down her fork and turned to me with an incredulous smile. "You're wasting your money—you should cancel the lease immediately and use the money to employ her full time."

My hands began to tremble and I plunged them under the table in an effort to control myself. In the silence that followed, I could feel my heart hammering. Then out of nowhere I heard my voice boom across the room. "I'm not cancelling the lease on her television. I don't need anyone to help me here. And Lucy is not just a black lodger, she's a human being and a friend."

Eleanor gave a short laugh. "I'm sure she's a very nice woman, Gillian. But you must be reasonable. You and Howell are married now, and it's his money as well that's paying for these luxuries."

I looked to Howell for his response, but he was dissecting his meat with surgical nicety and refused to be drawn into the debate. I tried to bring myself under control. "Why don't you tell your mother about your Soweto documentary," I said in a strangled voice. If she balked at the idea that we provided television for our lodger, I longed to see her reaction when her son told her that he had spent four months in Soweto in the company of black actors, gangsters and shebeen queens. Instead she was delighted.

"It could be an award-winner," she told him. "It's just the sort of thing the world is clamoring to see. Color! Exuberance! Showing everybody that blacks have a natural joie de vivre no one can put down."

I could see Lucy in her tiny room with its polished cement floors and the two-burner hot plate she used for cooking her meals; the bedspread she had crocheted through the winter months and her bedside table with its array of photographs, a tiny mirror and a jar of Ponds cold cream arranged just so. I thought of the quiet, careful way she let herself in and out of the house and the way she tapped her hands together when I made her a cup of tea in the mornings. I had seen the photographs of her daughters in their school uniforms and once forwarded a letter to her sister who had taken Holy Orders and was Mother Superior of a convent in Natal. She had lived with me for nearly six years and Howell knew how much I respected and liked her.

"Your mother has no right to tell us what to do about Lucy," I hissed to him after we were lying side by side in bed in the darkness.

"She comes from a different age, Gillian. Try to understand."

114

"Why do *we* have to be so understanding? Why can't she and all her phony friends just shut up and let us live our lives the way we choose to?"

Howell remained silent.

"I get the feeling you were siding with her on this issue," I said, unable to let go of my outrage.

"Of course we'll keep the TV," Howell said wearily. "Now, I've got to be up at six. I need some sleep."

"Howell, I'm not going to let this lie."

"Well, if you want to be so damn moral, why don't you just invite Lucy to live with us in the spare room?" he said. I sat up in bed, boiling with rage.

"Your mother told me I was 'spoiling it' for all the other women who didn't have enough money to pay their servants decent wages. I suppose so they can go on exploiting them with slave wages. Did you hear her?"

"And what did you say back to her? You told her that was all you ever set out to do. Spoil it for everyone else. You're very good at claiming the moral high ground, Gillian," he retorted. "Have you ever thought you could be wrong in the way you go about saying things?"

"I can't believe you're saying this, Howell. You know how we've talked this over. What's the matter with you? Why didn't you speak up for me at the table tonight?"

"Oh for Christ's sake, Gillian, get a grip on yourself. You're going off into one of your pious rages again. I handle my mother in my own way. She didn't mean any harm. To her it sounds as though you've got one hell of a bad conscience and you're trying to reverse all the ills of society on your own. You'll see. In the morning she'll have forgotten all about it."

"But *I* won't. You don't really believe in this, do you? You make movies because it's what you think you *should* be saying. You're a shallow, expedient opportunist and I hate you! I hate you and your whole damn family."

"And you're an insufferable prig. You know perfectly well where my principles lie. But if you don't like the way I live my life or handle my mother, you know what to do about it."

"And what's that?"

"Stay at home, or divorce me. We're not a match if you go on think-ing this way."

That drove me wild. "How can you switch like that?" I screamed at him. "Where do your morals lie? You're making documentaries about Soweto and taking time out at Omutara for rest and recovery. What the hell is going through your head?"

"That's *not* what this fight is about," he said with devastating final-ity. "I know where my morals lie. If you can't take my mother, stay away from her!"

"It's not that," my voice spiralled out of control. "It's you! I can't understand you when your mother's around. You lose your perspective. I hate it. I can't live with you. You're not the man I know. It's as if she has the right to dictate everything we do. Tell me where the hell I'm supposed to stand in this?"

"Oh, grow up," he said. "Just leave me alone."

The following morning I was sick with remorse. Sinking back into passive quiescence, I offered to drive Eleanor wherever she wanted to go and employed my sweetest wiles to placate Howell. I couldn't un-derstand why he remained cool towards me. *I* had got over the previous night's rage, hadn't I? Why couldn't he? I had tossed and turned most of the night, thinking about our future together, and his words had ter-rified me into submission. Leave him? I couldn't imagine life without him. I realized the rare moments of clarity allowing me to see things for what they were, were dangerous intrusions that could derail my life and my marriage if I allowed them to recur. I would have to use more control if necessary and see that they never happened again.

To show Howell how sorry I was for my outburst, I threw myself into entertaining his mother. I took afternoons off work to take her visiting and made sure she was as comfortable as possible in our home. By the time she left at the end of her seven-day stay, I felt noble and smug. I was also sitting on a cauldron's worth of anger. We had one last argument before I caved in completely. That was when Howell came up with the idea that we should think of starting a family as soon as possible.

"You hadn't talked this over before you were married?" Alma broke into my story.

"We had and we hadn't," I hedged.

"What does that mean?"

"It means that I hadn't had enough time with Howell. I wanted a closer bond before I brought a baby into the picture. Howell wanted a child straightaway. Like acquiring another piece of furniture, I thought."

Alma nodded for me to go on.

"I didn't want to give up work to stay home with a child when I hardly knew my husband. I wanted to build a steady, close relationship first—something that was rock solid and unlikely to falter. I hadn't given much thought to giving up work either. I always knew that I would if I had children. Not go back to work, I mean. Day care and childminders were fine, but I knew they couldn't care for a child the way a mother can. We never seemed to get very far when we began to argue about these things."

We had finished dinner and Howell had tilted himself back on one of the dining-room chairs. "I don't know what's got into your head," he repeated.

I steadied myself and sat down opposite him. I was not very good at this, but tonight I was sure of myself. I felt strong and calm.

"When we're here alone, we're great together. But I don't have enough of that. We've almost become strangers since we got married. Howell, something's got to change. If it doesn't, we don't have a future. I'm not prepared to start a family while we're still caught in a tug of war with your work and your mother."

"You're dropping me before you're dropped yourself, is that it?"

"Of course not! I just want us to get our priorities right as a married couple. We come first with each other. Not last, after work and family."

"I think you're being paranoid. You're trying to bully me into seeing things your way."

"Howell. We've been married nine months. I haven't seen you more than a couple of weeks in all that time. And that was only because your mother was staying with us. You want me to think about starting a family? Well, I have no intention of bringing up a baby on my own."

"You're just trying to find excuses not to get pregnant."

"I want a stable home life before that happens. I don't feel we've got it. I can't have a life with you while I come second to your mother and she sees herself as my enemy."

"She's not your enemy, Gillian. She just has her own ideas, that's all. I've explained all of this to you before."

"I guess what I need to hear is that I come first in your life now."

"What are you trying to do. Force my hand?"

"I'm your *wife*. I have the right to expect that I come first in your life. I'm telling you now that we can't make it unless we commit ourselves to becoming a couple."

He tipped his chair forward and looked hard at me. "You really mean that?"

"Of course I do."

"How long have we known each other?"

"Three and a half years."

"And you're willing to throw all of that away because of your insecurities?"

"I know I don't want to be in a relationship where I'm hanging on by my fingernails."

"Tell me something. Am I a decent guy?"

"You're a great guy. You're decent, honest and generous. You don't sneak around. You're restless, but I can live with that."

He looked hard at me. "I've never even looked at anyone else for as long as I've been with you," he said.

"You never gave anyone else a chance to stick around," I said rather churlishly.

"Exactly. I knew early on, not one of them was the right woman for me."

I sucked in my breath. "You've never told me that, Howell. I've never actually heard from you what I mean to you."

"So that's what this is all about. Why didn't you just come out and tell me at the beginning? You want me to tell you I love you and to shower you with attention."

I was hot with shame. "Stop it, Howell," I said. "Don't ridicule me."

He dropped his voice and stood up. "No, I'm not making fun. I do care about you. You're the only woman I've trusted in a long time. I can talk to you. I have fun with you. We share the same interests. You really are wonderful when you're not awful. But *I do not think I'm unreasonable about my mother or my work.* That's where it stands. If you don't like it, you know what to do."

"What's that?"

"Go get a divorce."

I sat there shocked and beaten.

"Okay. Are you clear about all of this?" he said, getting up to go.

"I believe so."

How we had ever crossed the barrier between friendship and marriage was an indecipherable mystery to me at that moment. I looked up at Alma who had listened to my tale in patient silence.

"Within the year, I had given up my job, moved to Cape Town and was pregnant with Emily. I feel pretty ashamed when I sit here and tell you how easily I gave in. But that's what happened."

"You gave up your academic career just like that?"

"It's a long story. Howell bought a house he fell in love with in Cape Town. Then he called me and told me. We had to sell the house we owned. When I put up a fight—about giving up our jobs and everything we had in Johannesburg, he told me once again that if I didn't like it, I could divorce him." I shrugged my shoulders. "I stuck with my marriage."

"So you, too, were suffering from moral ambivalence," she said.

"I suppose I was."

"No supposing. You were. You can hardly blame Howell for that," she answered.

"Why do you *always* take Howell's side?" I blew up at her. "It seems you always see his point of view first, not mine."

"You're quite wrong there. He gets as good as you in my sessions with him. Perhaps more. He's got as many things to work through as you do, and believe me the sessions with him are no picnic."

"I'm not so sure," I said, sulking.

"Gillian," she looked at me gravely. "Listen to me. I am a woman, just like you. But that does not mean that I will always take your side. I don't defend women who invite their fate and then call themselves victims. More often than not, the woman who screams blue murder when her partner plays true to type has chosen him above all other men. She *knew* who he was before she married him. How can she blame him for being himself? You're doing the same thing. You selected Howell in the face of a barrage of warning signals. Then you berated him for being difficult, for not showing you affection and for remaining bonded to his mother. You wore blindfolds because you were bedazzled and you wanted to keep this man at all costs. Don't blame him for being himself. Blame yourself for not accepting him for who he was. And is. It's the difference between your expectations and reality that created all your disappointments."

All I could do was nod miserably at the truth of her words. They embodied the core truth of everything I was to learn from her during our months of counselling together.

"And when I listen to you," she added, "I don't hear a man who didn't care. I hear a man who told you very clearly what you meant to him. Why didn't you want to hear?"

"I guess I wanted to see the proof of it," I said. "He always had this gift of getting around me with the right words. I wanted some of the right actions."

"And then?" she prompted. "You tell me you went ahead and had Emily." She sighed. "I suppose you're going to tell me it got a lot worse."

N • I • N • E

"What I hear is that you felt coerced into becoming a mother. Is that right?" Alma slid a box of tissues over to me and waited until I had finished mopping my eyes. I had been telling her how I had given in finally to Howell's insistence that we move to Cape Town, to live near his parents, and start a family immediately.

"It was the lesser of two evils," I told her stiffly. "Divorce or another chance at saving our marriage."

"You didn't want a baby?"

"Of course not. Not the way our marriage was going. But Howell had a way of making me believe that *all* my arguments for fixing up our marriage were angled against having a baby."

"Hold on a minute," Alma said. There are *two* statements there. You're saying that Howell *made* you believe something—is that right?"

"I've already told you about how he would do that."

"Could he make you believe *anything* unless you wanted to?"

"What's your point?" I sniffed.

"What we're talking about here is a nearly intolerable situation. A marriage that was clearly not working. A mother-in-law who didn't even want you to be married to her son. And instead of you seeing that and working your way through the problems, you chose the oldest escape route of all."

"Having Emily was an *escape?*"

Alma slapped her knees. "Of course! The time-honored escape route. There's no need to feel ashamed. The only shame you should feel was in the moral cowardice of refusing to resolve your problems *before* you brought a baby into this world. You weren't strong enough to walk away from Howell before you became pregnant. *Or* to insist that you work through your problems. You chose the easy way out. The alternatives were confrontation and standing up to Howell. And if that didn't work, perhaps being on your own again. *That's hard work!*" She threw me a grin as if to assure me she'd been there too and knew what she was talking about. "On the other hand," she went on, "there was Howell assuring you that if you did it *his* way you could still be part of a family. You do understand by now of course that your *great* fear is being on your own. Being responsible for yourself." She leaned forward towards me as though she was going to tell me her darkest secret. "I want you to know that it is everyone's greatest fear in life. Everybody's. Being on their own. So you see, you have no reason to feel ashamed that you chose the route you did. You simply put off the evil hour."

"You said I made two statements," I said to her. "What was the other?"

"That you didn't want a baby. Was that the truth?"

I looked squarely at Alma. "What do you think?" I asked her.

"The difference is whether you *ever* wanted children. Or whether you didn't want *this* one."

"No. I'm going to argue with you there. I don't think there's a woman alive who hasn't thought about having children. The only difference with me was that I never wanted to be a single mother. Not only for my sake. But for my child's as well. And I wasn't willing to risk starting a family simply because Howell said it would work. But the funny thing is that when I found out I was going to have Emily, I was ecstatic. I couldn't believe how lucky I was. Relieved as well. The decision had been made for me. There was no question I wanted her right from the beginning. Abortion is not an option as far as I'm concerned. But it was amazing to me that I fell in love with her long before she was born. The first time I saw her heartbeat on ultrasound, I think."

Alma looked at me from behind her creased and kindly seer's face. "There's much more to it, if you'll allow me to suggest," she said.

"Like what?"

"Well. Let's just think for a moment about your mother. Did she show you how to be a good mother? That's where we get most of our lessons from. If the signal she sent out was that motherhood and marriage is all work and no play, that's what you would have carried with you into your married life. When I listen to you, I don't hear much pleasure in your ideas of marriage and being a mother."

I thought back to my mother on the only days I had ever seen her really happy—Monday mornings in the little stone laundry built on to the kitchen of our house. With her hair curling in the steam, and an apron spattered with soap bubbles, she would lean into the tub of her machine and lift the fragrant, steaming bundles of washing, feeding them through the wooden wringers as if making an offering on an altar. The pounding of the machine and the rivulets of water cascading over the glass porthole of the old Bendix represented my mother's triumph over the filth a family brought in its wake. She had told me once in a moment of contemplation that *tons,* literally tons, of body fat and dirt were washed down the drains of South Africa every Monday morning. In her rapturous banishment of these evils, she was doing what she could to restore order and decency to her world, to hold at bay for this day at least, the torments that marriage brought in its wake.

Cooking, cleaning and running a household for eight had worn her down to a thin, sour shrew and when I asked her what it was like to have children, she had said without apology that too many children doomed you to a life of no reward. Out in the world, she sighed, you could earn your own money, forget time, travel and buy yourself decent clothes. At home, your life was eaten up by relentless drudgery. At the end of the day, the only thing to look forward to was the company of a man you did not love, and a basket full of darning. The message I took from her bleak philosophy was that children were the impediments that crippled opportunity and cut short your youth. When I went on to ask her with sly prescience whether she really loved my father, she had replied, "We are partners." Then added, "Though not always." My escape was school. There I was rewarded by teachers who took an interest in everything I did. Because work was the single activity I could count on to earn me attention, I grew up believing little else counted.

"Do you understand what else work accomplished for you?" Alma fixed me with a searching look.

I shook my head.

"I believe you do. Think back to the kind of rewards you got from working." She raised an eyebrow. I shook my head. I was stubbornly resisting her point. It was obvious that I had been able to buy independence, freedom from worry, the ability to make my own decisions. We had touched on these things before.

"Okay, I'll spell it out for you," she said. "It was all about control. You had maximum control over your life while you were making money and setting your own goals. Getting pregnant represented the other end of the scale. How much more out of control can you be than when morning sickness hits? It's the great leveller of womankind," she grinned with understanding. "And when you've been used to working, banking a salary, achieving some sort of competence in the workplace, pregnancy is like war. It's anarchy, a total loss of control. I think you were smart enough to know that. Also to see that you did not have Howell's wholehearted support to back you up. You knew that when you gave in to Howell's desire to become a father, you would also have to surrender the one area over which you had absolute control."

"My body?"

"Of course."

"And yet—when I knew I was pregnant, I just gave in," I told her. "I remembered the stories about all those mothers who had found the strength to lift cars off their children, and I understood completely where it came from."

"That may well have been your great ability to put the best face on things. And even if you did, the tragedy was that you didn't have the words to share this with Howell." She sighed. "It must have been a difficult time for both of you. There are critical junctures in every marriage where the bond between two people is either strengthened or the opportunity is lost forever. One of the most important of these times is during pregnancy."

I had a flashback to a day when I was just eight weeks pregnant and Howell had been getting ready for work.

"I can't get my head off the pillow."

"What's the problem now?"

"Can you bring me a glass of lemon water and toast?"

Howell flicked over his wrist to glance at his watch. "Why do you do this to me just as I'm ready to leave?" I heard his heels click down the stairs and his impatient voice as he pushed the cat out of the front door. A few minutes later he was back at my bedside. He put a cup and plate on the table next to my bed.

"Is this what you want?" he asked.

"What time'll you be back this evening?"

"Around seven. If I don't go now, I'll miss the train."

"Okay, then. Have a good day." He left without a goodbye and I listened to his footsteps receding down the garden path. I ate the toast slowly and sipped at the lemon water. Twenty minutes later I was back in bed again, my heart thudding from the effort of retching. Between bouts of nausea I slept deeply, knowing that this was the best thing I could do both for the baby and myself. I imagined this little being, no bigger than a comma, snuggling down and implanting itself even more firmly into my body and my heart. "I'll do just fine. We'll both do just fine," I told myself fiercely. "I'm here to take care of you." Then both of us would curl up, the one inside the other, into a deep, dreamless sleep that lasted the rest of the day.

In the late afternoon sunlight, I watched Alma tapping her fingers on the sheet of paper she used to scribble questions for me. Her gaze remained on the golden tomatoes ripening outside her windows. Then she turned back to me.

"I'm not unsympathetic to what you tell me," she said. "I want you to know that. But. And here's something I want you to think about. Your childhood could *not* have been all bad." She waited for my response. I didn't know what to say. "Otherwise you wouldn't be here," she added. "You would have snuffed yourself out in one way or another long ago." She ducked her chin at me, fielding my surprise. "But from what I can determine, it *was* pretty bleak. You don't talk much about kindness. I don't see your parents taking time to help you over your fears, or to show you how to become competent in the important things that matter in this world."

That was not quite true. I had a sudden memory of a time when I was seven or eight years old.

"Get *out* from under my feet," my mother told us a dozen times a day. "Why don't you go outside and play." When we fell and cut ourselves in the needle-sharp grass of the veld, we learned to ignore the sharp sting of skinned flesh, pressing eucalyptus leaves into the wound and proudly comparing bruises at the end of the day. "You don't know how lucky you are," my mother told us. "To have the freedom to play outside all day long and not have to work for a living."

There had been a war a dozen years earlier, someone said, and that was when my mother had lost her first husband. He had been shot down "up North" fighting the Germans and was buried somewhere in the Egyptian desert. My mother had planned to immigrate to Canada with him after the war, but those plans had been shattered on the day she received the telegram from the War Office. Two years later, at the end of the war, she had married my father, a handsome, soft-spoken man who had served in the signal corps and worked as a chartered accountant for the Chamber of Mines. She counted herself fortunate as a thirty-eight-year-old woman, especially one whose life had slipped through her fingers, to have found a man of good standing. My sister and I were her insurance policies. My father had longed for daughters and for the first years of our lives, he showered us with attention, driving us twelve miles to the Central News Agency in Rosebank every Saturday morning, so that we could choose any book we wanted to read from its well-stocked shelves. "You girls don't know how easy your life is," my mother would throw over her shoulder, as she bustled upstairs laden with ironed washing. "If you knew what we had to do without when we were young, you'd never ask for another thing in your lives." We were living in a newly built house on the outskirts of Johannesburg at the time, on an acre of muddy ground that had been cleared from the veld and sprinkled with a thin layer of topsoil trucked in from a nursery twenty miles away. The veld stretched forty miles in front of us to the blue hills of the Magaliesberge and had been a billion years in the making, my father told us. Overnight it had been scoured of its grass, trees and sagebrush so that twenty houses could be built in a row. My father tore out lumps of quartz the size of footballs to make rockeries, but the acrid-smelling *khakibos* still grew through the stones, refusing to be uprooted. My mother saved string and measured out sugar and milk, a wartime habit she kept right into old age. She turned sheets by snipping into the center and ripping the coarse fabric in two, sending a shower of soap dust into the air. Then she refitted the squares to each other, sitting at her sewing machine till late at night, her feet pumping the treadle and her hands guiding the worn material under the needle until the metal overheated and the hot smell of mineral oil filled the room.

But there were times when she did put aside her work for us. Every afternoon at five o'clock during the summer, savage thunderstorms would terrorize my sister and myself into cowering in a corner of our bedroom. The suburb we lived in had been built on top of the largest deposit of ironstone in the world and because of this, the blinding cracks of lightning that preceded the rain seemed to spring from our own front yard. I was certain we were going to be struck and that we would all be charred to paper in our rooms. I had seen a two-story thatched house explode and burn to the ground in minutes when I was four years old, the furniture inside buckling like taffy. "There, there," my mother would say, sitting on the floor next to us. "We have a lightning rod on the roof. You don't have to be afraid. Nothing's going to happen." Both my sister and I would cover our ears to block out the deafening explosions outside. First, there would be the initial strike of white lightning that lit the darkest corners of the house. Then both of us waited in terror, counting one, two, three, four, five, before the rumble of thunder that followed told you how far away the bolt had struck. Today, the center of the storm was five miles away. But what if it shifted? And what if the massive bolts were closer to home tomorrow? And what about the people who were being struck today? Wasn't it selfish to be glad it was their turn and not ours? "Would you like me to sing you a song?" my mother would say when I repeated my fears to her every afternoon. This was the one time she was never impatient with me. "You can sing with me if you like, and that way we don't have to hear the thunder." We sang hymns and *She'll be Coming Round the Mountain* and songs from when my mother was a girl, all at the tops of our voices, until the storm died away as it always did, as suddenly as it had begun, leaving only the sounds of birds in the veld and a thin steam hanging over the mud of the roads.

There must have been other kindnesses as well; Alma was right. Perhaps they came from the neighboring children whom we met up with every afternoon when our mothers locked up their houses until four-thirty. They did this to take a rest and to finish off household chores without their children in the way. This was our chance to break their ban on climbing to the top of the forty-foot acacia trees whose soft bitter gum oozed from the bark and stuck to your fingers even after a bath. We peeled twigs from chinaberry trees with razors sneaked from the bathroom, and cooked strips of stolen bacon in the veld over fires started with a magnifying glass. Once or twice we could not put out the blaze, and under threat of burning down a thousand acres of veld, as well as our houses, ran like deer to fetch help from the servants. *Fire,* we yelled at the tops of our voices and all of us—cooks, housemaids, gardeners and children—carried buckets of sand and old sacks to beat at the exploding grass that made our eyes water from its acrid smoke. At half past four, we went back indoors again, to exclamations of *just look at you, you're a mess* and *if this happens again you'll get the strap.* There must have been many kind words, but I couldn't recall them. Except from the black women who worked in our houses and let us sit with them on the grass outside the kitchen while they shelled peas, an enamel mug of tea alongside them, their aprons filled with pods and their fingers snapping the ends with smooth, dextrous movements. They talked among themselves endlessly, laughing and clicking their tongues, and I learned to understand enough to hear them say many times that the white madams were all a crazy bunch indeed, every last one of them. There they were every afternoon, locking up their silent houses and their well-stocked store cupboards and allowing their most precious possessions to run wild like animals in the veld.

"I was never a victim," I told Alma. "I'm not altogether incapable of looking after myself. I don't want you to get that impression."

She grinned. "On the contrary. I don't think you were ever a victim because you were so determined to survive. But a twelve-year-old—which is about where I put your emotional intelligence—has no idea of the skills she needs to survive."

"You're saying?"

"Simply this, my dear. You were a child having a child when you

128

had Emily. It seems that you had decided the way to survive in this world was to become intellectually competent. People would respect and protect you if you could prove you could read and write. No one ever told you the real secret is to get A's in life, and C's in the classroom." She cocked an eyebrow at me.

"I knew that!" I blustered.

"See?" she laughed. "You can't even bear to admit you didn't know that." She shook her head. "The kind of stuff you needed to know doesn't come from *Cosmopolitan* or a PhD. You hadn't been shown how to live life. Nor had Howell. And neither of you knew enough to be a parent."

"Trust me," I told her. "It was the steepest learning curve of our lives."

T ❖ E ❖ N

"You won't forget to collect my parcel from the post office, will you, love?"

In the subterranean light of our kitchen, Howell, close-shaven, thick hair tipped with silver and band-box spruce in a three-piece suit, bit into a slice of toast. It was 6:54 in the morning and I could tell from the way he was dressed that I would be on my own till late tonight. Along with the suit that would broker his day of power meetings, he exuded a subtle scent of cologne and all the robust energy of the handsome male animal he was. He wiped his hands on a napkin, straightened the knot in his tie and tore into an orange, releasing its pungent oil into the air. At the other end of the room, in fur-lined slippers, a dressing gown that had grown bobbles and hair that caught the light of dawn in unruly spikes, I fought the urge to scream *go get it yourself*. What I really felt was full-blown envy for the rewarding day he had ahead of him. Even the newspaper crackled as he snapped it apart, as if obeying some superior electrical charge. By the time I got around to reading it, butter smudges and milk stains would have blossomed on every page. Lately, as my pregnancy advanced, the natural world defied me on all sides. The clock played tricks behind my back. Spoons and cups jumped out of my hands and small tables lined up to trip me. I stared into the mirror at nipples like archery targets and feet that had spread like soft dough. I could no longer see them under my balloon-sized belly and the reflection that peered back at me with its skin like rose petals and expression of shocked amusement bore no relation at all to the person I was used to seeing.

At the beginning of my pregnancy, my sister had sent me Lars

Nilsson's book, *A Child is Born,* documenting the growth of a fetus in a series of remarkable photographs taken inside the uterus. I had stared in disbelief at images of blood pulsing along intricate highways of arteries and veins, tiny whorls that would become fingerprints, and nubs that would grow into hands and feet. As a child, my head had been stuffed so full of self-immolatory monks, bodies in trenches, war orphans and cities reduced to rubble, that now in contrast, photographs of the moment of birth seemed somehow shocking and indecent. But they had helped me come to terms with my altered state. I vaguely regretted my swift exit from the world of work, and in penance had attempted to write a feature article for a local magazine. But the effort had been enormous. As my body burgeoned outwards, my mind turned ever inwards and I couldn't concentrate on anything for long. I wished there was someone I could turn to who could reassure me that my secret obsessions and horrors were normal. I recalled with humiliation how other women in my family had been taught to deal with the rigors of pregnancy. There was the story of my great-grandmother, then a girl of nineteen, who, alone and pregnant with her first child, had made her way over two miles of rough veld to a railway track when her time came to deliver. There, in the dead of night and with no one to protect her, she had laid her head down on the metal of the tracks to pick up the vibrations of an oncoming train. With only minutes to spare when she felt its rumble, she had lit a brushwood fire in its path and by this simple act of courage and ingenuity had saved her own life and the life of my future grandmother as well. The story was handed down in the family as a parable of self-reliance and survival, my grandmother adding that her remarkable start was what had given her a spine of sterling silver. Ever after, the ability to endure hardship with grace was a virtue instilled in all her children. My grandmother's legacy equated more to stainless steel in my mother, but until I fell pregnant I was reasonably sure I had inherited an amalgam of both. Then, to my great shame, I discovered that I was the single child in the family who had developed a backbone of biscuit. Under duress from morning sickness, heartburn, backache and leg cramps, I crumbled. I was one of those shameful women to whom pregnancy does not come easily. I slept most of the time, in spite of good intentions to fix a room for the baby and keep the house in better order. I writhed in pain from cramps at night, and lurched between the bathroom and bedroom by day. Now, just over five months pregnant, I had settled into a bemused and shell-shocked state as morning sickness receded. I saw Howell for twenty minutes each morning and an hour again at night. After that, he retired to his study and I went to bed. We spoke little about how I was coping or what he was doing in business. I knew he was under pressure to pull together a scheme to renovate a city area that had lain dormant for years. He was the point man on the project and, with his obsessive attention to detail, was certain the undertaking was going to make us our fortune.

"If it comes off," he told me, "I stand to make half a million in commission alone. We'll pay off the mortgage and go for a trip round the world."

"With a baby in tow?" I asked.

"Of course. The baby goes wherever we do," he said. I allowed the dishes to wallow while I contemplated the idea. Howell pecked me on the cheek and left the kitchen to gather up his briefcase and umbrella in the hallway. I waited to hear his footsteps receding before I lowered myself gingerly onto the tender coccyx I had developed. I poured a mug of lemon tea and opened up the newspaper. Howell had a habit of removing whole sections at a time or tearing out ads so that pages were left dangling in space. By the time I got round to reading the inner pages, whole bits had gone missing. Just like me, I thought, as I struggled to make sense of that morning's lead story in the *Cape Times*.

"Don't you have any support systems at all?" my gynecologist asked at one of the twice-monthly checkups I had with him. "No mother, sister, cousins, close friends?"

I shook my head. We had been in Cape Town seven months when I became pregnant. My mother was two thousand miles away and didn't like to travel. My sister lived in New York. Eleanor's reaction when I had told her I was pregnant was *You're not!* and, superstitiously, I had avoided her ever since. Besides, she was back in Namibia for the rest of the year finishing off a new book.

"Know what I'd like you to do?" Dr. Findlay asked me. "I wonder if you'll consent to seeing a psychologist friend of mine. Not because I think you're in need of psychological care," he held up a hand. "Or do I? Well, yes, I suppose I do. From what I gather, Howell is not the most supportive spouse in the world at the moment. Got too much on his mind, I suppose. I'd like you to see Katherine Lyons twice a month. Just to talk really. To have someone to discuss these things with. I can give you all the medical advice you need. But I think you need another woman to talk to."

"A mother surrogate you mean?" I asked.

"Well, there's that to it, of course," he said. "Kate's wise. I'll have a word with her before you go. It would make me rest a little better at night, to think you had her on your side."

We liked each other from the moment we shook hands. Kate, short and round, with eyes as big as the bottom of Coke bottles, became the mother and big sister I didn't have. There was no pressure to be anyone other than myself when I was with her.

"David has spoken to me about you," she said. "I'm here to help in whatever way I can."

"Oh I'm fine," I trilled. "Dr. Findlay seems to think I could do with some female companionship, that's all."

"Have you ever been pregnant before?" she asked, gracefully ignoring my schoolgirl reaction.

"No, never."

"No miscarriages?"

"No. This is my first pregnancy."

"Unusual in someone your age. You're over thirty, aren't you?"

"Thirty-two," I confirmed.

"So it's all come as a bit of a surprise."

I dipped my head. How much of a surprise I couldn't bear to admit. "Do you and your husband talk about the changes you're going through?"

I looked up at her in astonishment. "No. Should we?"

"It's usual for couples to share what's going on, yes," she said.

"Well you see, we sleep in separate bedrooms. My husband, Howell, has a very stressful job and we both thought it would be best if I didn't wake him at night. I get heartburn and cramps."

"Who takes care of those?"

"I do," I said in surprise.

"Do you have anyone else to talk things over with? Friends? Neighbors?"

"I have David Findlay. And I see a bit of the other women who live around me. Most of them have children. They've been very good about dropping in."

"Excellent. Would Howell consent to see me with you if I asked him to?"

"Why?"

"Oh, just a little prenatal counselling. Wouldn't do any harm at all."

"I can't see him saying yes. But I could ask."

"I'm not wasting my time with psychologists," Howell told me bluntly. "I don't believe in them. They're a bunch of charlatans. Most of them have rotten marriages and pontificate about how the rest of the world should live. Tell Kate Lyons I'll pay for you to see her because Findlay seems to think it'll do you good. But I haven't got the time or patience to sit through one of those snivelling all-girl sessions with her."

"It wouldn't be all-girl," I said. "You'd be there."

"Out of the question. By the way, one of the chaps at work told me that his wife had joined a very good prenatal class when they had their twins. Based on yoga principles, I think. That might be a good place to meet people. Also limber you up for the birth."

"I plan to do it the easy way, I told you."

"Oh yes?"

"I'm saving up all my energy for the year after the baby is born. I don't believe in using it all up during birth."

"I don't know where you get your ideas from. But I think it would be a good idea to join this class."

The hall was huge, the size of a barn. Gritty linoleum floors and flickering neon lights distracted us from the serenity we strove to achieve. But much more unsettling was the attitude of the twenty or so pregnant women who attended the classes. Few seemed to evince the tranquillity that yoga espoused, and almost all displayed a slavish devotion to vogue theories of child-rearing that were then the rage of the day.

"Hope none of us is prone to epilepsy," I whispered to the woman next to me, pointing to the jarring lights above. Both of us were attempting the lotus position over bulging bellies. "Isn't this awful," she whispered back. "Look at us. Twenty intelligent women all wondering how the hell we landed in this situation."

"Be grateful you weren't Victorian. The only contraceptive they had was prudery."

"I thought it was a mistress," she said. Both of us began to giggle. "As for Dee-Dee . . ." she whispered, referring to our instructor.

"Mrs. Collinson? Mrs. Edwards? Are you paying attention?" the instructor called over to our corner. "Open up your centers of breathing. Imagine the golden life force streaming into you. *Push* open those joints. You want to open up like a lotus when your baby comes. *No* holding back. *Work* on those pelvic joints."

Next to me Robin began to giggle. "Do you know she had a tubal ligation after her second? Now she teaches for the sheer pleasure of knowing she'll never be back in the same position again."

"How d'you know that?" I asked.

Robin shrugged. "Cape Town's a village. Her husband's in the same practice as my brother."

Afterwards, a dozen of us stayed behind for fruit juice and cookies. Robin knew everyone and introduced me to the women in the group. So you're a *prima gravida* and a *prima para* all at the same time, one of them said to me.

"Excuse me?" I spluttered.

"Oh come on. First-time-over-thirty mother?"

"Oh yes," I said. "That's me."

"So. Where are you going to have yours?"

I mentioned the name of a small, private nursing home just outside the city. "They say the health inspectors found the place crawling with cockroaches on their last visit there," a blonde woman informed me.

"Where should I be going?" I asked.

"Anywhere they take the baby away at night," one of the women laughed. "That's why I chose the Queen Mary," I said. "You have your baby with you from the moment it's born."

"Get all the rest you can, sweetheart," one of the women said. "You're not going to sleep again for the next nine months."

At the next class, our instructor took time out to question us about the birth methods we had chosen. This was the early nineteen-eighties. Pain relief had been shunned as the evil conspiracy of a technocrazed patriarchy determined to deprive women of their God-given right to grunt, squat and sweat. As soon as they had delivered their infants, these same women would subject them to routines that would wilt a Marine. Many boasted about getting their babies to sleep through the night at six weeks of age. Others of toilet-training them at six months. A few were even proud of the fact that they would be back at work within three weeks of giving birth. "Why bother to have children at all?" I was stupid enough to ask. "Why bring them into the world if you're going to make them feel they're nothing but nuisances?"

"You've got to let them know from the word go who's boss," they told me, as though tiny babies were enemies that had to be routed at all costs.

"And you, Mrs. Edwards?" our instructor asked. "What method are you planning to go with?"

I had thought long and hard about this and there was no question in my mind. "I'm going for an epidural anesthetic," I said, "and if there's a problem, a C-section as well."

"Pain is all in the mind, Mrs. Edwards," she said.

"I sure as hell feel it in my coccyx," I told her.

Robin tittered. The class remained silent. Dee-Dee, svelte in her electric blue yoga suit, turned away from me and pulled up her spine.

"Everyone breathe," she ordered. "I want to remind those of you who have elected to have your babies the *natural* way, that natural childbirth is the *ultimate* orgasm." Next to me, Robin snorted. Dee-Dee turned her attention back to us.

"Mrs. Edwards, do you know that most epidurals require a forceps delivery?" I had heard so, I told her. "And you're willing to inflict this on your baby?" she enquired. "Do you know that a forceps delivery is like getting a cork out of a bottle with a pair of tweezers? Do you know what a mess that can make of a baby's brains?"

If brains were regularly mashed during forceps deliveries, I was sure the courts would be filled with malpractice suits, I told her. Knowing Dr. Findlay, I was willing to take the risk. But this heresy did not go down well with the more enlightened members of the class, and henceforth Robin and I were banished to our karmic downfall at the back of the room.

When I told Kate about these extraordinary sessions, she suggested that Robin and I team up at home to go through our stretching routines together. Robin lived in a small farmhouse in the Constantia Valley, and it was there that we set up a regular walk through the forest and into the mountains. We never managed serious exercise—we laughed too much whenever we got together. But I noticed that on the days when we had walked and talked our heads off, I had no cramps at night and I slept soundly until the next morning.

What I hadn't told Kate was that Howell had come home one night in early July with a face like thunder. The sour odor of tension preceded him through the house and my nose, now hypersensitive to smell, immediately picked up that something was wrong. I stood on the landing of the stairs as he walked out of his study.

"What's wrong?" I asked.

"I have three weeks to get all the options signed, otherwise I'm out of a job," he told me. "Brian's told me they're no longer willing to underwrite my efforts to pull off the deal unless there's tangible progress. The only problem is that not all the owners want to sign. Some of them live overseas. Others are holding out for bigger amounts of money. It's over. I can't do it in three weeks. I'm out of a job."

"Oh God, that's bad luck," I said. And then a feeble, "I'm sorry."

"What do you care?" he asked. "You're at home all day. You don't have to work or worry. All you do is wait for me to bring home the bacon."

"Not exactly," I told him.

"Oh yes? Well, how have you contributed in the past year?"

"I sold the piece on mixed marriages. And they say I can get on with the next story as soon as I'm able. If you're asking me to work, speak to Dr. Findlay. You know I nearly miscarried at twelve weeks. He's said no to anything more than yoga classes."

"You'll have to stop those. We don't have the money."

"I was going to anyway. I'll finish at the end of the month—they're paid for—and I'll go on doing exercises with Robin."

"What about Kate? Can you stop seeing her?"

I was surprised to hear how firm I sounded. "Absolutely not. She's my lifeline. I need her more than ever now."

Howell sat down in despair. All the luster seemed to have gone out of him. He rested his elbows on the table and propped his head on them. I felt a sudden surge of affection for him. "Don't worry, we'll manage somehow," I said, in spite of my heart knocking against my ribs. The old terror of having no money surged up inside me. Neither of us would be earning now. In turn, the baby kicked violently, knocking the breath out of me and making me double over with surprise. I stood up sharply.

"Now what?" Howell asked.

"The baby," I said. "She kicks like a little mule."

"How do you know it's a she?"

I shrugged. Somehow I was sure.

"I'll have to speak to my father," Howell said. "Ask him for a loan. I'll have to fly up and speak to him in person."

"Why don't you speak to him by phone?"

"You don't understand. I need to sit down with him, to explain things."

"Howell," I said, sliding into the chair next to him, "let's not go to your parents. Let's figure this out ourselves. We can find a way. You can go back to television if you have to. I can write another story. But let's do it on our own."

He stood up sharply. "No, I need a break," he said. I put a hand up to touch his arm, but he turned away. "I'll get on the phone to him right away. See if I can get a ticket out of here by Saturday morning."

"I don't like what I'm hearing," Kate said the next time I saw her.

"Oh, it'll be fine," I tossed off. I couldn't bear her to think I was whining. If I could keep cheerful, make a joke of things, I could keep her good opinion of me. It never occurred to me that I was paying to bore her with the details of my life.

"I can cope," I chirruped.

Behind her glasses, her eyes looked enormous.

"In the first session you had with me, you told me that you and Howell slept in separate bedrooms. You told me that was because you had heartburn in the middle of the night. What's the real reason?"

"The real reason?" I was dumbfounded. The real reason was that he didn't want to be disturbed by my nighttime complaints. When I had been up and down with nausea, both of us thought it would be better if he took the bedroom at the end of the passage. "That way both of us could get a good night's sleep," I concluded. "Come to think of it," I paused. "I was hoping . . ." my voice trailed off.

"Hoping for what?"

"When I told Howell's mother about our arrangement, I was hoping she'd say something to him about it. But all she said was, it's exactly as it should be. That Howell has a living to earn and he couldn't be expected to go to work if he'd been up half the night looking after me."

"And Howell went along with that?"

My voice sounded very faint. "Well, she didn't say it in front of him."

"Can you see why I think there's a problem?"

"Not really," I struggled to defend our position.

What she was saying terrified me. I didn't want there to be problems while I was pregnant. I didn't want her to uncover further swamps in our relationship. I was only learning now how to navigate what was in front of me.

"And where is Howell now?" she asked.

"With his parents. They're spending a week in Swakopmund on holiday."

"And you are—nearly six months pregnant—and on your own here?"

I looked up at her and suddenly the tears spilled over into my lap.

"I can't bear much more of it," I said in a whisper. "His mother hasn't done anything to show she's glad about the baby. It's as if she doesn't want me to have it. Howell treats me as though I'm some sort of an incubator. I asked him to rub my back the other night and he got pretty impatient with me."

"Has there been any other kind of violence? Physical violence?"

"Oh no," I laughed. "Howell hasn't touched me since just after the baby was conceived."

"You mean—no lovemaking since, when? January?"

I nodded, the tears coming faster than ever now. "He doesn't want to hurt the baby." I screwed a tissue into my eyes. "But it's my fault too. I just don't feel like it. I look so huge and misshapen."

"There's something very seriously wrong here, and I wonder why you've been denying it to yourself for so long. What are the benefits to you of staying in a relationship like this?"

"I can't get out now. I'm pregnant."

"My dear. You need to be your best for your baby. You need the support and love of your partner to be a good mother. You're not getting anything at all from what I gather. Is that true?"

I couldn't deny it. The long days on my own. Eleanor's indifference. The only people who had shown any feeling for this baby had been my sister and my mother. My sister had sent a box of bibs and jumpsuits from Bergdorf Goodman in New York, along with new maternity dresses and Lars Nilsson's book. Just days before, a layette of cardigans, shawls and caps had arrived from my mother, each item folded in tissue paper and smelling of baby powder. It must have taken her a month to knit the tiny clothes.

Kate got up and went through to her kitchen. When she came back, she put a mug of herbal tea in front of me. "I'm going to speak to Howell as soon as he gets back. I want to see him in here, at your next appointment."

"He won't come. He's already said so."

"Then you must leave him." Her words fell so swiftly in the room that at first I didn't register I had heard them. When I did, my head jerked up. "Leave?" I hiccuped. "I can't do that. There's nowhere to go. I'm going to have a baby."

"Then I'll speak to Howell myself," she said.

No, *I'll* speak to him, I thought. A little of Kate's anger had rubbed off onto me too. However blind I was to our situation, I had caught a glimpse that afternoon of who I had allowed myself to become. *I* can handle this, I thought, and forced myself to dial his mother's number in

Windhoek. I listened to the double burrs and imagined them echoing through the rooms, willing him to pick up the phone. To my surprise, Eleanor picked up the telephone herself.

"And how are you doing?" she asked sweetly. "No more backaches, tummyaches?"

"I'm fine now," I said.

"Still managing to sleep through the afternoons?"

"Yes," I answered shamefacedly. I remembered that she had finished a book while she was pregnant with Howell.

"Can I speak with Howell?" I asked.

"He's not here at the moment. Is there a message I can give him?"

"Well. It's just that I'd really like him back with me in case anything goes wrong."

"How far along are you now?" Eleanor asked. I could hear her rummaging for a piece of paper on which to write my message.

"Five and a half months," I told her.

She laughed. "Don't worry. The baby will arrive dead on time and nothing's going to go wrong at all." Had she really used the phrase *dead on time?* I couldn't believe my ears. Some of the courage I had drawn from Kate welled up inside me. I took a breath and tried again.

"I think Howell should be home with me," I said, holding the receiver tightly to my ear. "I think a husband's place is beside his wife when she's pregnant." A leftover hiccup marred the impact of my delivery. But I could hear that Eleanor was weighing up my words. There was a short silence on the other end of the telephone before she replied.

"Of course I do *too,*" she said. "When the wife makes it worth his while being with her."

I was floored. Had Howell said anything to her? I took a deep breath, shaking from my head down to my shoes. "Eleanor," I said, my mouth as dry as blotting paper, "you do not know your son the way I do. This marriage is not easy and I'm willing to take some of the blame. But I am *not* the only person at fault."

"Oh nonsense," she said. "Howell is the sweetest, dearest, most easygoing man in the world."

"You're not married to him!" I spluttered.

"I'm his mother. I *know,*" she replied.

"He is stubborn. He shows me no affection. He leaves me alone day and night. And I don't think any man who loves his wife would willingly leave her alone to be with his mother while she was pregnant."

"Well then, Gillian," she said sweetly, "you must look to yourself to see how you can remedy the situation."

I abandoned the last shred of pride and begged. "Is he there? Can I speak with him?"

"Didn't I say when we began that he was out? I'll tell him to call you as soon as he gets in."

It took me many years to understand what had made Eleanor who she was and why she refused to see the flaws in her children. As Alma pointed out, being able to recognize that her children were less than perfect would have meant denouncing her own efforts as a mother. And Eleanor wanted to look good at all costs. At the same time, I was too young to realize that she, too, had deep insecurities of her own. Trapped in a difficult marriage, she used her three sons to bolster her fragile ego, filling her life with activity to distract her from the realities of her situation. When her sons were small, she had shielded them with animal devotion from their father's outbursts against childish misdemeanors. In turn, Howell repaid his mother with unquestioning devotion. Her refusal to see any wrong in him made her the only woman he could trust never to turn on him or let him down. In his eyes, this put her beyond reproach.

The mystery factor in the equation was me. The reason I had steadfastly chosen to turn a blind eye to their bond was largely due to the tricks of perception I played on myself. But it would be another ten years before Alma pointed out how closely Howell resembled my mother and how he had become the perfect stand-in for the next round in the titanic struggle to win her love. Both were stubborn perfectionists. Both could be incisive critics. And both seemed to remain forever beyond my reach. I had believed that unswerving devotion would eventually prove to both of them how much I cared. But the flaw in this reasoning had to be pointed out over and over again before I acknowledged its truth. No matter how hard I tried, I was still too wrapped in my own narcissistic fantasies to see beyond the veil of misapprehension I had grown up with. And the same went for Howell. We were blind to each other's deepest needs. That is, until we were forced to work together for Emily's sake. And by that time, it was too late to retrieve our marriage. The circuits had been hard-wired for us in childhood and neither of us could have chosen differently. The same forces are still at work today, diminished but there, and now that we know about them we have a measure of control. Back then, Howell and I were mere straws in the wind.

Howell was rested and had eaten well during his holiday in South West Africa. As a result, he had agreed to see Kate with me.

"There's nothing a good haunch of venison can't cure," he laughed. But his good mood was dispelled as soon as he met her.

"Nothing I hate more than amateur art," he said derisively, as he sized up her ceramics collection in the waiting room.

"Howell," I said, jabbing him in the ribs. Just then Kate walked in and invited us into her study.

"So you're Howell," she said with a welcoming smile.

"And you're Kate," Howell returned, emphasizing each word precisely. I knew then we were in for trouble.

"Do tell me about South West Africa," Kate said.

"It's a land of samples," Howell replied, hauling out a response to humor her.

"I'm sorry?" Kate said.

"A land of samples. You know—no motherlode. Lots of mineral samples, but none of the real thing. Mining terminology."

"I see," Kate said, caught off guard. "Your parents have lived there all their lives?"

"My father went there when he was twelve. My mother was born in England. So it's their adopted land as well."

"Nice that you stay so close to them," Kate ventured.

"Yes," Howell said.

"And it must have left its mark on you as well," Kate said. "The country, I mean."

"I love the open spaces. The landscapes." This was a side of Howell he didn't talk about much and Kate took the opportunity to draw him out further.

"I've done some interesting work with children raised in wide-open spaces," she told him. "When you ask them to name their favorite colors, they don't go for the usual greens and blues like other children."

"Oh yes?" Howell pretended interest.

"They choose browns and golds. It affects the entire way they see life."

Howell nodded, not sure what to make of this piece of trivia. Kate waited, then pounced.

"May I ask whether you go back for the country—or for your parents' company?"

Howell looked at her with surprise. "Why, both, of course," he said.

She nodded, then took a breath. "You're close to your mother?"

"Yes."

"How does your wife fit in?"

The trap had closed and Howell hadn't even sensed its presence. But as soon as Kate posed the question, I saw his jaw clench. I looked at the floor, miserable with discomfort. The last thing in the world I wanted was a confrontation. Howell looked over at me.

"She has her place."

"First? Before your mother?"

"I wouldn't say that."

"Why ever not? I presume you know that the Bible says a man shall leave his mother and his father and cleave to his wife?"

"I've known my parents a lot longer than I've known my wife. I love my mother. If it hadn't been for her, I don't know where our family would be. My father was away a lot and my mother was the one who was always there for us."

Kate's eyes looked very big behind her glasses.

"You don't find it odd in any way that you are so close to your mother?"

"If you're implying that I'm homosexual, you're wrong," he said, preempting the usual accusation. "I love her and that's all there is to it."

I could feel the baby arch into a little ball inside me. This was a nightmare. I didn't want to hear these things.

"Children are not plants, Howell," I heard Kate say. "They can't be stuck into one place and artificially raised. They are the sum of all the influences and impressions that come their way from the day they are born. And a mother who will not release her son to take his place alongside his wife is not doing him any favor at all. In my opinion the closeness between you and your mother is hurting your marriage."

Howell was very cool in his reply. "In my family, I don't regard the affection between us as too close at all."

"But a man of your age . . . How old are you? Thirty-four? Should be out and away from his family."

"I was from the time I was thirteen. I was away at boarding school for most of my childhood. That's probably why I appreciate my mother so much."

Kate looked over at me. "Howell," I said, "we can't keep living our lives wherever they are. It's as if our whole life revolves around them. If we go on this way we'll have nothing to fall back on when they're no longer here. What will happen when they're gone?"

Howell looked hard at me, his face flushing with fury. Then he turned towards Kate. "I presume you heard that?" he said. "That's the kind of talk I get all the time. I think she wishes my mother was out of the way altogether."

"I didn't mean that at all," I said, realizing my words had come out all wrong.

"If you want to talk that way," he turned towards me, "I'm not staying around to listen. I'm leaving." He leaned down and made a show of tightening the laces of his shoes. Then he looked up at Kate. He smiled the charming smile of a guest taking leave of his hostess after a pleasant visit.

"If you'll excuse me," he said to both of us, "I'll be going now." I sat there numbed.

"What did I do?" I asked Kate, my insides churning with fear.

"My dear," she said gently, "there is only one thing you *can* do."

I looked at her expectantly. I knew she would have the answer.

"You *must* separate."

I didn't hear her correctly. Then, when the words rearranged themselves and my stunned senses decoded them, I was paralyzed with fear.

"We can't do that. I'm six and a half months pregnant!"

She shook her head. "My wish for you is that you go to a sanctuary until the baby is born. You cannot go on living in this barren relationship."

"I can cope. I know I can."

Suddenly the baby kicked me hard in the ribs as though to nudge me out of my paralysis.

"You're deluding yourself, my dear. A man who gets up and walks out on his pregnant wife is not thinking of her or of the baby."

"But I *need* him." The panic in my voice made me plead.

"You need his resources, yes. By law he is compelled to give you half of them. But staying with him is the equivalent of psychological battering. You have no security about what each day will bring."

Perhaps it was the excess of hormones in my body, but I began to cry in huge sobs, the kind you cry when you're a child and believe the whole world has collapsed around you.

Kate got up from her chair and crossed over to me. Balancing on the edge of my armchair, she put her arms around me and rubbed my back. "Cry all you like," she said soothingly. "I understand how difficult this time is for you." She allowed me to cry myself hoarse, then handed me a box of tissues and, holding my hand, repeated her earlier injunction. "There is *no* hope for this marriage. You must face the facts. At present, your husband puts his family first and you trail in second. My hunch is that he will assume the baby belongs to his family, not to the two of you. You will then become a very far-off third. If you want to save yourself and your baby, you must get out and make a life for yourself now."

Even as the words came out, I found myself erasing them from my mind. *This can't be happening to me,* I told myself. *I must find a way that will make everything all right again.* "Well thank you," I said stiffly. "But I can't accept what you say." I was lost in terror. On my own with a tiny baby? No money to live on. And no family to fall back on. The worst fear I had ever had was of being a single parent on my own. I felt as though I was drowning.

"You should get some rest," Kate said. "And try not to let this get to you." I thought that was the most inane remark she could have made under the circumstances, but convent manners made me thank her and pull myself together as I left her rooms.

Howell was waiting for me next to my car.

"Well?" he asked.

I struggled with my car keys and dropped them. Howell leaned down and retrieved them with an elaborate sweeping gesture.

"Kate thinks we should separate," I said.

He was silent for a moment. "Well, what do you think?"

"I can't go on this way, Howell. It's not good for the baby. I don't feel I have you on my side. Kate feels it will be worse after she's born."

"Nonsense. You're tired. Don't take any notice of her. You know these shrinks. They say things for effect. Why don't I take you out for a salad and then we can go home and get a good night's rest?"

I tried hard to hold onto the truth in the face of Howell's soothing words. In my desperation to make our relationship work, I lived only for the moment now, not allowing past incidents to intrude on my reason or ability to think. Here he was, calm, kindly and offering to take me out to dinner. Not for a second did I allow myself to remember that ten minutes before he had walked out on me. That Kate's words about coming in a poor third made ominous sense. Separation. Versus dinner out and a good night's rest. It was easy to see which choice I would make.

But my baby had a wisdom all her own.

An hour later, after eating a plateful of raw spinach, I made my way to the restaurant washroom. There, to my alarm, I noticed blood on my petticoat. I knew that a show of blood at six months meant trouble and, without waiting, found a public telephone and called David Findlay. In a quiet voice he asked how much and whether I had any backache. Just a couple of spots, I told him. All the same, he said, he'd like to see me immediately.

"Can you be here in fifteen minutes?" he asked. By great good fortune, we were five minutes away from his rooms and within that time he was cuffing my arm to take my blood pressure. Usually he hummed while performing this task. Tonight he was silent. I made a joke about the amount of spinach I had eaten but he ignored me, listening now for the baby's heartbeat.

"I'm going to put you on something to stop the bleeding," he told me. "This could be a spontaneous abortion, or a very late miscarriage." The baby was ominously still. I hadn't felt anything since the sharp kick earlier in the afternoon. Suddenly, I had a strong sense that whoever this little soul was, she was waiting for me to make up my mind, to take control of my circumstances and of her welfare as well. I had had enough of being told what to do, even by this well-meaning, competent doctor whom I trusted with my life.

"What are you putting me on? A hormone treatment?" I asked him.

"Yes."

I shook my head. "I won't take it. I won't do anything that could hurt the baby at this stage. If you're doing this for my sake, forget it. I won't lose the baby. I want this baby more than anything in the world and nothing will take her away from me."

"You run the risk of a miscarriage if you don't listen to me."

"I've never been more sure of anything in my life. But I tell you what I will do. I want you to book me into a nursing home for two weeks' bed rest. I won't move. I'll sleep and eat good food and give myself all the rest I can get. I promise you I won't lose my baby."

He turned away to fold up his instruments and I heard him sigh. "You know the problem with you pregnant women," he said. "Right now if I were to transfuse a pint of your blood into another patient, they'd go out of their minds. It's the hormones, you see. You have so many of them in your system at the moment, you're incapable of thinking rationally."

I grinned at him. "Don't worry about me. I know exactly what I'm doing."

Later that evening I checked into the Queen Mary Nursing Home on the outskirts of Cape Town. An old Victorian villa in a garden full of birds and flowers, it was a welcome haven away from the strife and tension at home. When Howell said goodnight to me, I told him I didn't want to see him for the next week. I didn't want friends to visit, and I didn't want telephone calls. I was going to sleep, eat, sleep some more, and forget about everything except my baby.

"Are you sure?" he asked.

"I've never been more sure of anything in my life," I told him. The baby was all that mattered now. And Howell was upsetting both of us. I wanted him out of here and as far away from us as possible.

"What about the cost?" he asked.

"Speak to your parents," I said bluntly. "This is their first—probably their only—grandchild." He nodded, pecked me on the cheek and turned away down the steps. At the bottom he turned and gave me a thumbs-up sign. I smiled back and walked through the doors to the room that had been assigned to me. There were French doors that opened onto a tiny patio with a pond and goldfish. My baby and I would be just fine here.

At four the next morning, I was awakened by a joyous tap dance on my ribs. The spirited performance went on for five minutes and after I had been jabbed hard enough to be reminded forcefully of her presence, my baby and I—as was our custom—curled up together for a good long sleep.

E · L · E · V · E · N

On a wet day in early September, I assembled the last of the cups, plates and forks on the dining-room table and walked through to the kitchen, balancing the load on my seven-month bump. Four of my neighbors had come for morning tea—my way of thanking them for the concern they had shown for me once news of my pregnancy had filtered through the neighborhood. All of us lived in mountain homes that were accessible only up steep stairways cut from stone. For this reason alone, there was a kinship among us. One of the women had delivered groceries when I was in bed with morning sickness. Another had sent around covered casseroles for Howell's dinner, knowing I probably wouldn't want to cook. Their thoughtfulness had grown into friendship, and I had asked them back to tea, not only to thank them, but also to ask for advice on caring for a newborn. All of them had children and we had laughed together about my first-time fears. My baby was due in seven weeks' time, and I planned to take these last two months easily. I had been back into the Queen Mary once again after my first two-week stay, and David Findlay had allowed me home only if I promised not to paint walls or lay carpets. I had never felt better in my life. Spring was around the corner, my baby kicked vigorously and the least I could do was to thank the women who had befriended me through the previous couple of months.

Howell was in and out of the house all day. He was energetically putting together a new real estate scheme that would bring long-over-due shopping facilities to our neighborhood, and his days were spent lining up prospective investors. In the middle of my tea he had emerged from his study, greeted each of the guests with a wide smile and stayed to sample chocolate cake and scones. Then he had pecked me on the cheek and said he was off to meet a contact in the city.

"Don't know when I'll be back," he said as he waved goodbye.

One of the women had brought along her baby-sitter, Grace Ncube, who had agreed to help me once a week in the house until the baby was born. The moment I opened the door I had warmed to her solid smiling presence and the firm grip of her handshake. This morning she had come along to get used to the house and to find out what needed to be done. My kitchen hadn't looked this orderly in months. She was there now, waiting for me to come through to pay her, the cups and saucers already washed, dried and back in the cupboard. I walked upstairs to fetch my purse, making my way back to the kitchen with lopsided steps. Grace sat at the table, shining and comfortable, placidly reading the newspaper. Suddenly I had the urge to sit down and talk to her. The companionship of women had been a godsend to me these past few months and I longed for more of it.

"Would you like another cup of tea before you go?" I asked. "And cake? They liked the cake."

Grace smiled. "I'd like juice if you have it," she said. I reached into the back of the refrigerator to pull out a pitcher of orange juice and to my astonishment felt a warm gush of liquid spill down my legs. I stopped short, not able to understand where the stickiness had come from, then realized what had happened. My waters had broken. They were puddling the newly swept kitchen floor with what looked like a bucketful of straw-colored liquid.

"Oh Grace," I cried out, "I'm going to have my baby right here." She was up in a flash and by my side. Then she spun around and collected all the dishtowels and cloths she could find in the room. She wadded them up and handed them to me.

"Between your legs," she said. "Put these between your legs." I sat down in a heap on the floor, weak from surprise.

"Where is your husband?" she asked. Seeing my stricken face, she added, "Don't worry. I have two children of my own and I know what to do." She glanced around the kitchen and my eyes followed her. Kettle, scissors, newspapers, towels. After all my careful planning, I was going to deliver my baby on the kitchen floor in the company of a woman I had met just three hours before. I began to giggle weakly. I didn't even know where Howell was. The other women had all left to collect children from school, to shop and to get on with their busy lives. None of them would be home till later this afternoon. At the same time, the thought flashed through my mind that ambulances no longer served this part of the Cape peninsula—too difficult to transport patients up and down the steep stone steps. Grace had left the room to fetch more towels from the bathroom, but was back within seconds with a pillow and blankets as well from the bedroom.

"What about your mother?" she asked. "I can call for her." I shook my head. "Sister, brother, friends?" she asked, her eyes widening in astonishment. It is unheard of among black people not to have an extended network of family members to call on in an emergency. "There's no one," I said. "Just Howell and me. Oh, and Doctor Findlay." She planted her hands on her hips and clicked her tongue.

"I'm going to help you upstairs, Miss Gillian," she said. "Then we can call your doctor." She reached down and put an arm around my waist. I leaned into her and stumbled to my feet.

"Grace," I pleaded. "Don't leave me." She clicked her tongue again. "I won't leave now," she said indignantly. "I'm going to help you bring your baby into the world."

We were halfway up the stairs when I heard Howell sauntering up the path, whistling brightly. I turned to Grace, not sure whether to let go of her or not. Somehow I felt as safe with her as I did with Dr. Findlay, sure that she knew as much as he did about delivering babies.

Howell stood at the bottom of the stairs staring up at us. He immediately saw that something was amiss.

"It's my waters," I giggled in shock. "They've broken. I need to get to a hospital." I was still leaking like a tap without a washer. And there had been no movement at all from the baby. Howell's reactions were lightning-swift. He reached for the telephone, called Dr. Findlay's office and asked Grace to collect the suitcase I kept packed beside my bed. Then he put me on the phone with David Findlay, whose calm voice helped me keep my head. What was happening? I asked. Would I lose the baby? He had glanced at my dates on a card in front of him, and his voice was cautious. "Let's just get you into a hospital immediately," he said. I felt no pain, no anxiety, just a sense of inevitability. Keep breathing, I told myself, falling into the pattern the despised Dee-Dee had taught in her yoga class. Leaving Grace to lock up, Howell walked me to his car, told me to lie down on the back seat and not to look up. The Queen Mary was fifteen minutes away. We were there in under ten. Howell put an arm around my waist and nearly lifted me off my feet in his haste to get me inside. I had felt no contractions and was dazed from the sudden events of the morning. I had no sense of time, just a strong conviction that everything was going to be all right. When the fetal monitor showed a strong heartbeat, I smiled up at Howell and patted his hand. But David Findlay had other ideas. While I lay hooked up to the monitor, he had called in to say that he was not happy about delivering a premature baby in a small nursing home without ICU facilities and that I would have to transfer to a bigger hospital.

"I've booked you into the Mowbray Maternity Home," he told me over the phone. "I know it's not what you wanted. But they have excellent facilities there." Howell helped me dress again and took me out to his car. It had been two hours since my waters had broken and still there were no contractions. White with anxiety, Howell made for the dusty, rundown suburb of Mowbray, where the city's largest state-run maternity hospital was situated. Run on segregated lines, the hospital was a byword for South African officialdom. Staff were known to process patients with ruthless efficiency, wards lacked any semblance of comfort and the corridors smelled strongly of Lysol.

"In here, Mrs. Edwards!" The iron-haired matron glanced at the clipboard in her hand. "Take your clothes off. Change into a gown, then we'll shave you."

"I don't want to be shaved," I said.

"You're in *our* care now. You'll do what we tell you to do."

"I will not. My doctor is David Findlay. He says there's no need for . . ."

"Take your clothes off. I haven't got time to argue."

The woman looked like two hundred pounds of boiled beef. As I stripped, the first contraction knocked the breath out of my body. I stiffened in shock. So *that's* what they meant by a labor pain. Oh God, I was a coward. If this was just the beginning, I'd never be able to stand this. I sat in the cubicle, shivering with fear. Somewhere near me I could hear other voices and debated whether to call out for help. Realizing I was only one of several women in labor, I decided to ride it out. Then the next contraction hit me like a hammer. This time the cry I let out carried over several wards.

The curtain in front of me snapped open. The admissions matron stood there blocking the light.

"What do you think you're doing?" she demanded.

"Get me a doctor. I want an epidural now," I demanded.

"There's no need to carry on like that," she barked at me in a thick Afrikaans accent.

"Just get me a bloody doctor *now*," I yelled at her.

"There is *no* need to swear like that in the Mowbray Maternity Home."

"Bloody well now!"

"You—a Christian woman—and you can't even bear a little bit of pain. *Sies.*" The disgust on her face was matched only by the force with which she jerked open the curtains around my cubicle. She bellowed for a nurse to take me to the delivery ward, and I found myself hobbling behind a young woman who marched briskly ahead while I struggled to keep the humiliating hospital gown and socks from slipping off and leaving me stark naked for everyone to stare at.

"How am I supposed to get onto this bed?" I asked the nurse. "I need a hoist!"

She put her hand into the small of my back and gave me a shove. Another pain struck and I drew in my breath sharply.

"Have you called for a doctor?" I asked. "I want an epidural *now*."

"He's on his way," she replied in a surly voice. News of my cowardice had spread like wildfire. I watched her reappear with a razor in her hand but by now I didn't care what was done to me and when, a half hour later, the anesthetist appeared, I was delusional with pain.

"You are definitely the handsomest man I have ever seen," I held my arms out to him. "Just take away this pain, and you can have anything you want."

"Not in your condition," he said kindly. Then he slid a needle into place and I felt the icy anesthetic flow down my spine. Ten minutes later, I was numb from the waist down. I was already six centimetres dilated and my baby was well on the way. Suddenly, Howell appeared in the doorway, crutches under his arms, his hair standing out at all angles from his head.

"Are you okay?" he asked.

"Just fine," I smiled. "What's happened to *you?*"

"I tripped up a flight of stairs. Cracked a bone in my foot. Findlay's on his way." He gestured with a crutch towards the spirals of tubing connecting me to a saline drip and epidural anesthetic.

"I see you've been given an epidural," he said. I nodded. "Can't feel a thing but you can see what's happening." The rhythmic flow of a contraction rippled across my abdomen, bunching up the muscles as easily as if I were making a fist and releasing it. There was no pain. I had even begun to relax and enjoy the experience, speculating on the impatience of the little being who was in such a hurry to be born. Howell sat next to me, glancing at his watch and fretting. David Findlay had said he would be in as soon as he could. Another hour passed before he appeared, loudly whistling *Annie Laurie.*

"A little unexpected?" he smiled warmly. "But I've been keeping a close check on your progress. The sisters tell me everything's going to be fine."

He had the grace not to chide me for refusing the hormone treatment that might have taken me to full term and not to nag me about what may have caused my waters to break. Instead, he set about calmly reassuring me, checking on the responses I had and wandering patiently from my ward to an adjoining room where another of his patients was in labor as well.

At 1:30 the following morning Emily was born. She came into this world without much difficulty, weighing a little under five pounds. She did not cry. Instead she wore an expression I shall never forget. As she was put into my arms, she looked deep into my eyes with a searching look that never wavered from my face. *So you're my mother,* she seemed to be saying. *And my future rests in your hands. I hope you're up to the job.* I was so struck by the grave expression on her face that I began to tremble uncontrollably. I couldn't see whether she looked like Howell or like me, but one of the first things I noticed was that she had my mother's hands, with their long fingers and perfect oval nails.

Suddenly I heard David Findlay call for an assistant. I looked up and saw Howell cradling Emily in his arms, walking her over to the other side of the room. He was crooning in a voice I had never heard from him before—gentle, reassuring and filled with love. I pulled my head up again to see David Findlay threading gut through a needle. *Third-degree tear,* I heard him telling the nurse. I could feel very little and had no control over the shuddering that shook my body. Trying hard to keep my wits about me, I made a supreme effort to call out to Howell, but a wave of cold swept through me instead and the room went dark. I slipped into a delicious warmth, far from clanging equipment and the bright lights above. Then the sister-in-charge slapped my face and shook my shoulders.

"Drink this," she was saying to me. "You can't sleep now. You must put your baby to the breast." All I wanted to do was sleep. But the sister propped me up with strong fingers that dug into my spine and put a cup of sweet dark tea to my lips. Where was Howell? I looked round the room and saw him far off in a corner. Emily was still in his arms and I saw an expression of caring on his face that had never been there before. The sister's voice rang out to him to bring Emily back to me. Dr. Findlay's hand was clamped over my ankle to still the violent shaking that racked my body.

"You must hold still," he said with uncustomary force. It was two-fifteen in the morning and everyone was exhausted.

"I can't. I'm sorry," I said. "It's not me. I don't know why . . ." and then I sank back again. I felt someone put Emily into the crook of my arm and my last effort was to hold her tightly to me. Then I blacked out beyond any hope of recovery.

Many years later, as I recalled Emily's birth for Alma, I was surprised at how much I remembered of that night. I had put the images out of my mind as soon as I sank into sleep, not wanting to remember Howell's apparent indifference right after Emily was born. Now they unfolded all over again, the pictures sharp and distressing in their detail. Kate Lyons had been right. Howell had "claimed" Emily almost immediately after she was born. I don't remember whether we even spoke to each other afterwards. I recall Dr. Findlay's face, his mouth set in a grim line and the matron's hard fingers in my back. I could see that David Findlay was aware of the strained relationship between us and even in this enterprise of becoming parents, I was aware we had failed as partners. But it was the expression in Emily's eyes that would stay with me forever. That and the fact that, in my few moments of lucidity, I knew I had lost Howell forever.

"Don't they look disgusting when they're born this small. Hairless rats." The voice on the other side of the curtain woke me with a start the following afternoon. Next to me Emily lay in a bassinet, one tiny finger propping up her face as though deep in thought. I had woken two or three times during the night, just to check that she was really there and to put a hand out to touch her.

"Good morning, Sister," I said sleepily.

"Good *afternoon*," she said. "Is this your baby?" She was accompanied by a second nurse who pulled back the curtains and squinted at my chart. The other seven women in my ward had gone to tea and the room was empty.

"The hairless rat is mine," I said.

"Well, she'll improve." She was unapologetic about the unflattering description she had used.

"I think she's beautiful just the way she is."

She dismissed me with a pitying look. My reputation as a delusional mother had apparently preceded my arrival in the ward.

"No getting out of bed," she pushed me down as I sat up. "You lost a lot of blood last night. We almost had to give you a transfusion, but your physician said not to." She shook down a thermometer and turned Emily over.

"You're taking her temperature?" I asked, surprised. The sister nodded. When she straightened up, she called loudly for her colleague. "I've got a thirty-four here, I don't like that. Get this infant into ICU immediately." I looked over at Emily and to my horror saw she was bright red, the first sign of hypothermia in an infant. I reached down into her bassinet and scooped her up, hugging her close to my body.

Her tiny hands stretched and clenched, the veins as clear as those on a rose petal.

"Why in God's name wasn't she put into an incubator straight away?" I flashed at the nurse. "Surely she's too tiny to be in here with me?" She ignored my question.

"*Answer* me, dammit," I said. She looked at me with hostility. Another birth-shocked mother causing trouble, I could see her thinking. I jumped out of bed, hitting the cold linoleum hard and startling Emily into wakefulness.

"You put my baby next to me, when it's obvious she should have been in intensive care? *How dare you do such a thing?*" The words streamed out of me. "*Now,*" I screamed. "Get her in there now. And I'm not leaving her for a moment. I don't trust *any* of you bitches."

"Mrs. Edwards. If you insist on interrupting the ward routine and using language like that, I'm afraid I'm going to have to confine you to a solitary room." The floor matron had appeared in the doorway and stood in front of me, hands on her hips. Her expression softened as she walked towards me.

"I know you've had an episiotomy and a tear. We have saltwater baths for that. Why don't you go along to the end of the corridor and take as long as you like in there."

"What are you *talking* about?" I asked. Was I the only sane person in this institution?

"Sitz baths. Salt water. For bruising," she repeated reasonably.

"And *I* am talking about my baby," I said, taking a threatening step towards her. "My baby *could have died from cold*. What are you all thinking of?" With Emily clutched precariously to my chest, I snapped the chart off the bottom of my bed and read out the details. "Baby Edwards—just under five pounds and you don't even think of life support? An incubator? What kind of *piss* awful place is this?"

The matron stepped over and put an arm around my shoulders. I could feel the familiar deep trembling starting in me.

"There, there," she said soothingly. At that instant, another nurse pulled down my gown, swabbed my upper arm and dug a needle into place.

"Get your filthy hands off me," I screamed as the sister plucked

Emily from my arms. Then blackness overwhelmed me.

Postpartum psychosis they called it, when Dr. Findlay came to check on me a day later. Fortunately nothing came of the episode. I had slept off my outburst, and awoke serene and calm to find Howell standing at the bottom of my bed, a basket of poppies in hand. Emily was sleeping soundly in an incubator in intensive care, her temperature stable and none the worse apart from a mild case of jaundice—normal in all premature babies. Her lungs thankfully were fine and she sucked ravenously at feeding time. In between sinking back into tranquillized sleep, I had breastfed her, sitting next to her incubator in ICU while I traced the line of her spine with my fingers. The bones were no bigger than seed pearls. I had looked at this complete and perfect little person as though she was not of this world, terrified that I might do anything to harm her.

Now that I had delivered her with little more discomfort than a foam rubber ring could alleviate, I was elated and filled with a surge of energy that made me believe I could do anything. I gave into forces beyond my control and forgot the world beyond, concentrating only on my baby and the miraculous changes in my own body. I remember a friend bringing Emily an antique dress, hand-sewn from fine lawn and over a hundred years old. And I remember my surprise when Robin put her head around the door of my ward, also wearing a hospital dressing gown. Her son, Jeremy, had been born a day after Emily and we flung our arms around each other like schoolgirls at the end of term. Eleanor flew down to Cape Town to inspect her first grandchild and appeared to be delighted. Her only misgiving was that she still felt too young to be called granny. "We'll have to think of an alternative title," she said. "But I won't worry about that now. It'll be a couple of years before she starts talking." She was wrong about that. Emily started calling her "Gaga" before she was eight months old.

On the tenth day, we were ready to be discharged. Emily's jaundice had cleared up and she had put on an astonishing eight ounces in her first week. I had taken the addresses of the other women in my ward, promising to stay in touch with each one and to compare the progress of our babies.

As I carried Emily down to our car, the nurses called out after me, "Enjoy your baby." Howell beamed broadly in the brilliant September sunshine.

"You make her sound like a lunch snack," I called back. We had made up most of our differences in the ten days I had spent with them. In that time, I had seen enough crazed behavior—my own included— to realize that their blunt discipline was grounded in a wisdom culled from many years' experience.

"Do you know why old people remember so much of their childhood and youth?" Alma was asking me. I had been telling her that I remembered very little of the next six months of Emily's life. I looked at photographs of the time with no more recollection of the moment than if they chronicled the life of a complete stranger. I did remember that Grace had been waiting for me when I came home from the hospital and that from the moment she took Emily into her arms, I knew that my child had found a surrogate mother in her.

"I'm going to be her other mother," she had stated. "God has meant it to be."

When I think back to Emily's first few months of life, it was Grace whose face I remember best. Grace who saw Emily's first smile and Grace who pointed out her first tiny tooth. Grace who mixed the *muti* that soothed her inflamed gums and Grace who carried her round on her back while I caught up on sleep during the day. It was also Grace who witnessed my frequent arguments with Howell. She never commented on them, but I could see the sympathy in her eyes for the fact that my husband showed little interest in anyone except his baby girl. She still worked for other families in the neighborhood, but I had given her the bedroom and bathroom in the annex to our house, and over time she was to become as much a part of our family as Emily herself, staying with us until we left to live in Canada nine years later.

I jerked myself back to the present and to Alma's voice. "I'm sorry, you were asking me why old people remember when they were young, but not the present. I don't know the answer."

She smiled. "It's because from the age of twelve onwards, we fracture our sensibilities. We overload our minds and bodies with too much to process. After that, few of us retain the ability to live in the present moment. When we return to it, we think ourselves lucky and call it an epiphany. The Greeks call it *kairos,* or a holy moment. Once we lose the ability to stay in the moment, it does not return easily. We need tricks like meditation, alcohol or drugs to get back to what a child does just by examining an ant on a blade of grass." She shook her head. This was one of her favorite topics and she often expounded on the need for regaining an integrated consciousness.

"*Get real,* we tell children. *Grow up.* Listen to us." She shook her head. "What a crime we do to them. What a crime."

"I'm sorry," I said. "Does this have anything to do with me bringing home Emily?"

Her eyes widened in surprise. "You don't see? Why, when I listen to you, it's a clear case. You, too, were shocked out of your mind. A premature birth can do that. It had to happen, of course. You needed something to wake you up. Both of you needed it. All the same, it shouldn't have happened on Emily's time. That was the shame. You know what Gloria Steinem says? *If men became pregnant, abortion would be a holy sacrament.* Mind, I don't go with abortion. There you are. You literally stepped outside of reality and went into a hypnotic trance. That's how you survived. But do you know? When I listen to you go on about your experiences with Howell, I'm beginning to hear—I *hope* I'm beginning to hear—just a little bit of objectivity at last? He's not all bad, anymore. You're not entirely an Angel of Mercy. And I hope you understand from your outburst in the hospital, that you *do* have a strong, assertive side to you. We might just get back to that when it all becomes clear again. When you regain the vision you lost. Well, that's enough for one day. Think about what I've said to you. Give it some thought. And love your child. She's the future. You've had most of yours already."

With that, she rearranged the pins in her hair and sent me off with a hug. As yet, I had only a faint glimmering of what she meant.

T · W · E · L · V · E

How would I paint this feeling? Sunshine thick as honey. Emily's silky head in the crook of my arm. A day full of finger pointing at new things, laughing when I pretend to bite off her fingers, shaking her head from side to side when I hold up an orange, and say, "Here's a banana!" Laughing over and over when I repeat the same silly joke. So many smiles and the lovely feel of her breath against the curve of my neck.

I had been dreaming. As soon as I opened my eyes I knew half the morning had gone. Outside, the screams of the gulls had tapered off, presaging early afternoon heat. I sat up on the edge of my bed, conscious that I had blacked out yet again the night before and overslept. From somewhere far off in the house I heard a crash. Then another, followed by another. I walked to the top of the stairs and made out the sound of glass smashing into glass coming up from the kitchen below.

"Howell? Is that you?" I called. The quiet, reassuring tones of Howell's voice drifted up the stairs, followed by Emily's gurgling laughter, and yet more crashes. I pulled on jeans and a T-shirt and ran downstairs, wondering what creative enterprise Howell was engaged in today. He and Emily were in the kitchen. She was sitting in a square of sunlight in the doorway, chewing on a wooden spoon, while Indaba, our stub-tailed cat, lay curled up next to her. Howell stood in front of a cupboard, picking out jars of baby food and dropping them one by one into a bin at his feet.

"What are you doing?" I laughed.

"What does it look like?" he answered.

"You're throwing out Emily's food."

"That's right."

Emily put out her arms when she saw me and I scooped her off the floor, hitching her onto my hip. I looked at him for an explanation.

"But why?"

"If you don't know why, there's hardly any good in telling you," Howell said.

"Well, there's logic for you," I laughed. My daughter coshed me good-naturedly over the head with her spoon, and looked deep into my eyes for a response.

"What on earth is your Daddy doing, darling?" I tickled her. Howell went on reaching into the back of the cupboard for more of the jars I had bought on a case lot sale, dropping them from on high into the bin.

"Now this is a doozy," he said, scrutinizing a label. "Monosodium glutamate, carob gum, sodium and sucrose."

I squinted at the jar. Two milligrams of salt. One of sugar. "Have you ever tried eating pumpkin without salt or sugar?" I asked.

"Emily doesn't know the difference yet. If she'd never had salt and sugar in her life, she wouldn't know the difference."

"Oh, Howell, be reasonable."

"No, *you* be reasonable, Gillian. I'm not having my child eat junk."

"Well, before you throw out all of these jars, why don't you parcel them up and donate them to a charity?"

Howell remained silent and turned his back on me.

"Oh *I* see. You don't trust me not to sneak a jar into Emily's mouth behind your back, is that it?"

"That's right."

"Do you mind telling me where this all started? Emily's a year old. I've been feeding her on this brand since she was nine months old. Why the sudden change of heart?"

"Don't you read?" he asked patiently. "Don't you know that factory food is preserved with every kind of carcinogenic substance under the sun? Can you in all conscience feed this to your child?" He held up a jar for my scrutiny.

"That can't be true," I tried reasoning. "There are chemists and scientists and nutritionists who would have blown the whistle long ago."

"You're so innocent, you make me despair."

Emily squirmed to be put down. On the lawn outside, our African gray parrot Cucu was screeching with raucous laughter, followed by a clicking *tsk, tsk* that imitated the African expression of disapproval. She had super-sharp hearing, and had taken to mimicking the regular arguments she heard between Howell and myself. Emily loved these displays. When I put her down, she crawled towards the cage, planting herself firmly in front of the bird, who craned to inspect her, her sharp yellow eyes dilating with curiosity.

"No touching," I warned as she scuttled off. Cucu's affections were mercurial and Emily had learned that pushing her fingers through the bars often invited a lightning-swift nip.

"*Gillian!*" the bird called in Howell's voice. "Gillian! Where *are* you?"

"Well, what would you like me to do?" I asked Howell.

"You could start by making Emily's food yourself. Everyone else seems to make their kids' food from scratch."

"Well, should I make some tea for us?" I asked, skirting the problem for the time being.

Howell glanced at his watch and scowled.

"It's past lunchtime. We could do with something more than tea."

"What's brought this on?" I chirped brightly.

Howell tossed two more jars of baby food into the bin at his feet and ignored my question. I glanced up at him while I was filling the kettle from the tap.

"Oh, and by the way," he threw in my direction, "we're using bottled water from now on. I don't trust the water treatment program in this municipality."

"Well, can we have a last cuppa before we do?"

"Please yourself."

Emily had crawled back to the kitchen doorstep to play with Indaba, who to her great delight was preening his whiskers and twitching the stub of his tail in time to her ministrations. She leaned forward to plunge a hand into his fur and to cuddle her face against his. The old cat rebuffed the indignity with a sniff, then delicately licked her hand.

I glanced round the bright kitchen, and in a surge of happiness left over from my dream, decided that the day was still worth retrieving. I made a snap decision to ask Howell what was really troubling him, took a deep breath and plunged in.

"Can we talk about what's happening?" I said. "Why the sudden blitz on the food and water? It would be nice if we could settle it and get it out of the way. It's such a lovely day and . . ." I saw the line of his mouth tighten and knew this was his way of shutting me out. Against my better judgment I tried again.

"You know how I hate wasting food," I said.

At last I had touched a nerve. He turned on me, his eyes green with fury.

"All you can think of is yourself, Gillian. Not what's best for Emily. You're always too lazy or too tired or too whatever the damn excuse is to cook from scratch. You'd rather see her poisoned than throw away a few jars of contaminated food."

On the bricks outside the kitchen door, Emily lurched in surprise as her father's voice boomed through the room. She thrust a fist into her mouth and her face buckled with fright. There were a few seconds of breathless silence before her wail cut through the afternoon silence. On the lawn, Cucu gave a warning cackle and launched into an ear-splitting imitation of Emily's cries.

"Now just look what you've done," I snapped.

"Blame yourself," Howell shot back.

At moments like these, I hated Howell with a fury that made me want to attack him. Fortunately, I was too exhausted to follow through on my impulses. Or perhaps fatigue was the armor I used to prevent me from facing our situation squarely. He was as inflexible in his views on child-rearing as he was contemptuous of any attempt to sit down and talk through our differences. There was nothing to talk about, he told me. He knew what he was doing. Besides, he added, he simply couldn't get through to me.

The nurse at the clinic had nodded sympathetically when I told her I wasn't coping very well. My sleep had been disturbed by waking every two or three hours during the night to feed Emily. And lately I had sunk deeper and deeper into exhaustion. Emily slept through the night now and had never looked back after her first precarious weeks. I was the one at fault. Once I had got over the initial shock of caring for a five-pound baby, a part of me had collapsed into inertia. I had become prone to sobbing in the supermarket, partly out of sheer delight at being back among people, and partly because I had no control over my emotions. One day I had watched the tears fall on a melon I was holding and, incapable of moving or of asking for help, had simply stood there while my sobs turned into laughter. *Nervous breakdown at the fruit counter* was the absurd headline that flickered through my brain, and I had scrambled to find a tissue while Emily gazed into my face. Lately, she had stopped smiling at these antics, knowing something was wrong. The tears came more frequently now and at the oddest moments—when I was sitting at traffic lights or giving Emily a bath, listening to old songs on the radio or watching the giant tailfins of baleen whales out at sea. I began to think I was going a little crazy. I cried on my own, suppressing my tears in front of Howell because I couldn't bear to hear his abrasive voice pulling me up. Once, when I had mentioned that the winter sea sounded like a broken washing machine to me, he had told me he couldn't listen to any more of my complaining. Did I really whine that much? To the outside world it must have looked as though we had everything a couple could want. A house in paradise, a daughter we loved, good friends and a promising future. Behind closed doors, we spent more and more time engaged in the kind of senseless argument that had blown up over Emily's food. These altercations never resolved themselves. In Howell's eyes, I was not doing well enough either as a wife or a mother. My way of handling defeat was to sleep it off and to put on a cheerful smile whenever I was in company. Privately, I had resolved by sheer force of will to improve no matter what kind of effort it took.

"What was happening there, Gillian?" Alma asked, easing me into one of the most difficult confrontations I had yet faced with her.

"Well, he was throwing all that food away."

"I understand that. How was he going about doing that?"

"I told you. Just tossing them out."

"Does that mean with anger?"

"No. Just dropping them into a bin. As if they were contaminated or something."

"But the point is that he hadn't discussed this with you. Is that right?"

"Right."

"You must have been rather surprised that he jumped into doing this without talking it over?"

"It was a pattern so long established, I don't know what I felt. I'm not sure how I would characterize my reaction. I've told you how I would feel murderous and then stuff down the feeling."

"Why did you stuff it down?"

"Well, 'murderous' is filled with rage and anger. That's what gets people into trouble. We've spoken about this before."

"Yes indeed."

"If I went around acting on how I felt, I could get myself into a lot of trouble."

"Howell would punish you?" She did not apologize for her interpretation of my words.

"Yes."

"How?"

"Freeze me out. Stop talking. Get up and walk out of the room. He had an expression on his face I came to know. All he would say was, "I have a phone call to make," or "I've got to get back to work," but I knew that if I pushed any further he might tip over into one of his furies. Or just go silent. There I would be yelling and going on about something and he would go dead quiet. I would go into overdrive. I had this frantic need to get him to speak to me again. To answer back. And he seemed to know that if he withheld this, I would fall to pieces. God, I used to hate him in those moments."

She was silent, her head to one side, her eyes searching my face.

"What?" I asked her.

"Go on," she motioned for me to continue.

"I've told you. That's all there was to it. He would leave. I would feel so furious, so confused, my heart would pound for hours. And then the next morning or that evening, he would reappear and things would be strained, but at least I wasn't being punished any longer."

Again she did not respond.

168

"You're making me feel silly," I tossed out at her. "Why aren't you saying anything?"

She took a deep breath and uncrossed her legs. "I'm not trying to trip you up in any way. Or to question what you're saying Howell did. But what I am hoping for is that there might be some connection in your mind between his manner towards you and something you've mentioned many times before to me."

"And that would be?"

"Think. You give me the answer."

"Oh God . . ." I slumped.

I hated these moments. What I still wanted from Alma was unqualified support. A nod of the head, an expression in her eyes that told me she was with me, a friend and sympathizer, not an inquisitor.

"Let me give you a clue," she offered.

"Go ahead."

"What was the payoff for you of never expressing your anger in any healthy way?"

"Well, I kept the peace." That was pretty obvious, I thought.

"At cost to whom?"

"Well, I guess to myself. I would rage inside and have to fight it down and hate the way I felt."

"And if you spoke up?"

"Chaos. Both of us ended up yelling. There would be doors slamming, long faces and silences. I used to hate it so much when my mother did that," my voice trailed off. I looked up into Alma's face. Her expression encouraged me to keep going.

"Get the connection yet?" she said.

That was it. A replay of the way it had been at home when I was a kid. I kept the peace there, too, because if I didn't, there was always the threat that I would be sent away. If I showed anger or reaction the punishment was clear. I would be expelled, shunned, sent off to boarding school, cut off. Abandoned.

"But now? How are things different now?" Alma nudged me along.

"I'm not a kid anymore. No one can tell me where to go. No one can discard me. Or send me away." I was reciting. I was not yet convinced of the truth behind the words.

"But wait a minute," she interjected. "Howell has threatened to do that plenty of times. And you always reacted in the same way you did towards your mother."

"I shut up, weaselled myself back into her good books and hated her all the more."

"I'll bet there were times when you hated her so much you could have killed her," Alma said. "And guess what?" She let a beat fall before she added, "Those were the times you were sweetest of all to her."

In the stillness of the room I analyzed the truth of that statement. She was right. That was absolutely what I did to both of them. *Why?*

"Because you are terrified of *your* anger. The more terrified you were, the more you covered up by going to the opposite extreme. And that's when you plotted sweet revenge. It's a classic passive-aggressive pattern."

I could hear the air in my lungs exhale as though the poison bottled up in there for so long was bubbling to the surface.

"The payoff to stuffing down your anger was that you could stay without being thrown out," Alma went on. "You didn't have to think for yourself. Or stand up and tell Howell this was the last time he violated your partnership. Or you would ask *him* to leave."

"If I'd had any guts I would have *told* him to leave. Never mind *ask.*"

"I like that," Alma said. "I like the confidence in your statement."

"Tell me more," I said.

"Anger is normal. It protects us against being violated by someone else's words or actions. When you suppress it, you give the other person permission to let loose their anger on you because they know there's no restraint on them. It's one of the reasons wife beaters can curb their tempers with police officers or with their bosses but not at home. When you accept another person's anger, you give them permission to return it. In a good relationship there has to be a balance of anger and restraint."

"What happened to all the anger I stored up in me?"

She drew in her breath and chose her words. "I feel it's still there. I hear it in your voice. I see it in your quick, sharp movements. I hear it in the kinds of things you bring up again and again. But I think what you've been describing when you talk about exhaustion and stuffing down your feelings is huge depression."

"I was depressed?"

"I'm not sure you aren't still. Depression is often anger turned against oneself."

"What do I do to get rid of it?"

"First, acknowledge it's there. Then figure out what most angered you—way back then *and* now. Then let go of the fear."

"What fear? I thought we were talking about anger?"

"The fear that is a part of the anger. The fear that if you express fury you'll destroy your own safety. On some level, you still don't see yourself as a functioning grownup. On a visceral level, you still feel you need to be protected. And yet all your life you've been taking care of yourself. You've been a wage-earner. You've given birth to a child. You've taken care of yourself all these years. No one else fed you, put clothes on your back, saved the money to give you the things you own."

"They *helped* me."

"Don't try to downplay your abilities, Gillian. Don't show so little respect for yourself. To be a competent, coping adult is the culmination of all emotional intelligence. It's what you will look back on at the end of your life and say *that's* what made it so much of a glorious achievement."

I thought back to the weeks after that Saturday when Howell had thrown out the baby food. There had been one other incident that I had kept buried in my heart all these years. Another of those things I vowed I would never forget or forgive. I had added it to my store of angers, nourishing and watering the growing list of crimes he had committed that I had never spoken out against. In my fury, I smiled all the more sweetly nowadays, but secretly I recited over and over like a mantra *Howell, I'll get you back. If it takes me the rest of my life I'll get you back, you bastard.*

Emily and I had gone on an expedition to the supermarket. The nearest mall was twenty minutes away, so our weekly trips had to be carefully planned.

That afternoon, we had arrived back home at about four-thirty. It was a glorious early evening in high summer and surfers were out in force, taking on the swells of a perfect sea. Down on the beach, throngs of people had brought along picnics and were spreading their blankets on the sand. I parked the car, propped Emily on my arm, looped the first two bags of groceries over the other arm and pushed through the wooden gate to climb the steps to our house. At the top step, I was surprised to find Indaba waiting for us, his tail twitching and his eyes wide with an intelligence I was unable to fathom.

"Say hello to Indaba," I puffed to Emily, out of breath from the climb. Then for her benefit, "What are you doing here?" Indaba spent afternoons in the shade of a gum tree, waiting for evening when the mountain mice came out to feed. I stopped for a breath and continued through the tunnel of greenery that led to the house. Before we reached the front door, I glanced towards the corner of the front lawn where Cucu spent the day strutting and preening on her perch.

"That's funny. Who could have taken Cucu indoors so early?" I said to myself. Evenings were Cucu's time for a gala performance, beginning with the national anthem and working up to a full range of neighborhood sounds, ranging from church bells to the squeaking brakes of the commuter train that ran on the tracks below. This evening the garden was ominously quiet. At the front door, I put Emily down on the polished tiles, dropped the bags of groceries next to her and reached for my keys. I let myself in, scooped up Emily and walked through to the kitchen.

"Where's Cucu?" I said to no one in particular. Emily looked at me, then shook her head as if to say *What's the answer?*

Howell was in his study and I walked back through the house, retracing my steps. A suspicion had already begun to form in the far reaches of my mind.

"Howell?" I knocked on his door.

"Who is it?"

"It's me." I pushed open the door. "Where's Cucu? I don't see her cage on the lawn or in the kitchen."

Howell stood up behind his desk and walked around towards me.

"She's gone," he said without preliminaries.

"Gone? Did she fly away again?" She had once escaped and spent the night on the altar of the chapel below us, only making her presence known during Holy Mass the following morning. The two sacristans who had captured her had no trouble in knowing where she belonged. She was famous throughout the neighborhood for the variety and exposition of her shrill expletives.

"No," he said carefully. "I sold her."

"*You what? Why?*"

"Calm down, Gillian, and I'll tell you why."

"Howell, she's been in our family for nearly twenty-five years. My father left her with me when he went to Zimbabwe. I made a promise to take care of her. How could you *do* this without telling me?"

"If you're going to get emotional, I can't talk to you."

"*How* could you do this without telling me? More to the point. Why can't you discuss things with me like an adult? You treat me as if I'm some sort of moron incapable of adult decisions."

"And you prove it when you get upset like this."

"Upset? *Upset!* What do you expect me to feel?"

Emily's eyes were huge with fright.

"Now look what you're doing to your daughter," he said. "It was because of her that I got rid of Cucu. If you'll just let me explain . . ."

"I don't want to hear. I've had about as much as I can take with you, Howell." He crossed the room and took Emily into his arms. Her mouth had begun to quiver at the force of the exchange between us.

"There, there, my darling. Don't worry. Mommy's just a little upset. I'm here to take care of you." She squirmed away from him and began to howl. "There, there," he said repeatedly. "Cucu could give you nasty respiratory diseases and I wasn't going to let that happen. It's all right. Mommy will see I'm right. I'm not going to let anything hurt you."

Outside on the veranda overlooking the sea, I sat in numb despair. Not only had he summarily got rid of a beloved pet, but he had decided yet again to go ahead with a plan he had only casually mentioned to me. His argument was that I was too emotional to reason with. How could he be so *underhanded,* I asked myself over and over again. He must have planned this to coincide with a time when Emily and I would be out of the house. And to crown it all, he had managed to turn it round to make me look crazy and unreasonable.

I sat there with the evening falling on our beautiful garden, jasmine scenting every corner, and Indaba at my feet, silent witness to the treachery of the afternoon. Inside, Howell had calmed Emily with juice and I could hear him clattering in the kitchen, searching for a glass for himself. I looked over at the corner of the garden where Cucu had laughed and strutted and sung for so many years and mourned her loss as though she were a child.

"You bastard, Howell," I said over and over to myself. "I hate you. I hate you with every ounce of feeling in my body." I sat there for a long time until the mountains turned violet and the sea reflected back the first stars. Finally, when I had managed to stuff down my anger, I got up and walked back inside to fix supper. I even managed a cheerful greeting for Emily. But the clock had begun to run down on how much longer I could go on living with Howell.

T ❖ H ❖ I ❖ R ❖ T ❖ E ❖ E ❖ N

"You're too isolated in that house. You need to get out and see people. Why don't you throw a little dinner party?"

Howell's mother was on the telephone to him one morning in October, just after Emily's first birthday. Howell's real-estate deal was hemorrhaging by the hour and he was talking to his mother about his options.

"I can't go on like this," he told her. "There's absolutely no reason why the investors should renege on the deal. I've promised them feasibility reports, environmental impact studies, the lot. They're just too scared to commit in the current economic climate." I saw him slump in his chair, tired and deflated. Lately, I had done what I could to keep the peace between us, maintaining the house the way Howell liked it, making Emily's food from scratch, and making sure he had little cause for complaint. But I continued to sleep long hours, and we still kept separate bedrooms, much as I knew this was bad for our marriage. The truth is, I preferred it that way. Resentment from unresolved arguments seeped into every exchange between us and, as a result, we had learned to keep our interactions to a minimum. We had fallen into a routine where Howell spent most of the day on the telephone in his study, while I looked after Emily and ran the house. At night, we sat down to dinner with little more to say to each other beyond polite requests to pass the salt and pepper. The one bright part of our lives was our daughter. On her first birthday, she weighed twenty pounds and made up for her parents' silences by babbling all day long to anyone who cared to listen.

To have someone to "talk" to, I began to keep a notebook. At first I wrote stories as birthday presents for children in the neighborhood. Then I scribbled down bits of conversations and kept notes on what was happening in our lives. With time, these grew into a journal that I looked forward to writing up nightly. The story I had written on mixed marriages had been nominated for an Excellence in Journalism Award. Perhaps there was a future for me there after all. One day, I came across an announcement for a travel-writing competition. The prize was a television set and VCR and the only rule was that entrants had to write about a destination served by the sponsoring airline. A television set was exactly what would help fill the long evenings when Howell was working, and I set my heart on winning it. I pulled out my notebooks and paged through the notes I had collected on St. James. From the day we had first moved into this suburb by the sea, I had begun to gather stories about its history. There were local fisherfolk who could still recall legends passed on to them about the whaling station their forefathers had established here in the seventeenth century. And in the last years of the nineteenth century, when Cecil John Rhodes and his millionaire friends had built the miniature palaces that dotted its mountain, St. James had been known worldwide as a watering-hole that attracted celebrities from the Prince of Wales to Rudyard Kipling. Gradually the scraps I had collected filled several notebooks. "Emily," I told my daughter, "I've set my heart on winning us a television. I don't quite know how we're going to do it, but I'm going to give it a pretty good try." The plan, however, did not meet with much enthusiasm from Eleanor.

"What are you up to at the moment, Gillian?" she asked at a family lunch some weeks later. Both she and Leo were in Cape Town to consult a specialist about the niggling coughs that had been troubling both of them since winter.

"I'm putting together something for a travel-writing competition," I told her. "The prize is a television and a VCR."

"And what will you write about?" Eleanor asked.

"St. James. Everything I can put together on St. James," I told her.

"Is that what they want?"

"You can write about any destination in the world that the airline flies to."

"Oh, but they don't want a place like St. James," Eleanor smiled. "They want Capri or Monte Carlo. Hong Kong or Fiji."

"I only know St. James," I told her. "And I've got enough to write a really interesting story."

"That's commendable, but there's nothing to say about St. James."

"Yes there is. Kipling wrote some of his best poetry here. And people say Cecil John Rhodes's ghost still haunts the house where he died, and there are any number of stories about the *Flying Dutchman,* the ghost ship out at sea."

"Trust me," Eleanor said, slicing into a ripe camembert, "no one will be interested."

Three weeks later, Emily and I pushed "The Private Pleasures of Millionaire's Mile" into the mailbox at our local post office. As the envelope disappeared, I crossed my fingers and said a prayer. I was proud of the story, but more importantly, it had given me the chance to get back to work. This alone was an achievement that helped lift the gloom I had lived under for so many months. Emily and I walked home with air under our feet. But the mood was shattered as soon as we saw Howell's face. After eight months of grinding work, his scheme had finally collapsed without any hope of revival. He met us at the front door, looking ashen and exhausted.

"I have an idea," I told him after he had confirmed his news. The best thing we could do now was to take some time out together. Neither of us had had a break since Emily was born, and this was the perfect opportunity for the three of us to get away as a family. But before I could get the words out, Howell went on to say that his mother had invited him away on safari to take his mind off things. She would be camping with a group of friends near the famed Skeleton Coast and this was a splendid opportunity for Howell to leave his worries behind and relax in good company.

"I've agreed to join them straightaway," he said. "Seeing my stricken face he added, "It's a once-in-a-lifetime opportunity, Gillian. Be reasonable. When the country goes independent, the place will be overrun by tourists."

"You're going without us," I said. All the joy I had felt minutes before had evaporated.

"Don't be silly," Howell said. "You can't take care of a baby in a place as barren as that."

I thought back to his words in the kitchen when I was pregnant. *"The baby goes wherever we do."* So many things had changed since then. Right now going anywhere together seemed unthinkable. "You're right," I said. I knew how hard he had worked. He deserved the break. But most of all I felt renewed fury towards Eleanor. She had undermined me at every turn and yet Howell still refused to acknowledge the role she had played in destroying our partnership. In the face of her granite opposition, our already shaky marriage was finally crumbling. Howell's decision only confirmed this.

The following night, he flew to South West Africa for a two-week break. Even before we saw him off at the airport, a mood of wild defiance had taken hold of me. When Emily and I walked back into the house, I snapped on every light, turned Fleetwood Mac up to maximum volume and sat down with my daughter for a feast of all the foods we liked best in the world. We started with bananas in custard, went on to baked beans on toast and finished with hot chocolate, marshmallows and brownies. That night while my daughter slept next to me, her hair shining in the lamplight and Indaba curled up at the foot of my bed, I scribbled notes for the day and for a brief and glorious moment had back some of the peace and well-being that had eluded me for nearly a year.

"Of course you must bring her along," Celeste had said on the telephone. "Hugh and I would love to see how she's grown." I put aside the silver ear clips and chose pearl studs instead. Then I stood back to judge the effect in the bathroom mirror. This was my first proper outing in months—to a real dinner party among six or seven adults. With Howell still away, I had leapt at accepting Celeste's invitation. She and her husband, Hugh, were old friends from varsity days. Both of them had made a career in journalism following the vagaries of their trade all over the country. At present, they were encamped in Cape Town to report on the sweeping changes rumored to be slated for the next session of parliament. For their Sunday night get-together they had rounded up a famous film producer and his wife, a visiting professor from the

London School of Economics, a fashionable antique dealer and my-self. I had looked forward to this evening as though I had been invited on a private tour of the Louvre, changing outfits three or four times and nervously checking the calendar to make sure I had the date right. At the last minute, just as I was walking out of the front door, weighed down with Emily and a carrycot, Hugh had called and whispered ur-gently, "Could you bring your whisky? I've just discovered Leon only drinks the stuff and we're out."

I lied. "Do I have any?" I asked, knowing I was keeping the last two tots in case I couldn't get to sleep at night.

"Of course you do," Hugh said firmly and put down the phone.

I had walked into the living room of Hugh and Celeste's cottage feeling like a twenty-year-old girl again with all the world at her feet. The film director, a shy man who made moody films, was talking to Hugh and the professor over in one corner, while his wife was deep in conversa-tion with the antique dealer.

"Are they flakies or crumblies?" the actress was asking, alluding to the degree of decrepitude shown by the antique dealer's elderly customers.

"Not a one who doesn't have the proverbial foot in the grave," the antique dealer confirmed, wrinkling her pretty nose. "But *filthy* rich. And *mean* with it. All looking for rock-bottom bargains for their god-children." The speaker had ice-blonde hair and the actress wore Persian pantaloons in pink silk. There was another woman who didn't say much but smiled a lot from behind her wine glass and next to her, Celeste, her long auburn hair caught up in coils of silver rope.

"This is Gillian Edwards," she said, rattling off the names of her other guests in turn.

"And this is Emily," I said, a little shy about the expression of sur-prise on the women's faces. I explained that my daughter was a night owl like me and liked nothing better than to sit on my lap until she finally fell asleep.

"Haven't you tried Vagellum?" the antique dealer asked me.

"It's wonderful," the other woman with the wine glass said. "Knocks them out in two-twos."

"I've been hearing about it since Emily was born," I said. "But I don't know what the long-term effects are." What I really wanted to say was that I didn't have the heart to dose up my daughter just to get her out of my way.

"The best idea of all is for Mom to get away for two weeks at a time," the dealer went on. "By the time she gets back, the little brats are so happy to see her they'll do anything not to upset her."

Everyone laughed. "How many children do you have?" I asked.

"Three very well-trained little buggers," she said. Didn't they miss her, I asked? Didn't the experts talk about separation anxiety when kids didn't see enough of their parents?

"You mean anxiety about not being separated long enough from them?" the wine-glass woman asked. Again, there was laughter. I felt inexplicably rattled. Emily's hand was curled around my neck in a trusting grasp and as she gazed wide-eyed at the newness of the scene, I could still catch the scent of soap on her from her morning bath, and hear her laughter as I had towelled her dry.

"Well, I'm still a learner," I said, aware I was appeasing these smart women. *Don't let it get to you,* a voice inside me warned. *This is not the time to climb on your soap box.* The antique dealer turned away coolly and changed the subject by asking whether anyone had visited the posh new supermarket in Constantia yet? There were rumored to be chandeliers in the aisles and grouse flown in daily from Scotland. I wandered over to where Hugh and Celeste were talking to the professor, a smoky-eyed Scotsman who had made short work of my whisky.

"Why *couldn't* we get the Olympic Games on television?" Celeste was asking. "I mean it all gets bounced off some satellite in the sky. Why didn't we just break the agreement and take whatever we wanted off it? Why do people have to stick to the rules all the time?"

"People tend to," the professor said. "They'd start refusing to refuel your planes at Heathrow and all sorts of nasties like that if you didn't."

"Oh God, sanctions are boring," Celeste pouted. "Don't you think so, Gillian? I haven't been able to buy a decent pair of Maglis in months."

I stood there with Emily perched on my hip, wondering whether I'd be able to contribute much during the evening. Somehow, discussions about supermarkets, sanctions and new shoes were not what I had anticipated. Or remembered.

Halfway through the evening, Hugh leaned over my shoulder to refill my wine glass and whispered, "You were once the second-smartest person I knew."

"You being the smartest," I replied.

"Of course," he said. There was a little crease between his brows. "Whatever happened to you?"

"I had a baby, Hugh," I said. "That's what happened to me." He pulled up a chair and sat down beside me.

"Five years ago," he counted off on his fingers, "you had financial independence, you were a good teacher, you were making a name for yourself, you were free." All true. I could have stayed in Johannesburg, finished my doctorate, and worked till Doomsday for tenure, I told him. Following Howell to Cape Town had been a calculated risk. Staying married, I suppose, merely compounded the flaw in my character he was referring to. I didn't dare tell him that Howell had scuttled off to find peace and rehabilitation in the silent stretches of the desert, as far away as possible from his tight-mouthed wife and wide-awake baby. I had told him that Howell was in Windhoek on business. I could only imagine the extent of his disapproval had I gone on to tell him that we had taken a loan from Howell's father, and that my sister had taken to parcelling up last season's clothes for me. To Hugh, my inability to conduct a coherent conversation was every bit as reprehensible as dressing badly and failing to do well in life. I listened to him as he recalled another version of me, the way I had been in our first heady years together at varsity. But it was impossible for me to reenter the mood of the time, however captivating his reminiscences, and while he was talking, my mind drifted to a dream I had had the night before. For some reason, it was clearer to me than the pink rattan dinner mats on the table in front of me, or the rasp of Hugh's voice in my ear. I had been looking up into the night sky, in my dream, when I had spotted the planet Jupiter, its bright red blood spot pulsing *like an egg*, I had told myself in surprise. Then, as I tipped the telescope and turned my eyes to another quadrant of the sky, the stars in the sight had slid down with it. *Oh yes, a starspill*, I had said. *I've seen that before. I know what that's all about.* In the dream, the rich, electric sky and the hot red blood spot had been extravagantly, luminously alive and I had been the orchestrator of their interplay. When I woke, the first thought I'd had was *I'm pregnant.* Then remembered I could not be—not with separate bedrooms at opposite ends of the house. And yet the images of the dream, so forceful and solid, had refused to fade, lurking at the back of my consciousness all day, their shapes and colors oddly reassuring.

"I'm okay," I told Hugh, bringing myself back to the present. "Don't worry about me."

"I'm not so sure," he said. "How long are you going to stay with Howell?" I looked at him in surprise. I had no idea he knew that things were so bad between us.

"Forever, I suppose," I told him. When I *had* allowed myself to think about leaving Howell, I had always stopped short, terrified about being on my own with no money, no courage and a baby who needed both a mother and a father for a fair chance in life. "Besides," I added, "I can't go out to work."

"Of course you can," Hugh retorted. "Millions of women do. I have friends who've been back at work three weeks after their babies were born."

"Not me, Hugh," I said. "I didn't have Emily to farm her out to caretakers. Her first three years, at least, are going to be with me." I was pleading my case, not taking a firm stand, and I could hear it in my voice. "I'm sorry," I told him, "I know I sound dull."

"Yes, you do," he confirmed. Then he bent down and kissed the back of my neck. "Don't worry, it'll pass." But what if it didn't, I thought? Weren't friends the people with whom you were allowed to be boring? Not Hugh and Celeste, I realized. It meant everything to them that their party hummed along, without breaks in the conversation and flow of liquor, without dropped dishes in the kitchen and postnatal friends whose conversation had dried up months ago. The talk at the table was all about recent trips to Europe and the fabulous Picasso retrospective and Chagall exhibition in Paris. The professor was expounding on millennial theories of wealth distribution in his latest book and the antique dealer was telling how she had sneaked a Chagall print past Customs by concealing it in a poster tube. Emily was asleep in her carrycot, exhausted after exploring the treasures of Celeste's eclectic living room. True to form, she had climbed back on my lap and sat there till dessert, when she had tucked her head into my shoulder and fallen asleep. The professor was telling the table in rotund tones that his speaking contract stipulated he always travelled first class or he didn't open his mouth. Hugh mentioned a column he had written protesting the destruction of a statue erected in honor of a black hero who had been murdered in one of the homelands. "I admit I wouldn't want my sister marrying a statue," he said. "All the same I do think it was going too far to pull it down." The company roared with laughter.

The film director sat with his legs crossed, saying very little and watching the group from behind steel-rimmed spectacles. When he uncrossed his legs, I noticed there was a hole in the sole of one of his shoes and remembered how much his films had tugged at my heart, though most of their picturesque Afrikaans was lost on my English ears. His wife had gained a reputation for portraying heart-broken city girls who wept on station platforms while steam from departing trains lifted the hems of her skirts. In Afrikaans lore, she had become the Anna Karenina of the Karoo. She was prettier and smarter than I had expected, smoking endless Gauloise cigarettes which she lit one from the other, pressing the tips together. She gazed at the professor from behind a veil of blue smoke and flattered him shamelessly. "Oh, was it you who wrote *Filthy Rich?*" she asked. "Did you hear that, Eban?" she turned towards her husband. "Oh, that's amazing." Understandably, she did not address much to my end of the table and why should I expect her to? I asked myself. All the while I was eavesdropping on her conversation, I had one ear tuned to pick up Emily's cries from the living room. Becoming a mother had probably weakened the muscles of my reason forever, and I realized that in this company I must have looked like little more than an empty paper bag. There wasn't much I could say that would engage their gauzy attention for more than a moment and certainly nothing I could share about the private world of small pleasures my daughter and I owned together. A part of me wanted to weep with fury—not sure whether the anger was meant for me or for them.

"Funny," I said to Hugh as I scooped up Emily to go home, "I was so looking forward to this evening." I had meant I was the one at fault, not my hosts or their glittering guests. But as soon as the words were out of my mouth, I realized I had arrived at a basic truth. I had no place among Hugh and Celeste and their friends. I had left them all a long time ago. My words caused Hugh to shrink back as though I had slapped him. Just two minutes before, he had put his arms around my shoulders and said in one of his nearly voiceless asides, "I think you're in an appalling position." Instead of concern, I had petulantly chosen only to hear disappointment in his voice. I wanted to shake him off and tell him, *This is real life, Hugh. Emily and me. My husband has gone off on safari with his mother and we are on our own. Reality is not retrospectives and duty-free cognac. It's boring but there it is. I'm a mother to my daughter and no matter how much you and the rest of society think it might be a good idea for me to reclaim my formerly smart life, this is where I am.* I fumbled for my keys, and Emily awoke with a start. Standing there in the spring night, I knew that after this evening, I really was on my own. Much as I had cared for Hugh and Celeste, I knew they were too fastidious to forgive me for putting a cold spoon in their soufflé. Besides, I wasn't even sure I would ever want a place again among these charming, tinkling creatures. I didn't hear from either of them for nearly six months. Not until the day Hugh called to say that the film producer had shot himself with his father's hunting rifle. He really had no comprehension of why Eban would do such a thing, he said to me. He had seemed perfectly all right on the night he and Celeste had given their dinner party. Hadn't he?

"You know what, my darling," I said to Emily as I tucked her into bed back at home, "we've got each other. What do you say to that?" I remembered the searching look she had given me right after she was born. *So you're my mother and my future rests in your hands. I hope you're up to the job.* Up till now, I had glossed over the differences between her father and myself, too scared to admit that our marriage was a failure. Hugh was right in one way. Five years ago, I had had a lot more guts than I did now. I had believed I held my destiny in my own hands. Instead, I had married Howell and put my future in his. Now I had to make the best of a bad decision. At the very least, he was a wonderful father to Emily. He spent long hours with her. Her welfare always came first with him. As for myself? I would have to come up with a better plan if I wanted to get back some self-respect. Tonight had taught me I could never go back to where I had come from. As yet, I had no sense of where the future lay. But the pulsing blood spot in the sky and the lovely star spill flashed again in my mind as I fell asleep and I knew that whatever they meant, they had left me with a sense of possibility, of new birth and fresh beginnings.

By the time the sky was light again, I had made up my mind. My marriage had no future. Emily and I did. Out of that simple equation, I was going to have to rebuild my life all over again.

F ❀ O ❀ U ❀ R ❀ T ❀ E ❀ E ❀ N

In the two weeks before Howell was due home, I looked for an apartment, found a lawyer and put my name down with an employment agency. I decided to wait until he had returned to give him my decision, knowing that if I told him over the telephone, it would sound like a threat. I wanted him to be in the same room with me so I could tell him face to face. I had told no one except my lawyer about my plans and hoped to keep it this way until our divorce was final. But life has a way of altering even the most fateful of our decisions, and before I could speak to Howell, we were confronted by news of a far more shattering nature than our own. Howell's father, back in Cape Town for treatment of a chest infection, was told that x-rays had revealed an advanced cancer in his right lung. Immediate removal of the lung was his only hope of survival. Howell and Eleanor flew back that evening from Namibia and were with him the following morning when he went into surgery. The surgeon who spoke with them afterwards was not hopeful. Months of radiation and chemotherapy might arrest the spread of the disease, but the brutal truth was that cancers of this type were irreversible. We were numb with disbelief. Howell, in particular, was devastated. This was the worst nightmare he could have envisaged. And it had come just at the time when we were irrevocably estranged. Respecting his feelings, I decided not to speak to him about divorce proceedings for the time being. The least I could do was to keep our home life running as smoothly as possible. With Leo still in intensive care, and Eleanor in a state of shock, Howell spent most days handling his father's business and accompanying his mother to the hospital to visit her husband. But just as we were coming to terms with the magnitude of this setback, an even more terrible blow hit the family. A routine chest x-ray taken during Eleanor's annual checkup revealed that she too showed a suspicious shadow on one lung. It had been a mere ten days since Leo was operated on and he was only now regaining strength after his massive surgery. With great fortitude, Eleanor decided to withhold the news from him. She too needed immediate surgery, but postponed this until Leo was back home again and under round-the-clock care. Then, she slipped quietly into hospital to undergo the same procedure. The results were devastating. Not only did she have the same cancer, but in a form that was far more aggressive than Leo's.

I went to see her two days after her surgery, and the small, frail woman who was hooked up to a tangle of drips and tubes looked nothing like the person I had done battle with for so long.

"Gilly," she smiled. "Come and sit down next to me." She patted the covers of her bed and I stepped over a length of tubing to hold her limp hand in mine. "I'm so sorry this has happened," I told her. "Tell me what I can do to help." It was the first time we had been alone in many years and I couldn't helping noticing, all over again, how beautiful her blue-green eyes were when she smiled. She gave the faintest shake of her head and said, "It doesn't help that you and Howell are thinking of divorce." I pulled back startled. So she had known all along. Howell must have spoken to her about our situation when he was alone in the desert with her. There was no use denying it, I told her. We had tried everything, but our life together had become impossible. She squeezed my hand faintly and said, "My only heartbreak is that I won't see Emily grow up." Of course you will, I wanted to say, as if I could reverse the nightmare unfolding for all of us. But I knew I would be lying if I gave her false assurances. Her surgeon had already explained the severity of her particular cancer to all of us. Not knowing what else I could do, I brought out photographs of Emily, Howell and myself taken in happier times and arranged them at the bottom of her bed where she could see them. But she could not lift her head from the pillow and for the first time ever, I saw tears of frustration in her eyes. "I can't sit up," she struggled to say. I held the photographs so that she could see them easily and she smiled with pleasure, particularly at one of Emily sneaking a lipstick from her grandmother's handbag and looking round guiltily in case she had been seen.

"She's the daughter I never had," Eleanor smiled. "Take good care of her, Gillian." I leant down and kissed her soft cheek, choking back my tears at the wasted years, the ill feelings and how I had overlooked so much of her magnificence. When she died, some months later, I found to my great shock that I missed her terribly. She had been tireless in making an adventure out of every day and I remembered with affection her enthusiasm for travelling to every out-of-the-way village and historical site in the Cape, the way she gathered information like a magpie, and the secret pleasure we both shared in exploring museums. She had shot buck on safari and camped with bushmen in the Kalahari desert, stood waist-deep in icy water to prise mussels from rocks and kept up a voluminous correspondence with everyone from American presidents to the struggling artists she supported. When I look at Emily now and trace the outline of Eleanor's features in her face, my heart lifts with joy that she has so much of her grandmother's spirit and fire in her. I often sit in one of her chairs and talk to her. As I do with Leo and my own mother, who died just a few months before both of them. If I had them back, I know now that I would look past every petty misunderstanding, choosing only to see the wonderful things about them that will endure forever.

Just before I moved out into an apartment two months later, a letter arrived in the mail with the news that I had won the television and VCR I coveted so much. My story had beaten out six hundred other entries and would be published in an upcoming issue of the airline's inflight magazine. Two months later, the editor of the magazine that had first made my sister famous asked me to write a short piece. Within the year, I had written two more for her and from these beginnings a new career began for me as a magazine writer. At first I wrote from home so that I could stay close to Emily. Later, when she was in kindergarten, I began working full time for the magazine that had first published my work. Some years later I was appointed its deputy editor. The custody agreement I had signed with Howell allowed us equal time with Emily after our divorce. She came home to me every evening and I took her to school in the mornings. Her father fetched her after lunch and she spent the afternoons with him, swimming, riding and playing with friends. Howell continued to work from home, and within the next three years would put together a brilliantly successful real estate deal. Our arrangement ensured that Emily was with one of her parents every hour of the day when she was not in school and continued to work well until Howell decided to immigrate to Canada four years after our divorce. In our agreement he had undertaken to pay for Emily's schooling, medical and clothing expenses, and I agreed not to ask for child support or alimony. I was already earning good money by then and the small sum owed to me by Howell from the sale of the property we had owned in Johannesburg was enough to purchase the two-bedroom apartment that was home to Emily and me for the next six years. Many of my women friends berated me for not putting pressure on Howell to pay alimony. But I have never regretted the decision. Howell did not have a regular income or much in assets at the time we divorced. And to force him into such an agreement while his mind was set on caring for his parents would, to my mind, have been immoral. In many ways the decision was the best thing I could have done for myself. It forced me back onto my feet and gave me back the autonomy I had lost so many years before. For the seven years after our divorce, whenever Emily was with me, there were countless hours when we fed the ducks and swans on the stream that ran past my apartment, floated leaves on the water, and I taught her how to swim, paint, draw and sing. I had never been happier in my life.

There was one other matter that had had to be settled before Howell and I could let go of each other, and that was Vanessa. She had heard early on through the grapevine that we were going to divorce, and I wasn't surprised when Howell told me she would be spending the summer as usual in Cape Town that year. We were still living under the same roof, just before I moved out, when one morning I was disturbed by the doorbell ringing loudly and persistently through my sleep.

I threw on a towelling gown, noting that it was just before seven, and made my way downstairs to open the front door. There on the doorstep stood Vanessa, her hair worked into an elaborate French braid, her body encased in a form-fitting running outfit and a look of shocked surprise on her face. She pushed her dark glasses up into her hair, cracked a brilliant smile and asked me whether Howell was at home. I stood there in disbelief. Since she had chosen to dispense with the formalities, so did I.

"Why?" I asked. "Why do you want to see Howell?" It was obvious; I didn't need to ask. She was back at last to reclaim him. I noticed that she was wearing more mascara and glossy lipstick than was usual for a morning run and made a point of resting my eyes on her wedding ring as it glinted in the sun. "Was he expecting you?" I asked.

She gave a breathless little laugh. "I just thought he'd be around and we could go for a jog," she said. She spun on her heel and began to walk away, calling back over her shoulder, "No problem. I'll come back later when he's up."

I took a step forward and called loudly after her, "No you won't, you tramp." She turned to face me, her mouth a little round *O* of shock. "What did you call me?" she said. Her words came out in a squeal.

"I called you a tramp," I said. "And that's exactly what you are. Howell is a married man. At least for the time being. And you are a married woman. Women who play around with other women's husbands and cheat on their own are tramps. Do I make myself clear?" She stepped towards me, lifted an arm and swung it back to slap my face. I caught her wrist, jerked it down and twisted as hard as I could. "I want you out of here now," I said. "If you come back, I'll be on the phone to your husband so fast, you'll be on the streets before I hang up. Got it?"

"You little bitch," she said. "Howell never loved you. The whole world knows that. And the way you treated his mother is disgusting. Just you wait till I tell everyone about you. You'll never hold your head up in this town again."

This is war, I thought. And it's been a long time coming. Okay then, let's settle it now for once and for all.

"No one's going to believe you," I told her. "Everyone knows you're incapable of telling the truth, even about what you had for lunch." She took another step forward and kicked at me with one of her power sneakers. But my guardian angel—and that's the only way I can explain what happened next—helped me grab her ankle, yank it upwards and with an especially vicious jerk, toss her butt-first onto the pathway. "Get up and get out of here," I told her from behind clenched teeth. As she scrambled to her feet, the prettiest sight in the world was Vanessa's jaw clanging shut. I wished there was someone to share it with. But many years later—in one of the coffee sessions Howell and I began to have together after seeing Alma—he told me he had watched the entire scene from an upstairs window. Had you invited her to go running with you? was the first thing I asked him. Of course not, he told me. But after he had stopped laughing at the sight of the two of us sparring like cats, he wondered why I hadn't stood up for myself in the same manner five years earlier.

"You know the rest of the story," I said, turning back to Alma. "I had a short relationship that didn't work out during the years on my own. I sent Emily over to see her father two or three times. I hated putting her in daycare while I worked and that's what eventually made me decide to come over here."

She looked at me quizzically when I had finished.

"Well?" I prompted.

"Well what?" she laughed, expelling a cat from the folds of her skirt.

"I always wish I'd done that to Vanessa right at the beginning of our marriage."

"Really?" She looked genuinely surprised. "Why?"

"I've just told you why." I was more sharp than I intended. "Howell was such a wimp when it came to the women in his life. He sacrificed me. If I'd stood up before, maybe things would have gone differently."

"Wow."

"Is that meant to be sarcastic?"

"You're still laying a catalog of wrongs at his feet. I repeat to you. You *could* have spoken out anywhere along the way."

"I told you. He threatened to divorce me whenever I did."

"Bullies always back down when they're put to the test. But I can't help thinking you enjoy telling your story."

"Why would I?"

"Oh . . . the drama of it. The villains. The tears, the suffering. The happy ending. It's an irresistible tale."

"What happy ending?" I asked, ignoring that she had implied everything could be fabricated.

"Well, after you left Howell you got out on your own, had an interesting career, made friends. You really came into your own."

"You make it sound like Godzilla's revenge," I said.

"Apt description," she said, cryptically.

There were times when I had the awkward feeling I was some kind of standup comedian recounting the tale of our marriage for an inscrutable audience of one. Alma always listened in silence and had little to say by way of comment. But her refusal to take my accounts at face value disturbed me. Perhaps our marriage had simply been stunningly dull. Or truly bizarre. Or perhaps my accounts came out too rich in the telling. I had no way of knowing. When I first began talking about my marriage, it was beyond my ability to see the part I had played in its dissolution or who I had really been. I found it easier to step into the roles of victim, martyr and outcast—all honed to perfection in the years I had spent with Howell. The most Alma would give back was a wry smile. She appreciated my attempts to keep her interested with my impersonations and descriptions, she told me, but if we were to get to a real understanding of what had happened, the unadorned facts would serve me better. Most of the stories were repetitious at any rate, she added. Many of them painted me as an undeserving victim, outraged that the situations I willingly walked into should have rebounded with such vicious results. Slowly, as I began to understand that I earned neither judgment nor applause for my well-turned accounts, I stopped trying to amaze her. I even risked showing a little of the person I really was when no one else was looking. I owned up to episodes of envy, spite, malice and glee. And still she did not rebuff me. I became bolder—even to the point of goading her once or twice, but she never lost her equanimity. And she gave as good as she got. At about the six-month mark, she began taking chances with me. She asked me to recast incidents from Howell's point of view. And made me imagine what sort of a daughter-in-law Eleanor had seen in me. She made me relive events the way Emily might have viewed them, and what ideas I might have passed on to her about marriage and motherhood. I put this down to a new confidence she had begun to show in me that I could stand the intense self-scrutiny this involved. All the same, I balked at the game.

I held on tenaciously to the idea that *my* views were sacrosanct and because they sprang from the hallowed domain of *my* feelings, were also unassailable. Weren't feelings the touchstone of the human spirit? I challenged her. Wasn't this what I had been taught to believe in all my life? Alma showed saintly patience. She took me back time and again to the fundamental events that had helped shape my life as I saw it. Little by little, she helped me step outside the charmed circle of myself and into the minds and under the skin of those around me. One day, right in the middle of this drill, I saw myself briefly and shockingly as an outsider might and did not like what I saw. Staring back at me was a shrill, judgmental windbag who had hidden behind self-righteous pronouncements culled from a ragbag of women's magazines, self-help movements and a well-nurtured sense of "poor me." The insight was shattering. After that, others came tumbling in thick and fast. I saw clearly how I had chosen to play out the drama of my life by recruiting Howell to replay the role I had devised with my mother, precisely because he, too, was so elusive. In time and with endless dissections of our marriage, Alma and I at last pieced together the puzzle of our partnership. How neither of us had escaped the influence of powerful mothers or been strong enough to stand up to them. How each of us had walled ourselves off to become invulnerable to more of the hurts and humiliations of childhood. How we had carefully chosen a partner who would not pry behind the intricate screens we had constructed. And how we had become people-pleasers to ward off scrutiny, hiding behind flashy jobs, glib repartee, and easily acquired opinions so that the world could never get close enough to see the timid souls beneath. Our partnership had been doomed from the first moment we recognized in each other two survivors from the same shipwreck.

Throughout all of this, Alma had made no comment at all about the unfairness of Howell's actions. I had thought she would be sympathetic to my tales of betrayal. Especially to this last account of Howell's defection to the desert. As far as I was concerned, Howell had pushed me to divorce him with his impossible demands and high-handed actions. After the baby food incident, the end was just a matter of time. I wanted to hear from her that my indignation had been justified. That Howell had indeed destroyed our marriage, stolen my best years and failed to stand up for me as his wife. Instead, she sat there just as she always did, doodling on a piece of paper, waiting for me to speak. And today, I was damned if I was going to. Wasn't she always talking about giving feedback? Well, I wanted some. And I wanted it *now*. Still she sat there, wearing the benign gaze of a dozy Buddha while the clock ticked on and all around us her house came alive with small sounds. This was costing Howell ninety bucks an hour, I fretted. Someone had better speak up soon or I'd start to get hives from the waste of money. Alma never budged. Okay, I thought. Maybe I had been a little *too* dramatic about things. Looking back, I could see what she meant about not taking responsibility for myself. Coming down to Cape Town, for instance, and giving up work on my doctorate, so that Howell could live near the sea and his parents. That had been a shock. But I could have transferred to Cape Town University instead of throwing away everything and blaming it on Howell. And the house he had bought without talking the plan over with me. I had been furious at first. But then, on the night we had moved in, there had been that full moon and a hot berg wind sweeping down over the mountains and while doors slammed and windows flew open, both of us had clung to each other and giggled, certain that the place was haunted by romantic ghosts. And, of course, Em had spent the first two years of her life there. And I suppose there were other happy times as well. But I damned well wasn't going to spoil my story by dragging in inessentials like that. The fact was that all these years later, I could still feel fury for the careless way Howell had brought our marriage to a grinding halt. Couldn't Alma see that?

Finally she cleared her throat and gave in. "Do you know what I hear when I listen to your stories?" she asked.

"Tell me," I said, triumphant that I hadn't been the first to break the silence.

She stroked down the velvet of her skirt and picked a piece of lint from the fabric. "There's a lot of *my* and a lot of *his* and not a lot of *ours* in them. Why don't you tell me what that's all about?"

"I have no idea."

"Too easy." She flashed the chink of a smile. "Try again."

I had two options here. I could rumble up a plausible explanation without too much effort. Or I could try to get hold of the point she was

195

making and take the chance that I'd fall flat on my face. In the past, on the one or two occasions I had taken her up on her open-ended invitations, I had found myself examining me from every point of view but my own. Why subject myself to more of these self-lacerating exercises? I thought. Worse still, I had no idea why I ended up feeling so hot and uneasy after putting myself through these hoops of fire. I wasn't about to shoot myself in the foot again.

"I really have no idea," I repeated. "What's your take on that?"

But Alma was not letting me off the hook that easily.

"Gillian," she said, leaning forward towards me, "I want to ask you a question and I want you to be as honest as possible about answering it." Her voice was gentle. She wasn't taunting me now.

"I'll try," I agreed.

"How do you see yourself? Are you a fairly straightforward person who gets through the day without too much fuss? Or are there moments when you feel caught up in intense feelings?"

"I guess the feelings part," I heard myself say in a whisper.

"Do you know where they come from?"

"Not really. Left over from the past, I suppose."

"And how would you characterize the feelings you have? Anger? Sadness? Feelings that you aren't worth much? Think before you answer too quickly."

"Fury. Hurt. Kicking myself for things I've done," I said at last.

"Any forgiveness?"

"Not much."

"A lot of stuff locked up in there that hasn't been released or forgiven in a long time. Is that right?"

That sounded like a fair assessment to me.

"Do you know how much that shapes the way you see life?"

"All I know is it uses up a lot of my time and energy," I admitted.

"But you hold on to them. Why?"

"It's me. It's what makes me the person I am," I said, shrugging my shoulders.

She shook her head. "History is not destiny. You can change or at least modify the way you look at life. And you can look fair and square at some of the choices you've made. See them for what they were."

"I don't know if I want to."

"Don't berate yourself. They were *all you were capable of at the time.*"

"You're saying if I had known better, I would have done things differently?"

She nodded. "You can't climb into the cockpit and fly a plane without learning how. The decisions you made reflected your level of wisdom *at the time.*"

She wasn't goading me now. There was compassion, kindness, even caring in her voice. "You know I follow Carl Jung in many aspects of my counselling." She looked at me intently. "Do you know what he says about people who cover up their suffering?" I shook my head.

"He says that the cover-ups they develop are always substitutes for legitimate suffering."

"I don't understand what legitimate suffering is."

"Facing the difficulties that are here for all of us in life."

"Why wasn't I able to do that before?"

"My feeling is that you were frozen in fear. You had no sense of belonging in your family. Then out of a sense of familiarity, you chose a family remarkably similar to your own when you married Howell. You had no sense of belonging there either. But the terror of being abandoned has stopped you from making better decisions about partners. You simply chose what you were used to."

"I was frozen in fear?"

"More like terror, the way I've been hearing it."

"So I'd do things differently if I let go of the stuff I'm bottling up?" I asked.

"You would be able to make much more informed choices, yes. You wouldn't be driven by compulsions or behaviors you devised to protect yourself when you didn't know better. Up till now, you've had no choice. You've been driven. From now on, you can *decide* how you want life to be for you."

I sat chewing my lip for a minute or so. What she said made sense. It was as if she had the ability to take me up above the landscape of my life, allowing me to look down on how things were related to each other, and to see clearly where the fault lines lay.

She swung her ankle up and down slowly before going on.

"When you married Howell, you let him into your life, but only on the understanding that he would never prise you loose from the habits you had built to shore up your insecurities. And for a time, it looked as though everything was perfect. Howell didn't question your obsessions. He didn't understand your fears. He was happy to go along with the arrangement until he got it into his head to move on. It was absolutely natural for him to explore, to extend himself. He gave up television with a snap of the fingers because he found a house in Cape Town he loved and wanted to move into. You must have known that this was one of the reasons why you married him. Because he could do things like that and you couldn't. Of course, he did choose to live next door to his parents, which didn't help either of you. But do you know what? It's interesting that both of you tell me about the same sorts of things when I speak to you."

"About what?" I asked.

"You both had the same goal. To be safe. You wanted roots and a home. For all his high-flying nature, Howell wanted the same things as you did."

"Without ever talking them over with me?"

"He *never* talked things over with you. Isn't that why you married him? He was the rambunctious, swashbuckling, unpredictable type. You *liked* the way he sprang surprises on you because you could never afford to be impulsive yourself. Going out on a limb might have meant ending up like your mother who had married your father on a whim and look where *she* ended up."

"So I have no right to be sore about our marriage?"

"Yes, of course you do. If both of you were operating from a foundation of respect, trust and intimacy with each other, you would have very legitimate grievances. But you weren't."

I stared down at the worn sisal at my feet. Alma went on. "The truth of it is that both of you have a real problem with sharing yourselves. I don't wonder that you talk about very little intimacy in your marriage. You couldn't even live under a single roof without staking out separate territories."

"You're saying I had no right to be angry about the things he did?"

"Gillian, if he had talked things over with you, it would have taken five years to get you from the kitchen to the hallway. Yes, it was wrong to go ahead and do the things he did without discussion. But you didn't want to talk. You wanted to stay put."

"What about moving back next door to his parents?" I was floundering now. I knew I had lost my case against him.

She laughed. "About the worst thing he could have done. Especially with your insecurities."

"Thank you."

"On the other hand," she held up a warning finger, "he brought you to a city that was beautiful, where you ultimately made a good life for yourself and where you could get away from some of the influences of your background."

"What about moving here?"

"Oh what about it," Alma snapped. "Do you think you deserve compensation for doing the right thing?" She waited for this to sink in, then added, "You're only angry with yourself for falling into the same old trap. Howell must be *very* persuasive."

I thought back to the surges of rage that would sweep through me during our arguments. I saw now with a shocked sense of surprise that they were not meant for Howell, but for myself. For failing to take care of myself. For being too afraid to talk openly. For being forced to grow up and take on adult responsibilities. With my dubious beginnings, I hadn't really wanted to grow up at all. I had wanted a companion who would live with me forever in my Doll's House.

As if reading my thoughts, Alma added, "The way to break free is to get out there and stand on your own. No Howell. No one except you. That way you find your own breaking strength."

"God," I said more sharply than I intended. This was more insight than I could tolerate in a single afternoon. Suddenly the clear outlines of my life looked blurred and broken. Worse still, I had a feeling about as comfortable as chicken pox that all the decisions I had made up till now had been cowardly and wrong. Every well-intentioned move was no more than a blind, groping, inept fumble.

"Do we have to go on with this?" I asked Alma.

"I can't push you past where you want to go," she said.

I hated having my courage called. "So you're not telling me Howell was right and I was wrong?" I persisted.

"No." She sighed patiently at my refusal to get the big picture.

"I get it. Neither one of us was right."

She grinned. *"Right."*

She waited for me to take this in, her hands resting palm upward in her skirt. She had ceded the thinking to me now, neither hurrying, nor prompting me to say what she wanted to hear.

"This really pisses me off, you know," I said finally.

She nodded. Her expression didn't change. "What you want me to tell you is that you were right to be furious with his high-handed actions," she said. "That you have just cause to hate him for the rest of your life. Instead, you're hating me for making you look at your own behavior, for seeing it all in a new light." I smiled. She was right. The muscles in my neck relaxed just a little. I *had* hated her this afternoon. For revealing my cherished grudges as no more than self-delusional defences. For refusing to take my side. For pushing me further than I wanted to go and for making me take a long, hard look at the crippled perceptions that had marred most of my life. At the same time, I realized in a rush of affection how much I owed her for sharing my shame without ever shaming me back.

"So," she said, reassembling herself on the sofa, "you have a picture of yourself as hard done by and misunderstood. What are we going to do to repair that?"

"I never said I was always right!" I barked back at her.

"Well, I'll reserve judgment on that," she smiled. "There's one thing that *would* have helped you think more clearly. If you'd been able to be open with your parents about who you were and what you believed in without being shamed, this would have strongly influenced the level of independence and emotional maturity you brought to your marriage."

"So you're saying that this kind of misunderstanding happens in *all* divorces?"

"Precedes all divorces, yes." She did not apologize for the generalization.

"In that case, if I wasn't so screwed up I could have married just about anyone and been happy."

"Precisely. And that is exactly what happens in the best of marriages."

"You're not advocating an arranged match, are you?" I laughed.

She shifted. "I have ideas that don't chime with Western thinking on this," she admitted. "I believe it's probably better to marry the girl or boy next door. For the simple reason that your stored experiences are familiar. I do not believe in passion as a foundation for marriage." She paused and looked steadily at me. "The real truth is that you fall in love for all the wrong reasons. You love for all the right ones."

"Tell me more about Howell and me," I asked.

She laughed. "Oh, you *are* a matched pair. You could be sister and brother. Or cosmic twins, you mirror each other so well. You both have the same frailties, the same inabilities to get beyond yourselves. And you refuse to like each other because you cannot accept these things about yourselves."

"If we got past the blocks, could we love each other again?"

She shrugged. "Real intimacy requires a profound respect for differences."

"Neither one of us is capable of that?" I asked.

"We grow into it. It is not a given."

I had come to this session yet again to unload my stored-up resentments against Howell's faults and failures. Instead, Alma had turned them around and made me see myself as never before. *Bloody hell,* I swore to myself as I walked home. If I had known this was what counselling was all about, I wasn't sure I would have begun in the first place. I had spent months bolstering my case against Howell as the insensitive monster who had wrecked my life. Instead, what I had seen clearly and without adornment, for the first time ever, was myself.

F ❖ I ❖ F ❖ T ❖ E ❖ E ❖ N

Then one day, eleven months after we had begun seeing Alma, a further miracle occurred. The first breakthrough came between Howell and myself. Just when it looked as though we would never quite catch the trick of understanding each other, he revealed a side of himself I had never seen before. From then on, the walls began to crumble. It was as though we had been moving through a blunted state of sensory perception towards each other and after this day both of us saw each other for the first time with brilliant clarity.

Up till now both of us had been unbending and accusatory in joint sessions. With nearly a year of drill behind us, we were still unyielding about revealing ourselves and clumsy with the rules of exchange. These were simple enough. During joint sessions Alma gave us permission to talk at length about our grievances. But the protocols were that we could not be violent or personally abusive. We were encouraged to stick to the facts, to be detailed about incidents and to play down the emotional content. If one of us had a particular grievance to voice, the other was asked to listen without interrupting, even if this took up most of the ninety-minute session. Cutting in, raising voices, name-calling, or "kitchen-sinking"—dragging in incidents that had nothing to do with what was being discussed—put us strictly offsides.

"Ask yourself what this particular incident is *about*," Alma repeated over and over again. "The complaints you bring up are surface manifestations of what you feel underneath. They're the scabs, the chicken pox, the fever. Be honest about your feelings. Don't give me the rationalized version of events. Once you understand your feelings, you can start dealing with the way you respond. Remember to take responsibility. '*I* feel furious,' not '*You* make me furious.' And the formula for expressing your grievances to each other is, *when you do* whatever it is, *I feel* this way *and then I go on* to do whatever it is. Stick to it! Take responsibility. Use your heads. Use your abilities. Start integrating what you feel with the way you handle your emotions."

She was like a ballet mistress choreographing two left-footed dolts in the intricacies of *Giselle.* "The rules are not meant to tie you down," she reminded us each time we saw her. "They are there to make things easier for you. They oil the wheels of interaction."

But the habits of a lifetime were hard to break. We blamed, refused to accept responsibility for the mistakes we made, sulked, stonewalled and sniffled. We were infinitely ingenious in devising excuses for accepting blame. Until Alma pointed out that the energy we used to deflect this responsibility could be better employed in building the fragile bond between us. How we had both managed to reach middle age without destroying ourselves and a good part of the planet around us baffled everyone.

"No, you can't blame your parents," Alma laughed when Howell told her it was his father's fault for being so repressive when he was a child. If his father had been more lenient, he may have been more open to reflection and self-criticism, Howell claimed. Alma was more general. "Put the blame on the twentieth century if you like," she said. "Two world wars, the Depression and a new world order have blown away all the old rules. Everyone has had to learn the protocols all over again. But they are universal. They date from the time of the Greeks and from Christ himself." Howell flinched. He hated being lectured. After a lifetime of being told what to do he had become sensitive to any note that smacked of *ought* or *should.*

Then came the Monday morning when all the rules slid silently into place. And for the first time ever, Howell and I understood what it was like to walk in each other's shoes.

He had taken his usual place across the room from me, ankles crossed, hands folded tightly in his lap. Alma took the armchair facing us, her distinctive knot of hair already escaping its pins and combs. As always, she gave us five minutes to gather our thoughts before the hard work of the session got underway.

"Remember to focus on what needs to be done today. Center your-selves only on what we're doing here. Remember you have a responsi-bility to Emily to be the best parents you can for her. Let that be your guiding motive whatever you say and do." She looked from one to the other. "Anyone want to take a chance on opening up?"

Howell and I sat tight-lipped. Angry words swarmed in my head from a row we'd had the night before about Emily's bedtime. I toyed with the idea of bringing this up, testing the words on my tongue be-fore I opened my mouth. I still struggled to express myself calmly and steadily in Howell's presence but, more verbal and more expressive than him, I always seemed to be the first to speak.

Today, he beat me to the draw.

"I'd like to talk about something that happened yesterday afternoon," he said. He cleared his throat and leaned forward in his chair. "It wasn't a huge conflict or anything, but I think it says a lot about the problems Gillian and I still have with each other." His tone was clipped and dry, the same voice he used whenever he had a complaint to make about me. Sure enough, his first words were cold and accusatory.

"I don't know what it is with Gillian," he began, "but she certainly knows how to push my buttons every time we're together." Alma looked at him steadily, giving him her full attention. Her open, even gaze often drew more from Howell than he intended to say.

"Yesterday we thought we'd try spending some time together," Howell went on. "For Emily's sake," he added. He cleared his throat again. "I bought a new Jeep last week and I thought it would be nice to take Emily and her mother for a drive. To see how we could all get along and so forth. Well, we stopped at a lake to feed some ducks and I noticed that when Em and Gillian got back into the car, Gillian was carrying a handful of leaves. It seems she'd got it into her head to give Emily a nature lesson or something because the next thing I know there's this caterpillar crawling round the car.

"Tell Gillian," she prompted him. "Look at Gillian and tell her what it was that upset you." He drew himself up and turned to face me, his expression tense and uneasy with what he wanted to say.

"I don't know what it is that gets into your head," he said, "but to bring a pile of mud and leaves into my new car and then let this . . . this

205

creature . . . get out of control while I was trying to drive in Sunday afternoon traffic . . . "

I had a nearly uncontrollable desire to giggle. The "creature" he was talking about had been a half-inch-long green worm Emily had christened "Lowly" after the character in Richard Scarry's books. She had found the tiny thing inching its way through the grass and, sensing that it was in imminent danger from the predatory ducks at the water's edge, had rescued it with infinite care. Seeing herself as the heroine of the afternoon, she set about assembling a home for the worm from leaves and a handful of grass. That was what I was carrying when we climbed back into Howell's new car. Unfortunately, as soon as the tiny creature was safe inside, it had revealed a fatal yearning to explore and, making its way along the top of the dashboard, had disappeared forever into the depths of the heating system. My attempts to rescue him with pencils and a tailcomb had evoked peals of encouraging giggles from Emily and a grim silence from Howell. I looked over at Alma for her response. As usual, Howell was overreacting, and I was sure she would point this out to him. To my surprise, she continued to listen intently to what he had to say.

"When I looked over again," he went on, "you were laughing as if this was some huge joke at my expense, and as usual, you demonstrated a complete lack of respect for the fact that you were in *my* car. I wonder what sort of example that sets for Emily?"

I searched Howell's face for some evidence of humor, but I could detect none. Wasn't Alma going to step in? Didn't either of them have any sense of the ridiculous? Let's get this into perspective, I was saying to myself. We're talking about a worm here, for heaven's sakes. This had gone far enough. I couldn't hold myself in check any longer.

"You can't be *serious!*" I spluttered, breaking all the rules of silence. "You make it sound as though I brought a boa constrictor into your precious car. This wasn't even a caterpillar. It was a half-inch-long green worm as thick as a bit of spaghetti! Why didn't you say something about it yesterday instead of saving up all your disapproval to make a grand gesture in here today?"

At last Alma intervened. "The thing to remember is that both of you have an entirely different perspective about what happened yesterday. Please respect that. You will never be able to accept another person as an individual unless you respect that they are organized differently from you. That the light falls differently for them." She turned back to Howell. "Before we find out what's really going on here, is there anything more you'd like to say to Gillian about this incident?"

"Yes, there is," he looked me squarely in the face. "I was angry enough to stop the car and ask you to get out. I wouldn't have cared if you'd had to walk all the way home and it took you half the night."

Again I looked back to Alma. Sensing how I felt, she turned towards me and put out a hand. "You'll get your chance to speak later, Gillian," she said. "Right now I wonder if there isn't more to what happened yesterday than a half-inch-long green worm."

"Howell," she said to him, "can you tell me about what was going through your mind while all this was happening?"

"When?"

"When Gillian got back into your car with the pile of leaves in her hands."

Howell shifted uncomfortably. Expressing his displeasure was one thing. Analyzing the emotions behind his response was another. Much of Alma's counselling focussed on pinning us down, making us probe precisely what had fuelled a particular reaction. Once we began to understand how much we were driven by ancient furies, her strategy was to slow us down, ask us to think, to keep breathing steadily and to extrapolate what the feelings were all about. In this way, with constant practice, we could begin to control our reactions. Eventually an uncontrollable impulse would become a considered response. Up till now, it had felt like an impossible new art neither of us had shown much skill in mastering.

"Well," Howell said, "it felt as though I wasn't even there. As though Gillian was simply taking over." He paused for a moment, then went on cautiously. "The problem is, I feel so angry when she does this, all I want to do is to lash out at her. I can hear myself telling her to keep her hands off me and everything that belongs to me. I want to yell *just leave me alone!*"

Alma's voice was gentle. "Can you remember any other time when you may have felt that way?"

Howell stiffened, as though he was listening to something just beyond the reach of his hearing. Alma let the silence stretch. He shook his head, staring at the floor. No one spoke and Alma shot me a look, warning me not to break the silence. Suddenly, as though someone had punched him in the back, Howell jerked forward and the words came tumbling out in a broken stream.

"When I was a child . . . when I was seven or eight years old something happened. Something happened that wasn't that important, but," he stopped short and held his breath, as if trying to halt the force of the memory flooding his brain.

"Don't hold back," Alma urged him. "Don't be afraid to find out what's there."

"I was out in the veld and I found a bird's nest," he said.

"Keep going," Alma encouraged. "Don't hold your breath in."

"I found this nest that had fallen in a storm. It was shaped like a bell, and it was made of grass and it had three eggs in it. They were blue and speckled and I couldn't believe the storm hadn't smashed them. I mean they hadn't even broken when the tree fell. It was a kind of miracle," he looked up at Alma. His words came out on the same flat note, as though all he wanted to do was to lay out in front of her the picture he had locked away for so long.

"I didn't touch them," he went on. "I knew a mother bird won't come back to her nest if she senses someone else has been there. But I kept thinking it was a miracle they weren't smashed. That it would be a terrible shame if she abandoned them. I was sure she would come back so I waited all morning. But by evening, she still hadn't shown up. So I picked up the nest very carefully and brought it home and wrapped it in an old shirt of mine up in my bedroom. Then I put it under a lamp to keep the eggs warm." He stared off at some point in the distance, seeing once again the makeshift orphanage he had set up so long ago.

"I thought maybe this was meant to be," he went on. "That it was my responsibility to look after them and hatch them because they'd been abandoned. That this was some kind of a test—you know the kind of things you think when you're a kid. So I thought *I'll hatch them and feed the babies with an eye dropper.* I knew where I could get some earthworms and then, I thought, when they're big enough to fly, I'll take them into the veld and set them free. And I had this belief that they would always come back to me. That they'd know who I was." He looked down at his feet for a long time before he spoke again.

"But I came home from school one day and found my brother had smashed them in with a hammer." He looked up at Alma. "By that time they were almost ready to hatch and all I could see was their tiny skulls." He stared down at the floor. Then he said softly, "I wanted to murder my brother. I wanted to smash his head in, just the way he had killed my birds."

No one spoke. Howell had never mentioned the incident. He rarely spoke about his childhood. And I had never seen him like this before. Not even when his parents died. Now his bowed head and crumpled body moved me profoundly. I saw that there were streaks of gray in his hair that hadn't been there before and that his hands were thin and blotched from all the years he had spent in the sun. I noticed too that the old cardigan he wore summer and winter had grown thin at the elbows and that his shirt sleeves were frayed at the cuffs. Suddenly, he, too, was infinitely perishable. I had the profound urge to reach out and touch him. To put my arms around him and hold him. If only he would let me. Why had he never allowed me to see this side of him before? Had everything about him been a role and a pose to protect the fragile and finite sense of who he was?

It was Howell's voice that broke the silence at last. "All of that happened a long time ago. It's over now," he said valiantly. He looked up at Alma, with a wan grin. "You're not telling me that's why I got so angry yesterday, is it?"

"The birds? No, I don't think that's why." She shook her head. "But the circumstances? Perhaps." He looked at her uncomprehendingly.

"Something that belonged to you," she went on, "something that you put a special value on, was treated with contempt and destroyed. When that happens—especially when it happens to us as children—we may feel that an integral part of us has also been violated. Children can't always make distinctions between what's out there and themselves. Where the boundaries stop and start. I imagine you believed there was some kind of magical attachment between yourself and your bird's nest. When it was destroyed, you probably felt a part of you was also. Your hopes of survival for the birds were linked to your own instincts to nurture and be taken care of. When you saw what had happened to them, that might naturally have evoked a rage to protect yourself as well. Can I ask you how your parents handled the incident?"

"My brother was just a kid. He didn't know what he was doing. They told me not to make a big deal out of it."

"How did you dispose of the eggs?"

"My father told the servants to get rid of them."

"So. When you expressed a natural grief about something that meant a great deal to you, you weren't given a fair hearing. Your brother wasn't helped to understand what he had done and you weren't even allowed to dispose of the eggs with some sense of ritual and respect?"

He shook his head. "You make it all sound so civilized. There wasn't a chance in hell that those kinds of things could have happened in my home."

"You're wrong," she said.

"Why?" he sounded surprised.

"Because you yourself showed that you knew about them. The respect and care you showed toward a couple of birds' eggs says so. I imagine that some of your rage and grief came from having the nobility of those feelings trampled on."

"It's no different for any boy," Howell said. "I bet you that any man alive today could tell you a similar story."

"And so the world turns," Alma sighed. "You do see that doesn't make it right? I'd like you to think about some of the strategies you devised from that time on to protect yourself. Especially from hurt and shock. Give it all the time you need." She reached over and touched the arm of his sofa, allowing him his privacy. Then she turned to me.

"Is there anything you'd like to say to Howell about what you've just heard, Gillian?"

My mind was racing. I was trying to make sense of a hundred incidents, habits, mannerisms and tricks of speech that I remembered so well about Howell. Suddenly all of them had a cryptic logic of their own. I wanted to turn to him and tell him, *I understand. I wish you could have trusted me enough to tell me about yourself. Why? Why couldn't you?* I already knew the answer. Simultaneously, as the fragments of our life together unravelled in my mind, I heard myself scream-ing at him to make himself more clear to me. To let me *see*—and al-ways, always—instead of walking softly in his sacred domain, driving him further away. I thought about his odd refusal to let me sample food from his plate. His irritation when I asked to borrow a sweater or a handkerchief. The careful manner in which he would lock away his papers at night, and the way his mother would tease him because when one of us tried to sneak up on him with a hug, he would spring away in surprise. There was his anxious overprotection of Emily, the bond with his mother, even his refusal to cut all ties with Vanessa. I had thought all these habits were evidence of a mean-spirited refusal to share him-self. I had never understood that they were formed out of a deep need to protect and preserve who he was. I remembered other incidents as well. If I had been able to understand them, perhaps they would have unlocked the key to his soul long ago. There was the time he had stopped his car on a busy highway in the Karoo to rescue a calf that had strayed into the traffic. I could see him now, lifting the terrified animal in his arms, cradling it with reassuring gentleness and lowering it over the barbed-wire fence back into its paddock. And another time, during a violent hailstorm, when he had run out into our garden to cover up my spring seedlings, grabbing anything that came to hand. I could still see the stones, as big as pigeons' eggs, bouncing off his head, and the smile he cocked at me as he squelched back into the house. *Well, at least your plants are okay, but could you have a look at the dents in my head?"* And finally, the one image that could still twist at my heart. The way he had held Emily just after she was born and so small she had disap-peared into the crook of his arms. The look on his face and the voice he had used to tell her how loved she was and how welcome she would be in this world.

I had erased all these memories from the composite picture I had formed of Howell, seeing only his cold anger and keeping the echo of our strident arguments alive in my heart. How might it have been if I had kept alive the Platonic ideal? How was it that I had lived alongside this complex, extraordinary being for so long without understanding all he was and all that he had become? For once, my own limitations cut me like a knife.

"Gillian?" Alma was saying. "Do you have anything to say to Howell?"

I turned to him but he was lost in his own thoughts. "I'm sorry," I said all the same. "I'm so sorry, Howell. I never understood any of this before."

Alma turned back to him. "Howell? Can you see that Gillian did not intend disrespect either for you or for your property? That she was merely ignorant of what drove you?" He gave the slightest nod. "And can you understand how you projected onto her some of the rage you felt when you were a child?" He nodded again. I realized how hard this must be for him. Rational and unemotional to the point of stoicism, he would be mortified to realize how much he had been at the mercy of long-buried angers.

As if reading my thoughts, Alma added, "I think it might surprise you, Gillian, that although you think you've had the tougher deal here, men can be very hurt as well."

Funny, I thought. Women learn to believe early on that they live at the mercy of men. That violence is perpetrated by men intent on doing evil to women. But what do we know of the violence done to boys who are forbidden to feel their own pain and heartbreak? Women know how to ask for help. Men are not even allowed to acknowledge the pain is there.

". . . and when we keep it safely walled off, "Alma was saying, "it's often our partners who pay." She looked at me to see if I had a response. "Well?" she asked.

This was a struggle for me. I had only recently plumbed the depths of my own rage. In the aftermath of Alma's skillful surgery, I was still trying to visualize what life could be like if I were finally able to free myself from those demons.

"I'd like to tell you, Howell," I stumbled, "that I broke many of the rules because I was ignorant of what they were. That's not an excuse, I know. But I want to tell you how sorry I am that I took away so much of the good life we could have had together. I didn't understand before. And I'd like you to know how much I respect you for keeping faith and for being here today."

Howell glanced up at me. For the first time ever, I caught a shy, quick grin of concession on his face. "Give me a chance to think about that," he said. "Okay?"

Later, over coffee at a restaurant near Alma's home, both of us were too wrung out to talk much. Usually, after joint sessions we would go our separate ways. Today, Howell had asked me if I would like to go somewhere for coffee with him afterwards. I sat at our window table in the early spring sunshine staring at envelopes of sugar crammed into a cup on the table. I wished I could find the voice to tell him all the good things I had remembered about him while he was telling his story.

"I guess she's a kind of fairy godmother in her way," I said finally.

"Who? Alma?" he said.

"Well, you know. She's given us a whole new perspective."

He grinned at me. "A lot of the credit goes to you, too," he said.

"To me?" I faltered.

"Sure. You've really worked hard. Mind you. I wouldn't say she's let me slack off either."

I laughed. "I'm starving," he said suddenly. "When did you last eat?" "Just before I took Emily to school this morning," I told him. "That's nearly five hours ago," he said, glancing at his watch. "Know what I feel like?" he grinned at me. "Do you remember when we were going through Scotland together and we stopped at a country inn and we were so hungry we started at the top of the menu and went all the way down through to the coffee?"

"And then you went back and started all over again," I recalled.

"The coffee tasted like rocket fuel," he grinned.

"But it kept us going all the next day," I said. Howell looked up at me with an enquiring look. "Have you got anything else you have to do this afternoon?" he asked. "Can you stay for a while?"

"I've got Emily to fetch at three," I told him.

"Tell you what," he suggested. "Why don't we have one of every dessert on the menu and then take some home for Em as well."

"I think that sounds like a wonderful idea," I told him.

S ❖ I ❖ X ❖ T ❖ E ❖ E ❖ N

We knew things were working well when we saw our efforts show up in Emily. The first sign was that she stopped biting her nails. Then, as we became more relaxed in each other's company, we noticed that she made her way through disagreements in much the same way we did. She began to speak up for herself with teachers, with friends and especially with a group who were picking on her at school. "It's not that I don't want to be friends with you," I overheard her tell one of the girls on the phone. "It's just that you make it so difficult for me to get on with you." She, too, had begun to reframe incidents, putting a more positive spin on her interactions with others rather than giving into the negative feelings that had flooded all of us in the past. This was part of the creed Alma had drummed into us: to empathize with each other and to practice good manners regardless of how we felt or of how heated our arguments became. Howell and I marvelled at Emily's ability to cool herself down, to pull us back on track when we veered off course, to cut through to essentials and to defuse arguments that could still flare out of nowhere. Learning how to reconfigure the poorly learned lessons we had brought with us from childhood, we found it was Emily who often took on the roles of pathfinder and cheerleader in our fledgling attempts to become a family again.

Now that we had discovered a new sense of appreciation for each other, the question came up in counselling about whether Howell and I should get back together again. Wouldn't that be the logical and happy ending for all of us? Howell might have been flippant when he told Alma we had too much of a good divorce going. But the realistic answer was that in ten years of living apart our lives had changed greatly, and we now had very different needs. Anyone stepping into our two homes would immediately see how unalike we are. Howell likes huge spaces hung with exuberant art. I like living amongst stuffed sofas, books and a jungle of flowering plants. Howell remains an ebullient extrovert. I prefer the company of a few cherished friends. Out on the court, he still returns a tennis ball with deadly accuracy. I watch hockey, basketball and golf, mystified that grown men and women give the best years of their lives to the precise placement of little balls. Then there is our ongoing debate about the origins of the universe. Howell believes we all evolved from single-celled amebae. I argue that someone had to design them in the first place. He remains an atheist. I am certain there is a Divine Plan and could not live without a spiritual component in my life. When Emily is with him, he still allows her the freedom to eat what she chooses, go to bed at any hour and decide for herself how much television she watches. I remain a charter member of *Mean Moms for Morals and Manners,* believing that kids need a strong center to push against—especially in their formative years. It's easy to see how our discussions can still reach boiling point. Living on our own we are free to be exactly who we are. And in respecting our differences, we give Emily permission to develop into the unique human being she was also meant to be.

All the same, there are one or two areas where Howell and I are still of like mind. When I finally became a landed immigrant in 1994, the first thing I set out to do was to find a permanent place to live. I had flown back to South Africa to vote in the first free elections of April 1994, to sell my apartment and to bring back the small amount of money I was allowed to take out of the country. In the months after my return, I began to look for work, and also for an apartment where Emily and I could unpack our belongings, hang pictures and make a home. But it was a disheartening task. After I had looked at nearly sixty apartments, I realized there was very little I could afford. Gradually, as he accompanied me on the fruitless quest to find an apartment below $100,000, my realtor had lapsed into silent sympathy and eventually, at the end of a three-month-long search, we had shaken hands and parted company. Back in Cape Town, I had owned my own apartment outright. Now it seemed that I would be back to square one again. I would continue to rent while I searched for work, hoping that, in time, prices would soften enough to allow me to buy. There had been just one condo I had fallen in love with. In a new building, off a street that was snowed in with cherry blossom, the apartment was a stone's throw from the ocean, overlooking a garden filled with trees and birds. But the asking price was more than double what I could afford and I had put the idea of it out of my mind. Howell disagreed with my decision to rent. He felt strongly that the sooner I found a home, the sooner I could put down roots and invest all my energies in finding work. I had not told him about my fruitless search, only that there appeared to be nothing I could afford. But with his usual cheery optimism, he refused to believe there was nothing suitable on the market. He himself had bought a house some months before and was busy unpacking furniture and hanging his art collection for the first time in several years. "I bet if I went out to look," he told Emily and me, "I could find something for your Mom in a single afternoon." Emily leapt to the challenge. "What'll you give us if you're wrong?" she asked him. "A trip to Disneyland at least," he vowed. Emily, who had accompanied me on a number of my futile searches, was certain the California trip was a done deal. That afternoon, Howell consulted his black books and the following morning met with a determined realtor who understood the urgency of his mission. "If I don't find a condo by this afternoon," he told her, "I'm in hock for a trip to Disneyland. You've got to help me out." At four that afternoon he called to tell us that his quest had been successful. "Tell your Mom I want her to see this place right away," he told Emily. I took the phone from her to copy down the address, and my heart did a somersault as I realized he had found the very same apartment I had fallen in love with a month before. "I saw it in early May!" I told him, shaken by the coincidence. "But it's *way* beyond anything I can afford."

"Just bring Emily along to see it," he said. "And let me do the negotiating." In the intervening weeks, the price had dropped by just enough to make the sale attractive. As soon as Emily and I stepped inside, we knew at last we had found the perfect place for the two of us to call home.

"Well? What do you think?" Howell grinned. After months of renting, even a room we could call our own would have been welcome. But this was beyond anything I had ever hoped for. This was the home I had dreamed of whenever I visualized us settled again. In a kitchen flooded with sunshine, there was room for a family-sized table where Emily could do her homework and I could write in peace. The living room was big enough to hold my piano and bookshelves. Outside, at arm's length from the window, a family of raccoons just happened to be making their way into the green depths of a poplar tree and on the lawn below, a sleek California quail, its quiff bobbing up and down, strutted like a matron at a garden party. I turned to Howell, my heart in my throat. "It's exactly what I've always wanted. But what about the price?" I asked. "I still don't think I have enough to make it." Before I could go on, he stopped me. "I realize how much it means to you to have a home of your own," he said. "I've done some thinking and decided to match your down payment. I'll grant you a mortgage for the remaining sum. It's the least I can do to help."

It was Emily who expressed my thoughts for me. "Dad," she told him, "you're a work of art." But it didn't stop there. There was a further surprise for us. On the day we moved in, we walked into a living room piled high with boxes from Eaton's. As Emily and I unpacked crockery, cutlery and glassware, sheets, towels, duvets and covers, a coffee maker, microwave, television, VCR, toaster and kettle, Howell looked on with amusement at our pleasure. I had sold all my electrical appliances before coming back to Canada and would have to buy everything from scratch all over again. "My housewarming present for Emily and you," he said. "Just to get you started off." I thought back to the days when I had longed to serve him dinner on our wedding china. Most of the crockery from that era had fallen prey to the ups and downs of fortune and I had never bothered with replacements. Now, by some stroke of genius, the plates I unpacked and held up for Emily's inspection were exactly what I would have chosen if I'd shopped for them myself. "How did you know?" I asked Howell. "If I don't know you by now, I don't think I ever will," he said. That night, we ate the first of many meals together in my new kitchen. Afterwards, when Howell had gone home and Emily was asleep, I ran my fingers along the gleaming white cupboards and leaned my head against them, thinking *I'm home at last*. So much of life plays itself out in a kitchen, I thought, and there really is no greater happiness than when two or three are gathered here together. It was here tonight that we had at last begun to make real reparation for the hurts of the past.

I set the table with breakfast plates and cups, calling to Emily to hurry up if she didn't want to be late for school. She had stayed up late last night to wash her hair and then to convene with the mirror and examine the angles an apparently wanton God had dealt her face. "I'm not pretty. Do you think I'm pretty?" she had asked me half a dozen times before going to bed. This morning she had slept through the rock 'n' roll alarm and yawned till tears ran down her face. Twenty minutes later I had found her still sitting on the edge of her bed, examining her feet with a meditative glare.

"I *hate* my feet," she said when I walked in to see what was going on.

"What have they done to you?" I asked in a feeble attempt to defuse Monday morning's moodiness.

"Be serious, Mom. They're so big they look like boats. You've also got big feet so I blame you."

"Guilty as charged."

"You don't have to be so *reasonable* about it."

"I can't swap them. I may as well like them."

"Well I hate mine."

"Fair enough. How about some breakfast?"

"It's not ready."

"It's been ready for a while."

"Oh, okay. I'm just getting my shirt on."

I walked into the kitchen and allowed my eye to be pulled back to the pattern of plates and cups against the plain wood of the table. In the moments of setting out milk, cutting bread, and lowering eggs into boiling water, there had been a sense of wholeness, of flow, each movement so deft and smooth, it was as though the nerves in my fingers not only obeyed my thoughts, but were in complicity with all the universe. The hum of the refrigerator, the rumble of water coming to the boil and the play of my breath on the glass of a window were all mantras to the morning. My daughter might not feel the same way I do, but I count it among the great pleasures of life to sit with her at this table, working through French verbs and Mayan glyphs, Neanderthal cave drawings and the rise of Mesopotamian city states. When I stir porridge, there is the thrill of wheat seeds sprouting in rich silt, the gathering and grinding of their kernels into flour, the storage in vats over the long winter months, so that out of this simple cycle whole cities and civilizations may be born. This is all that I want or need, I thought. All the times when I had longed to be part of a whole, an image had flashed into my mind not unlike the one in front of me this morning—an ordinary table set with plates and knives, light reflected from a window and someone beloved to share it with. And there she was, a yawn cracking open her face like a tent in a windstorm, yet every movement filled with the glorious coherency of youth.

"Don't look at me that way, Mom. I can absolutely tell when you're looking at my zits and it freaks me out," she announced.

"Your skin's looking much better," I told her, keeping my thoughts to myself. Lately, adolescent hormones had caused a crisis that called for swift countermeasures. Soap and water had brought the attack under control and calm had once again been restored to our shaken household.

"Well, it's got to be perfect for Friday night," she said. Friday night was when her choir group met with the boys' school for joint practice.

"Can you crack my egg open for me?" she asked.

"It's not hot. You can hold it."

"I know, but you do it much better than I can."

I picked up the boiled egg, cracked it in half with a knife and scooped out the yolk onto buttered toast.

"Yum. And salt. No. No pepper. Mo-om! You *always* do that. Does the phrase *I hate pepper* mean anything at all to you?"

I grinned at her. "But it tastes so *good*."

"Mom. You will have to get used to the fact that I may *hate* some of the things you love."

"Okay."

"You always say that. But you go on doing them."

"Be patient. I'm a slow learner."

"Marmee," she laughed. Then, after a long, thoughtful chew, "I love you."

It was a rare consent to have me back inside her magic circle again, to look one more time at the details so beloved to me. The ivory skin that turns to tallow when she's tired, just the way mine does; the dark brows, exactly like mine and the legacy of some distant ancestor neither of us will ever know. In so many ways she belies the sturdy origins of my own family with her full mouth, straight nose and wide hazel eyes under a cloud of thick, pale hair. Yet she will always be my daughter. A part of myself. In my hands and my care just as we had agreed to on the day she was born.

At her age I had been in boarding school, two hundred miles away from home, living among girls I had never met before in my life. We slept in prefabricated huts with tin roofs and asbestos walls wrongly supposed to retain heat when the temperature dropped to minus five at night. In reality, the only warmth came from the twelve bodies crowded into a room twenty by twenty feet and curtained off from the next dormitory by canvas sheeting. We were allowed two blankets each and an eiderdown from home as long as it was encased in a serviceable canvas bag. The floors were cracked cement, icy under our feet. As punishment for talking after lights out, we were required to scour out the cracks with our toothbrushes. Twice a week, we were permitted to take a bath, for fifteen minutes at a time in two inches of tepid water. But it wasn't the misery of feet that broke open from cold or the constant deprivation of small comforts that defeated me. It was the desolation I felt at being sent away from home. It was difficult to understand why my mother believed boarding school was a character-building exercise. There were good schools within five minutes of where we lived, and it was obvious I would be a square peg among girls who came from entirely different backgrounds to my own. I could not speak a word of Afrikaans. Most of my new school friends spoke it as their mother tongue. When I was exactly the same age as Emily, I had written home to my mother:

My Dearest Mommy:

I just want to tell you that I love you better than anything on earth, and that I'm dreadfully homesick. I remember you said I mustn't write to you and that I shouldn't say I love you when I had gone back to school. But after all, I do love you and I want to say just how much I do. I imagine you and Daddy sitting in front of the fire and I just want to tell you how much I wish I could be there with you. We've had three power failures tonight (so have I!) and had part of our supper by candle-light. I hope you won't be lonely—even if you do say how glad you were that I was going back to school. I really love you and the only place and thing I don't love is, well—look at the postmark. Please write to me. Goodnight.

It was as if a universe of malice had conspired to cut me off from everything I held most dear in life. In making her decision, my mother had chosen a school in a town as different as possible from anything I had ever known. There, among solid, rural girls who played smashing games of tennis and hockey, I learned the small arts of survival. On my first evening there, I learned how to catch flying ants, an essential skill if I wanted to supplement the dull boarding-school diet of cornmeal, bread and potatoes. "You've never eaten flying ants?" one of the girls asked me in disbelief. The afternoon rains had just cleared, leaving the red dust steaming and pocked with holes that disgorged thousands of winged insects. "Where have you been all your life?" Where I came from, I told her primly, we stuck to chicken and meat. *"Gaan kak in die mielies,"* had been her astringent reply. Being told to go shit in the cornfields was a veiled invitation, I knew, to join her in snapping up the ants as they squeezed from their underground burrows, pull off their wings and stuff several into your mouth at a time. You chewed quickly so that they didn't tickle your palate, and their peppery taste was almost as satisfying as the dried meat we smuggled in from home as tuck.

As time went on, I learned that the girls were much more kindhearted than their rough appearance suggested. They talked with great affection about the "folks back home" and the sheltered lives they led on the gold mines, where the mine manager was God and the "kaffirs" were the only problem. They shared *koeksisters* sent from their mothers' kitchens, dipping the syrupy twists of fried bread into sweet tea, and slapping their knees with pleasure at the treat. They breezed through science and math, teased me out of my city accent, taught me the correct fingering for Chopin's *Polonaise,* how to light a fire in the rain and what to say to a boy at a dance. They were all the family I had for two and a half years, and when I left to move to Zimbabwe with my parents, they gave me a pillowcase embroidered with name tags from every girl in the school. Later, when I bumped into them in Johannesburg, they had become doctors and engineers, nurses, teachers and excellent wives, the salt of the earth and a hardworking, feisty side of white South Africa few people care to acknowledge or show affection for.

"Mom, are you dreaming again?" Emily was asking. "I'm sorry to disturb you, but do you think you could possibly come back to earth?" She was standing in the doorway, her satchel over one shoulder at an angle I have told her will give her advanced scoliosis before she is fifteen.

"What's the time?" I asked.

"Ten past eight. If we don't leave now, I'm going to be *fa*tally late."

"You won't. I promise."

"Well, just remember there's photo radar now. You don't want to get caught. They feed your name into a giant computer in Ottawa and then they track you your whole life with electronic probes."

"Em, that's *not* true," I laughed.

"I promise you, Mom. I heard the seniors talking about it in the playground yesterday." I smiled at her.

"What?"

"Nothing." How can I tell her that she's still a child in so many ways, when in others she is not? On the way to school she practices a solo she wants to try out for and wavers when she hits high F. Her voice has a rich, bass note that always startles me when I listen to her speak. In the school parking lot, I help her assemble her books and lean over to peck her on the cheek.

"Mo-om! Not here," she protests. "People will see!" Then she leans over and gives my palm three quick squeezes, the old signal for *I love you.* I had better grab every squeeze and hug I can get, I think to myself as I back out. She won't allow me even to take hold of her hand anymore when we cross the street. Already there are posters of teenage idols on her walls and a locked diary I have vowed never to read on pain of death by instant stroke or blindness. And so, every day, I

223

make the silent, unspoken adjustments to handing over life to where it rightly belongs.

In the years since our divorce, I've asked myself countless times how we could have done things better. Ten years after the end of our marriage, I still wonder if there was something we could have done at the time to prevent our breakup. Knowing what I do today, I am certain that there is no greater wound we could have inflicted on a two-year-old than the destruction of her parents' marriage. And then there was the question of joint custody. At the time, we believed wholeheartedly that we were doing the best for Emily by settling on this arrangement. Today, I know it doesn't work. She has adapted well to keeping a bedroom in both homes, but inevitably a treasured possession is left behind, while the constant packing up and moving is enough to derange a nomad. We were also wrong in thinking that we could continue to give her the same quality of parenting as if we had stayed married. The whole of her short life has been defined as a divorced child. She has never lived with parents who show spontaneous affection for each other. Howell and I may have a friendship that is based on deep acceptance, but it is not a physical one and I believe a child needs to witness the constant exchange of warmth between her parents to catch the habit. She has seen us work our way through disagreements with greater and greater skill, but there have been many more of these times than there have been of easy, quiet moments.

I look at her and wonder what experiences of family she will take with her into her adult life. Her provenance as the child of families too shell-shocked to provide attention or affection will to some degree always mark her passage through life. At the same time, she carries within her my mother's superhuman determination to survive and Eleanor's gift for vitality and organization. She has also inherited my mother's tendency towards exercising small but vital economies. She keeps savings accounts and coin jars marked for short-, medium- and long-term goals and dreams up schemes to make money during the summer. Lately she has begun to sew and perhaps she will bring alive again my mother's gift for exquisite needlework. When my father died in January of 1996, we wept together as we remembered him. To Emily, he will always be the grandfather who would call to wish her happy birthday three days in a row because the time differences between Zimbabwe and Canada had become too much for him to decipher. For me, he will always remain the sweet-tempered father who carved my name into pumpkins in his vegetable patch so that I could watch the initials expand over the summer as if sculpted by magic hands just for me.

Perhaps Emily is not meant to be the musician or artist that Howell hoped for, but a financier with not a jot of sentiment about the books and paintings that fill the homes of her mother and father. What she will take with her into her adult life is sure trust in a father who has remained steadfast in each one of his responsibilities toward her and who has given her every opportunity to explore her world. Most important of all, she will remember him as a father who cared enough about his daughter to learn to get on with her mother all over again.

This morning, as I stop off at Howell's house for our ritual morning tea, I sense something is on his mind.

"I need to talk to you," he tells me as he takes down cups and lays out spoons on his kitchen table. He ends his sentence with a shy laugh and I know what that means. He's restless again. It's been a long winter, and the endless cold is difficult to bear for those of us who were born with heat in our bones. In South Africa the months from October through to April are uniformly brilliant. The skies are the color of new denim and the constant machine-shop whirr of cicadas reminds you that yet again the temperature is in the nineties outside. This past December has been particularly hard on Howell. His bones ache with the cold and he longs for open stretches of sun-baked land. This time, however, I am adamant. We have agreed to stay together in one place for Emily's sake and I won't move her yet again. For three terms running she's earned Honors with Distinction at school. Another move would be disastrous just as she gets ready to move up to high school. I am sympathetic but steadfast.

"You may want to take time out down in Arizona," I suggest. "Give yourself a month-long break. And there are good deals to Hawaii at the moment. What about going there?"

"I don't really want to be away that long," Howell says. What he means is that he will miss Emily too much to be away for more than a week on his own. We agree to let the thought ride. In the past, we would have been at each other's throats by now, each claiming that the only point of view worth considering was our own.

In a good divorce, there are few rules or expectations. Every day is a reinvention, and Howell and I are not experts, only novices in charting the way. But like a good marriage, a good divorce is also grounded in kindness, flexibility and long-term goals. As a quintessential baby boomer who grew up believing I was entitled to more and better of everything, I am profoundly thankful that Howell and I chose to work through our broken relationship to find new appreciation for each other. Rediscovering care and respect for the man I was once married to has been a necessary rite of passage that has allowed me to let go of our past with goodwill and blessings.

I don't think we could have achieved this in South Africa. There is still too much political and personal turmoil in the country to allow the existence of a moral framework that puts the rights of children first. And it is this single precept that is the cornerstone of our agreement. Emily's rights supercede our own. There is no exception to the rule. We have had our chance and broke faith with the promises we made. We have no right to inflict further misery on her because of our failures.

The other key lesson I learned from Alma was that forgiveness is essential to the covenant we have made with each other. In her view, forgiveness is the act of giving up all rights to revenge. And now that I understand where my old angers came from, the furies that shook me seem to have died down like a March windstorm. In their absence, I am surprised to realize how much I still care about Howell. After all, who else would bring me strawberries out of the blue, or a chocolate heart on St. Valentine's day (though strictly speaking I don't qualify). Who else would go out of his way to find me buttons for a blazer on a business trip to London or accompany me to an x-ray session to give me support? No one else has meant as much to me in my adult life, and it's warming to know that the spark my sister saw in him so many years ago has proved to be a steady flame. All the same, we know from Alma that emotional relearning will be a lifelong process between the two of us. In our final session with her, she graded us B-plus and said, "I imagine both of you will be very nice people when you've finished growing up."

We are all of us mere footnotes to our parents' histories unless we break away and write new stories of our own. In mine I plan to say that whatever else I did with my life, I made one undeniably good decision. I chose the right father for my daughter.

ABOUT THE AUTHOR

Ian Reeves

After spending most of her life in South Africa and Zimbabwe, Gillian Tucker settled in Canada in 1993. She has written for magazines in New Zealand, England, the United States, Canada, and South Africa, and she is the former editor of a South African publication. Her writing focuses on biography and personal nonfiction. She lives in Victoria, B.C., and shares the care of her daughter with her ex-husband.